A Relentless Spirit

Catharine Ladd, Southern
Educator, Entrepreneur,
and Author, 1808-1899

A Relentless Spirit

Catharine Ladd, Southern Educator, Entrepreneur, and Author, 1808-1899

Patricia V. Veasey

For Patty,
Thank you for your interest
in Chatharine Ladd's
Story, Best regards,
Pat Veasey

Cover art and design by M. C. Churchill-Nash
Book design by Maureen Ryan Griffin
Author photograph by Lifetouch

Published in the United States of America by

FLOATING LEAF PRESS

A division of
WordPlay
Maureen Ryan Griffin
6420 A-1 Rea Road, Suite 218,
Charlotte, NC 28277
Email: info@wordplaynow.com
www.wordplaynow.com

ISBN 978-0-9802304-8-2

This book is dedicated to my parents,
Isabelle and Mike,
who taught their daughters to love reading, be curious,
and ask questions.
And to the women who encouraged me along life's journey:
Aunt Jo, Aunt Patti, Aunt Vance, Aunt Lynne, Aunt Lavoy,
Aunt Mimi, Aunt Peta, Aunt Louise, and Aunt Phyllis.

This dedication includes my friend Nancy Craig,
a believer in the book who knew I would see it to the end.

Table of Contents

Author's Notes

Whereas many facts about Catharine Ladd's life are irretrievable, what is clear from the available information is her relentless spirit in the face of loss and gender prejudices of her time. She proceeded forward in providing an education for young women, in building community, and in supporting the arts, especially in literature and the theatre. I discovered a Catharine with high energy and a sharp wit who, for one example, founded a drama troupe, produced and wrote plays, designed scenery, and painted the scenery herself. From the onset, the question was whether to attempt a biography of a person with few sources for documenting her life, yet not lose her story as an important chapter in the history of remarkable Southern women.

Her circumstances of loss were known. In February 1865, at the end of the war, Catharine Ladd's house in Winnsboro, South Carolina, burned at the hands of Union troops under Brigadier General Slocum. She had been widowed the previous year, and now had no place for her family to live. She had six children: two daughters at home, one daughter in Florida staying with friends while recovering from illness, and three sons away at war. Her writings of over thirty years were gone, as were all paper documents of records including those of operating a school, teaching materials, books, letters, and whatever possessions she and her husband, George, accumulated over a lifetime. As was the case throughout the South, evidence of her past life was gone. Nonetheless, family oral history about George and Catharine Ladd fascinated me and prompted me to know their story, especially that of Catharine before the war. I was not discouraged, so like Catharine, I relentlessly forged ahead. It was an extended research journey of two decades.

I visited repositories like the South Carolina Department of Archives and History and the University of South Carolina's Caroliniana Library in Columbia, the South Carolina Historical Society in Charleston, and the Southern Historical Collection at the University of North Carolina in Chapel Hill. I read many secondary sources for historical context, including *The Secret Eye: The Journal of Gertrude Clanton Thomas, 1848–1889*, edited by Virginia E. Burr; *The Diary of Miss Emma Holmes, 1861–1866*, edited by John F. Marszalek; Christie Anne Farnham's *The Education of the Southern Belle*, a definitive history of female education in the antebellum South; Walter Edgar's comprehensive *South Carolina: A History*; and a new view of American history by Jill Lepore, *These Truths*. Sam Thomas, Curator of the T. A. A. Cobb House, acquainted me with Henry D. Grady, the famous Georgia journalist and orator who coined the phrase, 'The New South' in 1886. His speeches were published in 1910 by editor Edwin Dubois Sherter and are online at Hathi Trust. My editor kept me apprised of new works in historical fiction: *The Invention of Wings* (about the Grimke family of Charleston, South Carolina), by Sue Monk Kid, and *The Last Painting of Sara De Vos,* by Dominic Smith, were favorites of mine. A recent biography of Harry Truman, *The Accidental President,* by A. J. Baime, proved that biography can be readable. Reading gave me time to breathe, to think, to consider ideas, and to admire good writing.

Slowly, information about Catharine and George Ladd accumulated that looked promising for a book, although there were gaps in the story. An editor wisely advised that combining the stories of Catharine and George was too ambitious. I decided to write an article about George's known paintings and to concentrate the biography on Catharine. This resulted in a detour that yielded important information from the Museum of Early Southern Decorative Arts (Winston-Salem, North Carolina). While exploring their Craftsmen Files for George Ladd as an itinerant artist in the South, a cross-reference to Catharine Stratton Ladd's family surfaced. Her mother, Ann Collins Stratton, was an heir to Ann's stepfather John Collins, a successful house carpenter and land owner in Richmond, Virginia. In his files were a death notice, his will, estate settlement notices, and family names. Catharine's maternal family spread before my eyes. This rich source opened an entire family history and several unsolved mysteries about Catharine Ladd, but not about George.

Another serendipitous experience revealed more about George Ladd's career. While searching the collections of maritime museums (as a teenager George was a seaman), I discovered a previously unknown portrait in miniature painted by George Ladd in the Newport News Maritime Museum (Virginia) collections. George Ladd signed his painting, and, previously unknown to the curator, the case contained a lock of the subject's hair. The portrait was of Matthew F. Maury, the "Pathfinder of the Seas." These experiences encouraged me to focus my article about George Ladd on his work as an itinerant portrait artist in the South. The journal of the Museum of Early Southern Decorative Arts, JESDA, published the article in 2018. It can be read at http://www.mesdajournal.org/2018/correct-likenesses-george-ladd-itinerant-miniature-and-portrait-painter/.

The biography of Catharine Ladd fell naturally into a thematic form with three parts: Catharine as an educator, Catharine as a community activist, and Catharine as an author, with each section written in chronological order.

Investigation into female education generated a wealth of information from curriculum postings in newspaper advertisements, family letters, family papers with school accounts, surviving examples of schoolgirl art, examples of student academic work, medals for student progress, images of academy buildings, and documentation of students and teachers in the United States Federal Census records and the South Carolina Free School Act (1811) Commissioners' reports. By combining biographical information, the United States Federal Census records, and newspaper advertisements, I built a chronological account of the places George and Catharine lived from their marriage in 1827 to their final home in Winnsboro, South Carolina. I began to understand the nature of antebellum female education and Catharine's importance as a teacher and principal.

Catharine's work as a community organizer and activist was most evident once she and George settled in Winnsboro, South Carolina, in 1843. The documentation for this phase of her life came from Civil War records like the Ladies Relief Association of Fairfield, letters home from soldiers, and from the local newspaper. Most of the known Ladd activity described in the newspapers during the war was about Catharine and her sons, with very little about George, though it was documented that he and Catharine submitted a design for the Confederate national flag in 1861. (This information was not published or known as a fact until Devereaux Cannon Jr. explored the topic in the twentieth century.) Legal documents did identify activity of George serving in paralegal functions and buying and selling real estate. After the death of George at home in 1864, the widowed Catharine remained an organizing force in her community, promoting the rebuilding of the town of Winnsboro. Her pursuits were publicized in the Winnsboro newspaper. Those accounts provided an intimate and poignant snapshot of how widowed Catharine Ladd and her children, and one Southern community's people, scrounged to make a living after the war.

The final section, about Catharine Ladd as an author, was the result of an extended search for her extant works of poetry, short stories, plays, and essays. A surviving scrapbook owned by a descendant contained some copies of her writings, including hand-written copies of her plays, poems published in the Winnsboro newspaper, and newspaper articles about her life. Most of this collection was from the post-war years. A former editor at South Carolina Press, Alex Moore, led me to a source for locating early writers' works. Using Catharine's contemporary biographical entries as a guide, in which her writings and her pen names were discussed, I searched both original and online publications of the mid-nineteenth century, using her pen names and her actual name. *The Southern Literary Messenger* (Richmond, Virginia) published the earliest examples of her poetry in the 1830s. This publication's history was well-documented and provided specific information about contributors like Catharine Ladd. Later these findings were confirmed by a search of digitized collections through https://babel.hathitrust.org and the University of Michigan.

An important link from a descendant proved pivotal in the early years of my research while I served as the director of education at Historic Brattonsville, where Catharine Ladd started Brattonsville Female Seminary. Michael Crocker, a Ladd descendant, visited Brattonsville with some original documents that he wanted help in identifying. There were several family letters, a hand-sketched funereal memorial on paper, and a hand-written essay.

In the family letters was the account of the death of George Ladd in July 1864, written by son A. W. Ladd. Two other letters were essential links to the Ladd and Stratton families. One was a letter from Boston from George's brother, William H. Ladd; the other from Lynchburg, Virginia, from Catharine's cousin, Emma

Dabney. It was providential that these three letters, which were so pivotal to the family story, found their way to me. The hand-written essay corresponded to those described as being written by Catharine according to a biographical entry by Mary T. Tardy in 1869. It was a thrilling moment to see and read the essay, signed by what looked like a cipher for Catharine Ladd's initials, CL. The descendant donated it to the Culture and Heritage Museums. It is one surviving example of Catharine's politically themed writings about promoting white labor in the South, the failure of slavery to generate profits by producing cotton, and the lethargy of white male voters after the war.

I went on to locate at least one example of each genre of writing undertaken by Catharine Ladd. As no complete collection of Catharine's writings was ever known to be published and the full extent of her writings may never be discovered, I decided to include a list of her known pieces in the book's Appendix.

The importance of Catharine's writings lies in how they opened her heart, mind, and soul to the reader. In the first sections about Catharine as an educator and community activist, the sources reflect her actions and movement—in other words, her physical self. We learn where and how she taught school, and what she did in the community. We find out about the birth of the Ladd children through genealogy and the census. However, the lack of any of her personal letters or a journal written by her leave the reader ignorant of how Catharine felt, what motivated her actions, and any details of her private life.

The inability to communicate feelings was a societal prescriptive for women in the nineteenth century: women had few outlets for personal expression other than through female friendships and writings. The diaries and journals of upper-class Southern women like Mary Chestnut, Emma Holmes, Ella Clanton Thomas, and others confirm that women suppressed their personal feelings and opinions in deference to decisions and control by fathers, brothers, husbands, and even sons. Literacy for women was reserved for the educated minority. Women had few legal rights, especially concerning property. Therefore, knowledge of Catharine as an author serves as a vital and unique part of this biography. The revelations show us a real person whose body had a mind, soul, and heart. Although Catharine's literary legacy was small in volume compared to the professional women writers of her time, her works reveal a talented, imaginative author. We learn through her writings about personal tragedy, betrayal, a sense of humor and fun, racism, political opinions, and personality traits. We see that, in some instances, her feelings and actions were at odds.

Naturally, there were mysteries that remained unanswered. The created Ladd family story included "myths" about Catharine's Richmond childhood as a playmate of Edgar A. Poe, where Catharine and George lived and when, her activities during the Civil War, and her creation of the Confederate flag. Of course, there was some truth in the myths that needed to be demystified. The discovery of the true stories was much more compelling than fiction, and these are all addressed in the book.

As described previously, Catharine Stratton's maternal genealogy was uncovered accidentally. Her grandmother was married three times, the first time to an unknown man who was the father of Ann Collins, Catharine's mother. Ann Collins grew up in a large family of stepbrothers and sisters of her own mother's second and third marriages. The death of Catharine's father by drowning was a family story, but undocumented. She may have had siblings. There are no facts about how Catharine Stratton and George Ladd met in Richmond, Virginia, and married. Catharine's widowed mother, Ann Collins Stratton, lived with George and Catharine until her death in Winnsboro in 1856. Yet, strangely, there are no stories, incidents, or family information about Ann Stratton. There are no memorials or poems written by Catharine to her mother. The only mention of her was in a letter by son A. W. Ladd about his father George Ladd's death, stating, "His resting place is side by side with grandmother, in the old Methodist church yard."

In the first ten years of marriage, Catharine and George were separated for long periods while he pursued patrons for portrait painting. It was the nature of itinerant artists to be absent from home, but Catharine expressed emotions of disappointment in love and possible betrayal in her poetry, writing of those feelings even at age eighty-nine. An indiscretion in their relationship hurt Catharine deeply. At the time of George's death at home in July 1864, two of the daughters were at his side, but not Catharine. A. W. Ladd related in his letter that his father had lain unconscious for several days, but despite that fact, a wife normally kept a close death watch. Admittedly, it was a time of war, but no obituary of George Ladd was printed in the newspaper. George's will, written in 1859, left all property and all decisions to Catharine, which was highly unconventional and contrary to common law in South Carolina. Was the will negotiated by Catharine against their personal history?

As was common in the nineteenth century, children frequently died young, and Catharine wrote of death's grief. The Ladds may have lost a first child, as suggested by the presence of a male child under age five in the 1830 United States Federal Census (Fayetteville, North Carolina) who does not appear in subsequent census accounts. Catharine and George raised six children. Two children predeceased Catharine: Annie Ladd Neil died as a young married woman soon after the birth of her only child in 1875; Charles Henry Ladd died of tuberculosis in 1880.

In the period between the Revolutionary War and the Civil War, education for women flourished in female academies built throughout the nation. Although these were largely for women of the wealthy and professional class families, town and rural schools also provided a basic education for others. In the South, wealthy land owners began academies on their plantations, and the Presbyterian church sponsored academies in towns and cities. The first American college for women was founded in the South in 1839, Georgia Female College (Wesleyan College) in Macon, Georgia.

Christie Ann Farnham wrote the definitive text on antebellum education for Southern females, *The Education of the Southern Belle* (1994). I relied heavily on her work for a background on antebellum female education.

To explore the realm of female authors in the nineteenth century, I read the works of English authors like Mrs. Hemans, Mrs. Sigourney, and of American writers. In *Women Writers and Journalists in the Nineteenth-Century South* (2011), Jonathan Daniel Wells wrote about the consequences of an educated, literate female population in the South, prompting a demand for journals, magazines, and newspapers with fiction and non-fiction on a variety of topics. *Godey's Lady's Book*, with Sarah Hale as its female editor, published a monthly magazine with poetry and prose, book reviews, and articles from history, geography, philosophy, literature, and religion, along with domestic skills in sewing with instructional patterns. Catharine Ladd contributed at least one poem to *Godey's Lady's Book*. Daniel Wells also wrote *The Origins of the Southern Middle Class* (2004), which gave some background that enabled me to see where George and Catharine Ladd fit into the picture. All the above works were documented studies citing many individuals, academies, and periodicals, but they failed to mention Catharine Ladd, her academies, or her writing as a newspaper correspondent, poet, playwright, and essayist. She was also left out of the series *South Carolina Women: Their Lives and Times* (2009–2012).

Throughout the research, I was unsettled about how to share the sparse information about enslaved individuals in the Ladd household. I was frustrated by not having any direct information about the Ladds' relationship with these enslaved persons, specifically how George Ladd acquired them, what duties and skills they demonstrated daily, and other indications. Like any other interpersonal relationships, the communication between owners and the enslaved was a complex matter. I wish I had access to this information on the Ladds, but I did know something of other families.

Most of my research in nineteenth century female education in the South involved many hours of reading family papers in archival facilities. These family papers were largely those of plantation owners in the Carolina Piedmont, including Springs, Bratton, Spratt, Torrence, and Davidson. There were family letters, legal documents including wills and inventories of estates, and some bills of sale for enslaved people. It was a stark education in the facts of life in an enslaved society. What follows are some things I learned.

First, the enslaved were almost never mentioned in letters unless there was an illness or epidemic, that is, something of financial concern or consequence to the white family. The enslaved were basically invisible; they did not exist in society on the same level as the white family. This was an example of how owners of the enslaved engaged in self-denial of slavery. Their children would, however, in writing letters to home from school, like the popular Salem Girls' Boarding School, almost always include a greeting to the servants or hands, or an individual by name. Likely the one greeted was the child's caregiver from birth.

An 1862 Civil War letter from soldier Floyd Jackson in Winchester, Virginia, to his mother in Winnsboro, South Carolina, exemplifies how complicated individual situations were. Floyd mentions his enslaved cook, Bill. Bill was sent from the Jackson home to assist Floyd at his war encampment.

In this ending to a letter to his mother, Floyd sends his greeting to his siblings and to the enslaved at home.

> Tell Warny & Eddie that I will write to them. Give my love to all and kiss Inez. Howdye to the blacks. I remain
> Your affectionate Son,
> Floyd[1]

Floyd Jackson referred to Bill in his letters and forwarded on Bill's messages to those at home. In this instance the enslaved man Bill sent his *howdye* to those back home and is possibly literate, unless Floyd reads and writes messages home on behalf of Bill.

> Bill is well he recv'd Marima's letter and will answer it as soon as possible, sends howdye. Give my love to all and write soon.
> Your Affectionate Son,
> Floyd[2]

And,

> Bill is getting on finely and sends how-dye to all. [3]

Second (and this is reflected by my using the language of the nineteenth century when giving examples from the public record, like the census or wills), the enslaved were not called slaves by their owners, but instead, "negroes," "servants," or "hands." Using the word servant was part of the state of denial.

Third, the nature of these complicated relationships prevented the owners from admitting that the enslaved were not loyal members of their family, indebted to the owners for their existence, but were instead always desirous of freedom whatever it brought. On the other hand, some enslaved persons believed they were truly cherished and loved by their owners, when in reality they were never seen as equals on that level.

The famously known Civil War diary of Mary Miller Chestnut, *Mrs. Chestnut's Civil War*, edited by C. Vann Woodward, and those of Ella Clanton Thomas and Emma Holmes, written by women of the wealthy class of Southern families, all voiced a dislike, disapproval, and condemnation of slavery. Each of these three women knew she faced a different future for herself of employment and domestic labor but was relieved to see the end of slavery. With an education and moderately good health, these women had privilege in their favor, as opposed to an uneducated and perhaps unskilled former enslaved woman.

Consider however, an example of a skilled woman, Mrs. Keckley, formerly enslaved, who had purchased her freedom. By 1860, she had a thriving dress-making business in Washington, D.C. Her clients included Jefferson Davis's wife, Varina, and other wives of cabinet officials. In 1861, Mrs. Keckley became the confidant and exclusive dress maker for First Lady Mary Lincoln. Their close relationship ended badly after Mrs. Keckley published an intimate account of the Lincolns in the White House, and later sold some items from Mrs. Lincoln's wardrobe, albeit for philanthropical reasons. This is only one of many situations of complicated interracial relationships.

I included in this book what was known about the ownership of enslaved persons by George Ladd. Catharine Ladd did not own slaves herself but had supervision of those engaged in her academies. It is unknown if Catharine or others taught any of the enslaved how to read and write. It was forbidden by law to teach the enslaved to read; nevertheless, there are stories from the WPA

Slave Narratives [4] (Depression Era interviews with former enslaved persons) that some did teach themselves to read by exposure to classroom materials and books like Webster's *Speller*. After the war, literate African Americans became teachers in their segregated schools. The facts I did learn through various sources were noted and inserted where most relevant in the discussion. I could not change the historical facts on record but was motivated to include everything that I learned for the sake of truth and accuracy.

Catharine Ladd's story was lost in the twentieth century for several reasons. Her works were never published in their entirety. Her name as an author was often disguised as a pseudonym in periodicals where her writings survived. Her family descendants were confused or not informed of her early life. No one explored the public records for facts on the George and Catharine Ladd family. Without stories and facts from local sources, a researcher would have trouble uncovering Catharine's history. That is why I took on the task: I enjoyed sorting the myth from truth, tracing down details, and learning about female education in the South. I am hoping to put Catharine Stratton Ladd's name back into the annals of history.

In the end I pursued the story of Catharine Ladd for compelling reasons, summarized here.

The lives of George and Catharine Ladd provide insight into how educated individuals without inherited wealth pushed boundaries of class and gender to build commercial and social networks, acquire property, achieve middle-class status, and adapt to circumstances in the South before and after the Civil War.

The expanse of Catharine Stratton Ladd's life over the nineteenth century in the South gives readers access to an array of experiences from one woman's point of view. Traveling to various locations in search of teaching positions from Virginia to Georgia, while at the same time being a wife and raising a family, offers a remarkable view of her work and domestic spheres. As an author, Catharine's writings provide insight into her thoughts and emotions that add dimension to her actions.

Her life reveals how a Southern woman participated in her community daily, and how she maneuvered around barriers to women's freedom of expression.

Catharine's gifts as an author of poetry, prose, plays, and as a journalist, remain today in the surviving published and unpublished examples of her works. By expressing her opinions, emotions, and observations she opened herself to further understanding on a personal level. She also shared her sense of humor in writing and producing plays for a post-war community that needed entertainment. Her legacy as a Southern female author was not in her status professionally or in the volume of works published, but as an individual who wrote and published in mostly a regional market.

Our understanding of local history expands with an examination of individual uniqueness. As an example of that uniqueness, Catharine had financial resources in reserve after the war, perhaps partly freed for her use upon the death of her husband. Although the means remain unknown, Catharine used her money for the public good by investing in the revival of buildings in the town of Winnsboro. The property deeds documenting her transactions are a matter of record.

Catharine Ladd's experience as a middling sort who provided leadership in her community increases the "depth and nuance" of "gender, work, and region," so aptly expressed by Emily Bingham and Penny Richards in "The Female Academy and Beyond: Three Mordecai Sisters at Work in the Old South," found in *Neither Lady nor Slave: Working Women of the Old South.*

Catharine's actions forged the way for women's progress in education, voting, and property rights. Harvard Professor Jill Lepore, author of a recent view of American history in *These Truths*, stated in an interview on PBS that before women could vote, yet while they held the higher moral ground, they told men how to vote. Catharine was a model for the future of feminism. She influenced hundreds of young women to seek lives as educated women, capable of independent action and thought.

Catharine's long, remarkable life spanned the nineteenth century. After a life of generosity to family and community, Catharine, like many before her, lacked material security and good health. Her situation in no way discounted her many accomplishments and contributions to the education of women, to the recovery of her beloved community of Winnsboro, and to the literary volumes written by women with a voice for gender equality. With this biography her place of influence is renewed.

Prologue

Winnsboro, South Carolina, 1861:
A Flag for the New Republic

When Catharine Stratton Ladd was a sixteen-year-old schoolgirl in Richmond, Virginia, she saw the Marquis de Lafayette emerge from his horse-drawn carriage and approach her class. He then, according to her own written reminiscences, grasped her outstretched hand as he proclaimed success for the new American republic. Now, in 1861, this same republic of George Washington's was torn apart by civil strife.

At her home in Winnsboro, South Carolina, Catharine must have felt compelled to answer the call of the Provisional Congress of the Confederate States of America for a flag design suitable for a different new republic.

Here is what is known: Catharine Stratton Ladd, a Southerner from birth, and her husband, George Ladd, a New Englander, submitted a design proposal for the Confederate national flag in February 1861.

Just two months later, on March 4, 1861, the Provisional Congress of the Confederate States of America adopted a flag design chosen by the Committee on Flag and Seal. Within hours the first flag was made and raised in Montgomery, Alabama, an event recorded by Mary Chestnut:

> We stood on the balcony to see our Confederate flag go up.
> Roars of cannon, &c&c [etc.] . . . Miss Tyler . . . ran up our flag.[5]

On March 6, 1861, Mrs. W. W. Boyce of Winnsboro wrote in her diary:

> Heard the startling news that our forces are to attack Fort
> Sumter tomorrow. Received a letter from Mr. Boyce in which he
> gave me a description of our new flag. The flag to the Boyce
> Guards is to be presented on Friday by Minnie.[6]

On March 8, 1861, Miss Emma Holmes of Charleston, South Carolina, made the following entry in her diary:

> . . . The flag which has been adopted by the Confederate States
> has a red field with a white stripe, dividing it equally, the white
> and red being the same width. The blue union on the left
> extending to the lower red stripe and containing a circle of seven
> stars, thus:[7]

Emma Edwards Holmes, Diaries, 1861–1862 [8]

On April 17, 1861, the *Edgefield Advertiser* proclaimed:

> On Saturday last we had the honor of presenting to the Town
> and District of Edgefield, through our patriotic Intendant, a
> handsome Confederate Flag. It is now flapping its brilliant folds
> at the top of the staff in the centre of our plaza, and commands
> the involuntary homage of all who behold it. [9]

This new Confederate national symbol that was being hoisted onto flagpoles in the South—where did it originate? Witnesses seemed unconcerned, but scholars have varying opinions about it. In 2004, Devereaux D. Cannon Jr., an expert on Civil War flags, presented a paper to the North American Vexillological Association, "The Genesis of the Stars and Bars," reconsidering his former conclusions about the origin of the design for the Confederate national flag.[10]

Since the early twentieth century a controversy over who created the flag design centered around two men: Nicola Marschall and Orren Randolph Smith.[11] In his new essay, Mr. Cannon credited inspiration for the design chosen by the committee to husband and wife George and Catharine Ladd of Winnsboro, South Carolina.[12]

The Committee on Flag and Seal of the Provisional Congress of the Confederate States received over two hundred proposals for the national flag, motivating the committee's chairman, Mr. William Porcher Miles of South Carolina, to admit that not all proposals could be acknowledged. On February 10, 1861, William W. Boyce, a South Carolina delegate to the Confederate Congress, received proposal No. 64:

> ...by a lady with whom I am well acquainted; a neighbor of mine, who resides in the picturesque town of Winnsboro, Fairfield District, S.C. She is a lady of remarkable intelligence, whose path through life has been illustrated by all those virtues which adorn the female character.[13]

This lady was Catharine Stratton Ladd, who wrote that the proposal was a:

. . . flag for the new Republic designed by Mr. Ladd, which is
simple, as all national flags should be. It is tri-colored, with a red
Union, seven stars, and the crescent moon.

It was all the design of Mr. L., with the exception of the
stars in a circle or wreath, and placing the crescent moon among
them, which I thought would be a fit emblem for our young
Republic; and by placing the stars in a wreath others could be
added forming a larger wreath as the other States come in.[14]

George W. Ladd flag design [15]

There are two differences between the Ladd design and the final
one: reversal of the red and blue colors and the removal of the
crescent moon in the circle of stars in the canton.

Mr. Cannon observed, "No other submission, however,
included a canton[16] and only three stripes or bars in either the

traditional American color arrangement or the reversed colors suggested by Mr. Ladd."[17]

In the end the committee chose a simple design, but as Mr. Cannon noted, the Montgomery *Daily Advertiser* "tells us that the flag 'was the work of the committee appointed by Congress, none of the designs sent by individuals as models having been thought suitable.'"[18] Or, as Mr. Miles professed early in the decision-making, "otherwise why have a committee?"

Confederate National Flag, 1861 [19]

In "The Genesis of the Stars and Bars," Mr. Cannon gave the reasons he supported the Ladds' proposal: it fit the committee's design requirements; it had elements that became part of the final design; it was documented as being submitted to the committee; and most importantly, it was not the design of a single individual, but a design adapted by the committee to fit their stated objectives.[20]

In 1861 in Winnsboro, South Carolina, George and Catharine Ladd were well-established residents. George was an itinerant portrait artist with a successful regional reputation. Catharine was the founder and principal of Winnsboro Female Institute, a published writer, and a community organizer.

In his article, Devereaux Cannon Jr. addressed, using information from Ladd oral family history and Catharine Ladd's biographical entries, the compelling story that Catharine Ladd designed the first Confederate flag, setting the facts down and forming his argument on behalf of George as well as Catharine. Persistent stories like this one handed down about Catharine and George Ladd reflect their complex yet previously unexamined lives that deserve confirmation and revelation. The historical contributions of Southern women whose impacts have been forgotten, or lost altogether, warrant discovery.

Thankfully, many facts are known about the woman who submitted her husband's design for the new Confederate national flag. Virginia educator and writer Catharine Stratton married New Englander George Ladd, an itinerant portrait artist, in 1827. Moving throughout the Southeast for the next decade, they established female academies, and George solicited patrons for his artistic services. It proved a successful partnership that achieved a prosperous living for their family before the Civil War.

Their financial success was in part attributed to their secondary careers: Catharine's as a writer and George's as a teacher and store clerk. Known as an eccentric and outspoken member of her community, Catharine published essays on politics and education, poetry, and short stories under various pen names. During the 1850s their academy, Winnsboro Female Institute, enrolled and educated hundreds of girls. George and their older children, then educated and matured, accepted roles as instructors in the school while Catharine served as the principal. Her contributions to female education in the antebellum South were felt from Virginia to Georgia.

The life of Catharine Ladd provides insight into how an educated Southern woman without a material inheritance pushed boundaries of class and gender to build commercial and social networks, adapt to change, acquire property, and achieve middle-class status in the South before the Civil War. Catharine proved that a woman—even as a widow during Reconstruction in the South—could have a voice and assert nontraditional roles.

Catharine's outspoken voice was often heard in her community, whether supporting enlistment in the Confederate army or urging citizens after the war to rebuild their town and resist negative voices.

Her pen beyond the community was anonymous, sometimes revealing a haunting melancholy attributed to private circumstances of her life that remain unproven. This was characteristic of the disparity between the public and private face of Southern females of the antebellum South.

Her life revealed the complexity of women living in her place and time. Listed in four contemporary biographies and seven in the twentieth century, Catharine's important contributions, once known, were forgotten. Her identity merits a new consideration in the annals of American women's history.

Part One

Catharine Ladd as Educator

Encounters with Truth and Myth:
Lafayette and Poe
Catharine Ladd's Early Years in Richmond

Facts about Catharine Stratton's genealogy are clouded in mystery and innuendo. The paternity of her mother, who grew up with the name Ann Collins, was not only unknown, but her inheritance was withheld, a fact revealed in the will of her stepfather, a man named John Collins. Her maternal grandmother, Catharine Collins Dabney, for whom Catharine Stratton was named, was married three times and had children by all three unions. Of her three husbands, it is known she outlived the last two.

Catharine Stratton was not born in time to know the two grandfathers who raised her mother, but she did live in the household with her maternal grandmother, Catharine Collins Dabney. Catharine Stratton grew up without knowing a father, as a child hearing the story of his accidental drowning. She may have had a brother, but there is no mention of it in the family history. Rather, Catharine and her widowed mother survived with a strong-willed grandmother and her extended family.[21]

Catharine Stratton was born in Richmond, Virginia, by 1808, the only child[22] of Ann and James Stratton. Her father disappeared before 1820[23] while putting out to sea from Norfolk, Virginia, although the circumstances cannot be confirmed. Catharine

Stratton's mother, Ann Collins Stratton, was the child of Catharine Collins Dabney's first marriage to a man whose name and circumstances are unknown.

It is certain that her grandmother's second husband was John Collins, a prosperous house carpenter and land owner of Richmond, Virginia.

The following facts chronicle what is known of Catharine Stratton's maternal family history in Richmond.

First is a glimpse into drama and intrigue. John Collins's will in 1794 named his children Ann, Jane, John, and Adam, all underage, as heirs, stipulating that:

> Item, should Ann Collins the daughter of my dear wife by her former husband acquire her fortune which I think is at Present unlawfully withheld from her in that case the said Ann Collins is to relinquish her claim to what I have herein bequeathed her which is to be divided among the other Children.[24]

What is known is that by 1798 Catharine Collins married a third time, to Humphrey Dabney, her deceased husband's apprentice, who thereon became guardian for the Collins children.[25] John Collins thought well of his apprentice, leaving Humphrey books on architecture and instructions to purchase out of his estate a chest of instruments with a silver plate inscribed "John Collins to Humphrey Dabney."[26] [27]

Following the death of John Collins, Humphrey Dabney exercised the trade of house carpenter, joiner, and lumberyard proprietor from 1795 to 1808.[28] In 1804 he advertised having 60,000 feet of lumber and "a valuable Negro woman for sale."[29] In 1805 he was elected magistrate for the city of Richmond.[30] Humphrey Dabney died before July 1809, [31] leaving his wife widowed again.[32]

In 1809 Catharine Collins Dabney gave public notice that she was closing the estate of her second husband, John Collins. In that same year the real estate of John Collins was distributed to his heirs, including Catharine Stratton's mother, Ann. "And to pay James Stratton and Ann his wife[33] the sum of $85.00: thirdly, we allot to James Stratton and Ann (daughter of said John) his wife's lot No. 6, [valued at $1000], they having sold their moiety of the lot No. 331 to Catharine Dabney."[34] At this settlement of real estate the total monetary value to James and Ann Stratton was $1,085, not including the sale of half of lot No. 331 to Ann's mother.

According to the 1810 United States Federal Census, James Stratton lived with his wife, Ann, and two-year-old Catharine in Richmond City.[35] Ann's widowed mother, Catharine Dabney, resided next door as head of household. The Dabney family included six children: a male under ten years [Albert G. Dabney]; a male age sixteen to twenty-six [possibly Adam Collins];[36] two females under ten years [Mary Ann and Susan H. Dabney]; two females ten to sixteen [Katherine and Sarah Dabney]; and one adult female age twenty-six to forty-five [Catharine Collins Dabney, age forty-five].[37] The other children, Jane Collins McCabe and John Collins (II), were living independently by this time.

In 1820 the Dabney household, with Catharine Dabney as head, included two females whose ages corresponded to Catharine Stratton and her mother. They now resided in Henrico County, Virginia, not Richmond City.[38] There was no male head of household, nor was James Stratton listed separately as a head of household in Henrico County, indicating the absence of father and husband. Clearly, between 1810 and 1820, Catharine Stratton's father became absent, perhaps deceased. She became part of an extended family that included her mother and her maternal grandmother, with no male head of household. Therefore, in the years between 1794, the date of John Collins's will, and 1820, when

a census was taken, their household varied from the widowed
Catharine Collins living with four underage children to the
remarried (and re-widowed) Catharine Collins Dabney living with
her widowed or single daughter, her granddaughter, and the Dabney
children.

According to John Collins's will, Catharine Collins Dabney and
her daughter, Ann Collins Stratton, as heirs, had some monetary
resources to assist their survival as widows with children. That is,
we can surmise, the Richmond tenement lots and houses inherited
from John Collins generated rental and sales income.[39] It is also
known that, in 1820, Catharine Collins Dabney as head of
household owned two enslaved persons: one male and one female.

There was additional income from the sale of John Collins's
personal property in Richmond, including plank, scantling, and
other articles of stock, and his plantation in Buckingham County,
Virginia, three-fourths of the proceeds of which sales went to the
children and one-fourth to his wife, Catharine. The final settlement
of the Collins estate was fifteen years after his death, as he had
stipulated in his will, when all of the children had come of age
[twenty-one].

It seems that the Dabney estate was not as beneficial to his heirs
as the John Collins estate. Newspaper notices from Humphrey
Dabney's estate settlement suggest that because neither Catharine
Dabney nor anyone else claimed the role of executrix, there may
have been debt.[40]

This fact, along with combined family living quarters,
exacerbated the difficulties of being women who were left to
manage financial affairs of deceased heads of households. Without a
reliable income, women faced financial hardships, and yet female
employment was limited to a small number of acceptable
professions, like teaching, millinery and dressmaking, and writing.

In these circumstances widowed mothers often moved in with married children.

In 1830 Catharine Dabney was head of household in Richmond City with three unmarried children in residence,[41] but in 1840 the census record suggests she lived with her widowed daughter Jane Collins McCabe. The 1840 United States Federal Census shows a woman seventy to eighty years old (Catharine Dabney was seventy-five) living in the household of Jane Collins McCabe in Loudoun County, Virginia.[42] With no further census records listing Catharine Dabney in 1850, it is assumed she died sometime between 1840 and 1850. There is no record of her burial place or date, or that of her late husbands John Collins and Humphrey Dabney.

Evidence found in the census records showed that the immediate and extended Collins/Dabney/Stratton family lived in and near Richmond until Catharine Stratton's marriage in 1827[43] to George W. L. Ladd. Her mother, Ann Collins Stratton, lived with George and Catharine Ladd until her death in 1856 at age 73 in Winnsboro, South Carolina. A letter written in 1866 from Emma Dabney[44] in Lynchburg, Virginia, to her cousin Albert Washington Ladd[45] in Winnsboro, South Carolina, indicated that Catharine's maternal family remained in touch throughout the years. In the absence of other documentation, these facts are the scant resources chronicling Catharine's early years. Late in her long life Catharine Stratton Ladd composed sentimental poems about her childhood that embellished her experiences of growing up, fatherless, in Richmond.

The capital of Virginia from 1779, Richmond was a center of politics and commerce during the period when the nation moved from an agrarian to commercial economy.

Richmond from the Hill Above the Waterworks/engraved by W.J. Bennett from a painting by George Cooke , c. 1834 [46]

With a population of nearly 6,000 in 1800,[47] Richmond was a port city on the James River where political and commercial people of importance walked to the capitol or courthouse and were easily recognized by its citizens. Thomas Jefferson, with his French architectural collaborator Charles-Louis Cle'risseau, modeled the capitol building after a Roman Temple in Nimes, France. The capitol was completed in 1800.[48]

It is possible her mother, Ann Collins, taught in a female academy in Richmond, an accepted vocation for a widow with some education.[49]

> Teaching was almost the only respectable calling open to women, and they also were inclined to look upon it as a temporary arrangement. Nevertheless, the teacher of mental ability, of high character, of attractive personality, was not only esteemed in Richmond, he—or it might be she—was even revered.[50]

At various times in her life Catharine Stratton Ladd testified in published accounts of her meeting the Marquis de Lafayette in Richmond in 1824. At that time Lafayette was on a Southern tour celebrating the anniversary of the American Revolution and the new American republic. The written reports of Lafayette's tour were detailed in newspapers, journals, and Congressional records, including his daily schedule and travel routes through cities and the countryside, celebrations, and speeches. Catharine's memories of her experience closely corroborated the written accounts.

The James River docks were busy with commerce, exporting tobacco and importing manufactured commodities from New England and Europe. Richmond boasted a theater where Shakespeare, Sheridan, and American plays, some written in Richmond, were performed regularly until 1811, when a spectacular fire destroyed the building. On the second evening of Lafayette's visit in 1824, citizens witnessed the arches of Capitol Square festooned with greenery and illuminated while fireworks were set off. Afterwards Lafayette attended the theater.[51] From 1811 to 1837 concerts and the circus were popular entertainments in Richmond, along with exhibitions of paintings such as "The Conflagration in Moscow" that were visited during the day and illuminated at night.[52] Growing up in Richmond exposed Catharine to a culture that sparked her imagination and creativity. Her observations of politics, commerce, and entertainment had lifelong influences on her teaching, writing, and civic involvement.

Catharine was educated in Richmond, for her ability to teach the English course, painting, and fancy needlework attested to her own formal education.[53] This fact of an education also proved that her family had the desire and financial means to provide Catharine with tuition, perhaps boarding, and money for school supplies. A typical fee schedule for the best female boarding academies in Richmond could cost two hundred dollars for a ten-month term, including boarding and ornamental subjects.[54] In 1820, when Catharine was twelve, she and her mother lived with her grandmother Dabney's family outside the city of Richmond in Henrico County. If she were a student at, for example, the MacKenzie school for young ladies or Mr. and Mrs. Turner's female school in the 1820s, she would have been a boarding student, but there is no documentation for this. Catharine Ladd's advertisements for female instruction showed that she taught fine arts—essential offerings in the eighteenth century and popular into the nineteenth century.

For example, her advertisement from Charleston, South Carolina, named ornamental subjects.

> Mrs. L.[add] acquaints the Ladies, that she intends taking a SCHOOL for teaching the art of Colouring and Painting Flowers, Fruit, &c. in a new method, called Poonak Painting, taught in six lessons. She will also teach Painting on Velvet and Paper in the usual way, likewise Embroidery, Bead, Wax, Shell, Chrystal, Ebony Work, &c. Charleston Courier, 1828. [55]

Friedrich Bruckmann Portrait of Edgar Allan Poe, printed in 1876.
"Courtesy of the Edgar Allan Poe Museum, Richmond, Virginia."

In 1811, Edgar Allan Poe along with his sister Rosalie moved to Richmond with his mother Mrs. Elizabeth Arnold Poe, an actress with Mr. Placide's company. Mrs. Poe died in December of that year. Edgar and his sister, Rosalie, were taken in by families in Richmond. Edgar went to live with Mr. and Mrs. John Allan. From that time until 1815, Poe resided in Richmond with the Allans, where he received instruction from William Ewing at Ewing's Academy (males only). Catharine was three to seven years old during the years 1811 to 1815. In 1815 Poe went to England with Mr. Allan for five years, returning to Richmond in 1820, thus making the claim of being a childhood playmate of Catharine, at least from her age of seven to twelve, impossible.

Although a study of the facts of their parallel lives in Richmond revealed that a childhood friendship between Catharine and Edgar Allan Poe was unlikely; however, it did bring to light where their paths may have crossed in Richmond academies.[56]

Poe attended Joseph H. Clarke's/William Burke's English and Classical School from his return until 1824. While a student there, Poe joined the Richmond Junior Volunteers who welcomed Lafayette in 1824. A possible crossing of paths for Catharine and

Poe may have been at the Monumental [Episcopal Church] Sunday School[57] when Lafayette was there in 1824.

> In the other churches of the city, also, the secular Sunday Schools must have been strong, for in 1824 Lafayette received four hundred Sunday School children on his visit to Richmond. It is possible that after returning from England in 1820, Edgar Allan Poe attended the Monumental Sunday School for religious instruction.[58]

While the stories about Catharine and Edgar Allan Poe's childhood friendship were disproved, recollections of her meeting with the Marquis de Lafayette were valid. Catharine claimed that she was among the Sunday School children who received Lafayette in Richmond in 1824, when he made a formal visit to the city. One of Catharine's reminiscences recalled vivid details of the Marquis de Lafayette's visit, which was interpreted in many texts like this one:

> On the next [second] day took place the formal parade and the speeches of welcome at City Hall. . . On the third day General Lafayette received the children of the Sunday Schools of the city, was presented to the pupils of Mr. and Mrs. Turner's Harmony Hall School and was made an honorary member of the Virginia Bible Society.[59]

Sixteen-year-old Catharine recalled standing with her Sunday School Union[60] class in review at Capitol Square when Lafayette worked his way down the line shaking everyone's hand. Her class presented Lafayette with a token of their esteem. Lafayette held her hand as he spoke of the sacrifices of Revolutionary War heroes and predicted the United States would become a great republic.

Catharine never forgot that experience, and in her ninetieth year in 1898 was able to state with alacrity in *The Richmond Dispatch* that

Lafayette's prediction had come true—the United States "now stands unrivaled in the world in size, strength and power."[61]

Gilbert du Motier, "Marquis de Lafayette" [62]

The circumstances under which Catharine met her husband, George W. Ladd, remain unclear, but it is certain that George Ladd traveled south to Richmond, Virginia, from his native New Hampshire after living and perhaps studying painting in Boston. With her marriage to Ladd in 1827, Catharine Stratton and her mother journeyed with him to Charleston, South Carolina.

Catharine Ladd: Beginning as Educator and Female Academy Founder, Charleston, South Carolina, to Macon, Georgia 1828–1838

Catharine Ladd used the opportunities she gained from her education in Richmond to forge a career in teaching. She set her sights on female academies where girls of the upper class learned basic academics and ornamental skills for social advantage. From the beginning, Catharine proved her abilities in both academics and fine arts by advertising subjects in all departments. She started in Charleston, South Carolina, with ornamental subjects and, with experience, increased her proficiency in teaching academics. She emphasized the importance of a collegiate course while continuing to offer ornamentals as long as they remained popular with parents. Although education for women evolved slowly, "The antebellum South was an innovator in collegiate education for women, which was explicitly designed to be the equivalent of men's colleges."[63]

From the early period of the New Republic[64] to the Civil War, the education of South Carolina women beyond basic reading and writing was limited to the children of the upper class. The growth of the new nation brought with it an increase in female boarding schools. An educated daughter was considered an asset to her family. Parents believed education enhanced her social status and improved her prospects for marriage, a constant concern of affluent land owners. The education of women reinforced a national ideology termed the cult of true womanhood or republican motherhood, which placed the responsibility for children's moral instruction on women.[65] Women were molders of their children's character, forming a son's future as a responsible citizen and modeling a virtuous path for daughters. Teachers like Catharine Ladd embraced the opportunity to influence children within a moral compass and an awareness of civic virtue.

Engraving, "Keep within Compass and you shall be sure, to avoid many troubles which others endure," 1785, London [66]

Local female academies were established either in the homes of prominent citizens or in schools built by subscription. Beginning in the 1790s, elite Southern female academies adopted the English course of study that was already offered in male academies. This particular course of study for males included arithmetic, bookkeeping, geography, history, elocution, English grammar, rhetoric, logic, and Greek and Latin.[67]

In the American South, a curriculum based on the classics remained a permanent feature, distinct from its Northern counterparts. Female instructors added astronomy, botany, Latin and French, and ornamental branches or polite subjects that included music, drawing and painting, and embroidery.[68] In the South, instructors were often recruited from institutions in the North, the most noted of which were Emma Willard's Troy Female Seminary founded in 1821 in New York and Mary Lyon's Mount Holyoke founded in 1832 in Massachusetts. The fiscal stability of rural Southern academies was a constant problem, given a lack of infrastructure and the tenuous nature of the business, resulting in a transience of both schools and teachers.

The school year of a female academy followed a predictable schedule: the year began in January after an enrollment announcement in the local papers in the late fall of the preceding year. Two sessions of five months each divided the year: January to May or June, and June to October or November. A spring break with a May Day celebration occurred, then in the fall a Christmas break followed examinations and graduations.[69, 70] Oral exercises or examinations were open to the public, with an announcement and a subsequent report in the newspaper about the students' performance. The end-of-year report by prominent citizens praised the students and confirmed the reputation of the teacher and her instruction, as well as encouraged continued enrollment. This was followed by a timely announcement for the January term.

Female academies in the antebellum South generally fell into one of three categories of organization: a proprietor/principal, a board of trustees, or a sponsoring by a church. These were not mutually exclusive. Catharine Ladd experienced all these arrangements throughout the Southeast from 1828 until after the

Civil War. The predominance of Presbyterians in the Carolina Piedmont and their commitment to education provided a favorable climate for the growth of both male and female academies. As a teacher and principal, the organization of her academies paralleled changes in female education the antebellum South. By 1850 female institutions increasingly offered a four-year curriculum of advanced academic studies.

Regardless of the type of organization, all academic institutions depended for their success on the income from tuition.[71] The following summary of the Ladds' experiences clearly illustrates this path, beginning with Catharine's teaching in Charleston, South Carolina, to her becoming principal of Winnsboro Female Institute; from a lack of sufficient tuition to a fiscally profitable operation.

George and Catharine ran an ad in the *Charleston Courier* for painting and teaching from December 1828 through January 1829.

> Portrait and Miniature Painting.
> Mr. Ladd,(from the North) most respectfully informs the Ladies and Gentlemen of this place, that he intends to remain here for a season, and would be happy to devote his professional services, to those who may want LIKENESSES, Old PAINTINGS cleaned and repaired equal to new.
> Mrs. L. acquaints the Ladies, that she intends taking a SCHOOL, for teaching the art of Colouring and Painting Flowers, Fruit, &c. in a new method, called Poonak [sic] Painting,[72] taught in six lessons. She will also teach Painting on Velvet[73] and Paper in the usual way, likewise Embroidery, Bead, Wax, Shell, Chrystal, Ebony Work, &c.
> Specimens can be seen, and terms made known by applying at No. 101 Broad-street, opposite St. Andrew's Hall.[74]

As an addendum to the advertisement titled *Portrait and Miniature Painting*, Catharine proposed a school where polite subjects of schoolgirl art would be taught. These included Poonah and theorem painting; fancy needlework in silk thread and beads; and ornamental designs in shell, wax [flowers and fruit], crystal, and ebony.

Wax work floral arrangement under
inverted glass bell on wooden stand [75]

In the advertisement the Ladds stated that "specimens can be seen," meaning portraits, repaired paintings, and schoolgirl art work. Most of the ornamental techniques originated in the seventeenth- and eighteenth-century European tradition of female instruction and remained popular until the mid-nineteenth century.

As the proprietor and instructor, Catharine was an entrepreneur who did not own a separate building for the school and who relied on her own resources to organize the curriculum. Catharine's widowed mother, Ann Stratton, who was born in 1783 in Virginia and who lived with the Ladds, was available to assist her. Catharine arranged a teaching schedule by the number of responses and spaces available "at No. 101 Broad-street, across from St. Andrew's Hall," their residence.[76]

The city of Charleston offered entertainment that appealed to Catharine's imagination: theatre, concerts, exhibitions, museums, and the circus. The availability of newspapers, magazines, and books provided access to the current political news, art prints, and publications. According to biographer Mary T. Tardy, [77] Catharine contributed to the Charleston newspapers and to journals edited by William Gilmore Simms. In January 1829, the inauguration of Andrew Jackson as President was a celebration memorable to Catharine in her later life.[78] In spite of the Ladds' accessible location in Charleston, they failed to gain an adequate income from school tuition and portrait painting. In March 1829 the name George Wm. Ladd appeared in the *Charleston Courier* on the dead letter list[79] and in October of that year an advertisement for *Portrait and Miniature Painting* appeared in the *Newbern Spectator* (Newbern, North Carolina).[80] There were no advertisements for Catharine's teaching in Newbern.

After a brief stay in Charleston the Ladds located in Fayetteville, North Carolina, in 1830. George Ladd's advertisement for painting appeared in the Fayetteville, North Carolina, newspaper several times.

> Mr. LADD. PORTRAIT, MINIATURE AND
> ORNAMENTAL PAINTER. Specimens can be seen at his
> house on Bow street. [81]

Fayetteville, North Carolina, on the Cape Fear River, was in Cumberland County with a population of 3,500 in 1820, just second to New Hanover County (with the port city of Wilmington). Fayetteville experienced the "Great Fire" of 1831, "one of the worst in the nation's history." Although no lives were lost, most of the homes and businesses, along with the best-known public buildings such as the old "State House," were destroyed.[82] If the Ladds were still in residence then, they may have been driven out.[83] In July 1830, George W. Ladd had unclaimed letters in the Fayetteville post office.

Catharine Ladd did not advertise as a teacher in Fayetteville, North Carolina. If she taught at an established school, her name was not published. What is notable in the 1830 United States Federal Census record is an entry in the George Ladd household for a male child under five years. The other entries correspond in age to George Ladd, Catharine Ladd, and Mrs. Ann Stratton. This may mean that George and Catharine had a male child by 1830. Son Albert Washington Ladd was born six years later October 15, 1836, in Chester, South Carolina, the first surviving child of record.[84]

It is interesting that, in the 1830 census, a George W. L. Ladd was also listed in Ricks District #4, Nash County, North Carolina, as head of household with no other household members recorded.[85]

> Mrs. Ladd will open a School on the first Monday in January, 14 miles from Raleigh, on the Northern Stage Road. The situation is healthy and pleasant with good society. [86]

A board of trustees hired Catharine to open a female school, Rolesville Academy, northwest of Raleigh, North Carolina. An advertisement in *The Star* (Wake County, North Carolina) newspaper, confirmed that Catharine Ladd was principal of Rolesville Academy that opened in January 1833; her pupils were examined in June 1833.[87]

She was in residence there at least by the fall of 1832, knowing that it took some time prior to the December 1832 enrollment advertisement for Catharine to find living quarters and prepare a school for her pupils to be examined in June 1833. The board received applications for this academy that offered an English course of study with an ornamental department. This reflected the addition of courses in geography and English grammar in female academies that were offered in male academies in the 1830s. The primary department at Rolesville Academy encompassed reading, writing, arithmetic, grammar, geography, and marking [plain needlework]. Advanced classes were natural and moral philosophy,[88] elements of chemistry, ancient and modern history, and rhetoric. Ancient history and rhetoric both included a study of the classics. Ornamentals offered were embroidery, painting, and music. With this experience Catharine taught and supervised a full range of academic and ornamental subjects. It is not known if she received tuition payments directly, had a fixed salary, or if she had assistance, including that of her husband.

It is undocumented if George lived in Rolesville while Catharine conducted Rolesville Female Academy in 1833 and 1834.[89] However, George Ladd's talents were relevant in teaching art as well as instructing other ornamental subjects like filigree work, bronzing, and gilding.[90] The second session began June 24, 1833.[91] No further advertisements were located after 1833, seeming to confirm the transient nature of female academies. A school run by a board was subject to fluctuations in ownership, board members, and principals, factors that often shortened its existence.

After this time until June 1838, residences for the Ladds remain speculative, within the following facts: A son, Albert Washington Ladd, was born October 15, 1836, in Chester County, South Carolina. In addition, two portraits were completed and signed by George Ladd during that time. One painting was a signed bust-length portrait of William Rosborough, 1835, a resident of Chester County, South Carolina; the other was a signed portrait in miniature of Matthew F. Maury about 1835, a resident of Fredericksburg,

Virginia. The combined evidence of the Rosborough painting signed by George Ladd and the birth of a child in Chester, South Carolina, indicated their presence in Chester in 1835 and 1836.

There remained the following gap of undocumented residences for the Ladds: in 1831 and 1832; from November 1833 to October 1836; and for the year 1837, with the question if and where Catharine taught during those years. During the early years of their marriage, George Ladd lived in Richmond, Virginia; Charleston, South Carolina; New Bern, Fayetteville, and Nash County, North Carolina; and Macon, Georgia. These locations were also the urban centers favored by successful portrait painters along the Eastern seaboard. Of those places, it is known Catharine Ladd lived with George in Charleston, Fayetteville, and Macon. During the first ten years of marriage, the Ladds seldom stayed more than two years in one place and were living apart for periods within those years. Catharine's mother, Ann Stratton, was a household member who could provide stability and child care. This was particularly true after the birth of their second son, Charles Henry Ladd, on April 1, 1838, in Macon, Georgia. Catharine continued to teach at the same time.

It is unknown how the Ladds travelled from one location to another, whether they travelled together, how George and Catharine decided where to go, or whether they secured employment before their arrival. Transportation by boat was possible in all the places they lived, due largely to the necessity of getting the staple crop of Southern agriculture, cotton, to Northern markets in an efficient manner. Steamboats and schooners sailed the rivers to the sea. Cargo boats had a few cabins reserved for passengers. Travel by horse-drawn coach along dirt roadways, often impassable due to rain, was tedious; plank and macadam roads were few. It was in 1833 that the first steam engine railroad (in the world) was completed from Charleston, South Carolina, to Bamberg,

South Carolina, but it would be years before train travel was commonplace in the South. Southern travel was a long journey regardless of how you went. For example, taking a cargo steam boat from Macon, Georgia, to the coastal port at Darien, Georgia, was a five- to six-day journey in a season of plentiful rain that made rivers navigable. From Darien the boat sailed up the Atlantic coast to New York City.

Undoubtedly the Ladds utilized nineteenth century networking with family, friends, and patrons to exchange information on employment opportunities by letter or direct conversation. In a study of Presbyterianism and female education in the Carolinas, it was clear that the clergy established networks that provided teachers, curriculum, and supplies from the North to the South.[92] In the North, there were placement agencies and personal networks used by graduates of reputable academies such as Troy Female Seminary to locate available teaching positions, many of which were in the South.[93]

Except for his portraiture in 1835 in South Carolina and Virginia, the evidence of, or absence of work, confirmed that George W. Ladd led the typical life of an itinerant portrait artist, that of being away from his wife and family for long periods of time. The separations were intensified in the rural antebellum South by a lack of infrastructure that posed barriers to transportation and communication, as well as a Southern society that could be closed to outsiders like New Englander George Ladd. Itinerant portrait artists in the North settled successfully in small towns and villages where customers were available within the surrounding area. Even the acclaimed Samuel F. B. Morse found in the international city of Charleston that his early success beginning in 1818 faded by 1821 despite family connections and talent.[94]

If George Ladd did find patrons during the 1830s, the economic returns from his investment could not have met his family's needs, especially weighed against the cost of travelling and boarding. Typical fees for the itinerant artist ranged from $1.50 for an individual portrait to $20.00 for a pair of paintings.[95] For a married man in the antebellum period, being unable to provide for his dependents would normally cause the husband shame, and he might forbid his wife employment in the "public" sphere.[96] "By working for money, a woman shamed male relations, exposing their powerlessness to support or subdue their social and sexual dependents."[97]

For example, Jacob Mordecai operated the Warrenton Female Academy in North Carolina as a family enterprise; however, the Mordecai daughters who taught in the academy were not compensated, nor given access to the financial success of the academy in 1818 when their father sold it for $10,000. Rachel, Ellen, and Caroline Mordecai served as teachers and managers of this and other academies for over five decades. Caroline, who remained single, later moved to Tennessee and Alabama where she ran female academies into her sixties. "Indeed, in 1854 she said she felt 'something like degradation' when collecting tuition money, a statement that brought her full circle to the impropriety of paid work with which the Mordecai women had contended since 1809."[98]

The future success of the Ladds in achieving middle-class status over the course of thirty-six years of marriage indicated they disregarded some societal norms and adapted to circumstances to meet their financial goals. As seen from the record of their travels and advertisements, Catharine was not hesitant to secure a position wherever she could achieve it, with or without George.

Catharine Ladd also received compensation through an occupation that was acceptable for women in the nineteenth century, that of a writer. Some female poets managed to save their family from poverty by this profession that paid well by the standards of the time, if one could bear the pressure demanded by the press.[99] Publications of the day were filled with women's contributions in poetry, short stories, and essays. Some journals were led by female editors, like Mrs. Hale of *Godey's Lady's Book*. Catharine contributed to literary journals, newspapers, and journals on education. Her life's work was recounted in ten biographies of Southern writers published between 1870 and 1999. [100]

In June 1838 a newspaper article in praise of a Presentation of a Standard "from the young Ladies of Mrs. Ladd's school," confirmed Catharine's location—and excellence as a teacher—in Macon, Georgia:

> The Macon Volunteers under the command of Lt. James A. Nisbet, received a Standard on Tuesday afternoon from the young Ladies of Mrs. Ladd's school. The colors were presented by two young ladies of the school, and a very beautiful address delivered by E.A. Nisbet, Esq. which was appropriately replied to by Lt. Nisbet. The Standard as a work of art, is highly creditable to Mrs. Ladd: the design is felicitous, and the execution excellent. The fair donor has [secured] the gratitude of the corps, for her patriotism in conferring this splendid present, and their admiration of her skill for the beautiful manner in which the work was designed and executed.[101]

The school had to be in existence for some sessions prior to the ceremony for Mrs. Ladd and her students to prepare the flag and presentation, although the name of the academy was undetermined. The astounding fact was that it was just two months earlier, on April 1, 1838, when Catharine Ladd delivered her second son, Charles Henry Ladd. Undoubtedly Catharine relied on the security of her mother's assistance during labor. "Whenever circumstances allowed, a woman's principal support came from her own mother. Southern mothers regarded parturient care of daughters as a natural duty, and most assumed this responsibility."[102] According to the newspaper accounts, Catharine continued her involvement with teaching along with her second pregnancy at age thirty, an unusual situation for a married female in the antebellum South.[103]

George Ladd announced the opening of his painting room above Mr. Oldershaw's store on Cotton Avenue in Macon in April 1839, and in May a testimony of his work as credible proved that he had already painted the likenesses of some Macon citizens. His residence was not documented previously in Macon, with the exception of the birth of a son in April 1838.[104]

In January 1839 Catharine Ladd taught ornamental subjects at the Macon Female Academy, whose principal was Mrs. Napier. Catharine Ladd also placed a separate advertisement.

> Mrs. Ladd having declined taking the Vineville Academy, has the pleasure to announce to the ladies of Macon, that she will open a regular Academy for the instruction of Drawing, Painting, Music, &c. at the Macon Female Academy.[105]

Parents of prospective students could apply with Mrs. Napier "or at the residence of Mrs. Ladd on first Street, near Judge Holt's."[106] This suggested the question of whether Catharine Ladd were previously head of Vineville Academy, for instance, when her pupils presented the regimental flag in June 1838.

Macon Female Academy was the final instance where Catharine Ladd worked as a partner or under another head of academy, although she had limited experience on her own in Charleston and Rolesville. The reputation of Catharine as a teacher grew through the years, enhanced her advancement, and placed her in a bargaining position to negotiate her situation. In 1839 the Ladds made an important move to York District, South Carolina, under the sponsorship of planter Dr. John S. Bratton. Catharine Ladd started the Brattonsville Female Seminary that began its winter term in January 1840. From the time Catharine established the Brattonsville Female Seminary until she retired from teaching, Catharine was always the principal of her academies. Advertisements for academies founded by Catharine Ladd name her as the principal. As Christie Farnham noted in *The Education of the Southern Belle*, reputable academies with female principals were not the norm after 1820.[107]

Catharine Organizes
Brattonsville Female Seminary

A national reform movement in the 1830s generated regional dialogue on many topics; education was one subject of interest. Articles that debated methods of discipline, instruction, and the merits of female education appeared in local newspapers. It was during this period that Catharine Ladd established Brattonsville Female Seminary on the plantation of a family with a strong Presbyterian heritage.

Homestead, plantation house of Dr. John Bratton c. 1825.
Photography by Mike Watts, Culture and Heritage Museums,
York County, South Carolina.

By 1839 the Brattons of York District, South Carolina, achieved what few families in the Carolina backcountry could boast. Dr. John Bratton, youngest son of Revolutionary patriarch Colonel William

Bratton, built the first large plantation house in the area, increased inherited land holdings, invested in cotton production, raised crops and livestock, collaborated with in-laws in a plantation store, and operated a sawmill, all with enslaved labor.

John and Harriet Bratton wanted to further the education of their seven daughters, ranging in age from five to fourteen. The oldest Bratton daughters needed advanced study, while the younger girls required a primary course. Dr. Bratton felt the time was right to remodel his father's log home for a teacherage and schoolroom. He believed it could be an academy for his daughters as well as neighboring girls if he secured a qualified teacher. Yet these ambitious plans were occurring at a time when cotton prices were falling, and the economic climate was depressed. Once again, the Brattons were ahead of their neighbors, seeing the financial advantage of a school at Brattonsville where boarders, neighboring girls, and even the younger Bratton sons[108] could be instructed. The boarding school option would be an incalculable expense for seven girls.[109]

Whereas many of their relations and neighbors sent their daughters to the Moravian Salem Girls' Boarding School in Salem, North Carolina, for at least two years,[110] the Brattons preferred to keep their daughters at home. John and Harriet Bratton's interest in educating their daughters reflected the prevailing notion of the planter class, who regarded education as a means of upward mobility. As well, their Presbyterian heritage carried with it an emphasis on the importance of education.[111] Dr. John Bratton's offer was attractive enough for Catharine Ladd to accept the principalship of a new girls' school; Mrs. Ladd named it the Brattonsville Female Seminary.

> To distinguish their level of coursework from that of ordinary academies, the term female seminary came into use. . . . A few

educators wanted to offer college-level programs, but they chose
not to use that title, either believing colleges to be inappropriate
for women or that society was not yet ready to accept them.
Instead, they called their schools female institutes or collegiate
institutes. [112]

The transformation of a former story and-a-half log residence
into an academy and home for the Ladd family was typical for rural
academies in the Carolina Piedmont. The log home built by the
founder of the Brattonsville community, Colonel William Bratton,
stood on the family property before the Revolutionary War. The
home also served as a tavern in the post-war period, being
strategically located at an intersection of several colonial roads.
After the deaths of William and Martha Bratton [1815, 1816], their
youngest son, Dr. John Bratton, and his new wife, Harriet Rainey,
resided there until the early 1820s, when they completed a Federal-
style home across the roadway. Following that time various family
members occupied the story-and-a-half log building. Dr. John
Bratton hired a contractor to remodel his father's home for its new
function. They plastered the interior walls; added glass-paned
windows downstairs in the parlor and two narrow windows high in
the west wall upstairs (for light); inserted a paneled front door with
glass highlights; re-floored the downstairs; and added a south wing
for the school room with six large nine-over-nine glass-paned
windows, a fireplace, and attic space above. There was an existing
small log building with a chimney and shed room in the yard on the
north side, as well as additional outbuildings.

The new occupants, the Ladd family, consisted of three adults:
George, age thirty-seven; Catharine, age thirty-one; and Catharine's
mother, Ann Stratton, age fifty-six; as well as two children, son
Albert Washington, age three; and son Charles Henry, age one. In
the 1840 census the Ladd household included two enslaved females:
one child under ten years and one adult between twenty-four and

thirty-five years.[113] When and how George Ladd acquired two enslaved females is unknown.

The circumstances of how the Brattons contacted and hired Catharine Ladd are not documented, but the Ladd family moved into the remodeled Colonel Bratton home at Brattonsville in the summer of 1839. It was a first experience in plantation living for the Ladds. They had resided in Southern cities like Richmond, on the James River; Charleston, a port city on the Atlantic Ocean; Fayetteville, North Carolina, on the Cape Fear River; and Macon, Georgia, on the Ocmulgee River. The new perspective and isolation must have been an adjustment for the Ladds. Brattonsville was located at the junction of several important roads, so having a store that also served as a post office and news center for the community was a natural advantage for the Brattons.

The Brattonsville store ledger provided a record of the Ladd residence in the summer of 1839. An analysis of the items purchased by George Ladd from the Bratton store in June 1839 through December 1841 shed some light on their lives and work.

Mrs. Ann Stratton's[114] name appeared late in June under Mrs. McNeel's store account. Dr. and Mrs. J. W. McNeel [Elizabeth] were Chester County neighbors of the Brattons, thus it appeared that Mrs. Ann Stratton boarded with the McNeels at that time.[115] Ann purchased five yards of lace. Then in early August Mrs. Ann Stratton, listed under George W. L. Ladd's[116] account, purchased a silver thimble.

Later in August the Ladd accounts showed an entry for Mrs. Stratton, who purchased a pair of children's shoes and five yards of brown linen [hempen cloth, a coarse fabric].[117] The only other purchase specifically under Mrs. Stratton's name was in September 1839 for [Hyson] tea.

George W. Ladd's store credit made him responsible for settling the account balance. Catharine Ladd's name was not listed as a purchaser or on a separate account, although other females such as Mrs. McNeel were recorded as purchasing items under a spouse's account. Items purchased under the G. W. Ladd account beginning in August 1839 were housekeeping objects, food staples, and supplies associated with the academy. In the household category were kitchen and dining goods for setting up housekeeping.[110] While most purchases were utilitarian, several luxury items such as a looking glass and Mrs. Stratton's silver thimble were on the accounts.

Food staples such as sugar, coffee, tea, spices, and condiments were regular purchases. The record does not clarify if the Ladds' enslaved females prepared meals for the family or students at the academy residence, or if they took meals at the Bratton's plantation home.

From their arrival in 1839 until January 1842 the greatest quantity of goods purchased by the Ladds were textiles used for household bed linens and clothing. Examination of the detailed list underscored the important role of seamstress for most women in the nineteenth century. Items included household textiles[119] and those used in the classroom for plain sewing exercises, for schoolgirl art (canvas for theorem and landscape painting), and for fancy needlework. Some of these textiles were suitable not only for the students' plain sewing, but for personal clothing and other projects,[120] as seen in the following transcription.

Textiles/sewing/needlework supplies

12 skeins Zephir [German wool for Berlin needlework]
12 yds bleached homespun
9 yds calico
4 7/8 yds copperas cloth
2 1/2 yds apron check
4 yds calico
2 flour [flower] patterns [Berlin work]
2 yds white homespun

3 ½ yds calico
3 yds. homespun
3 bolts cotton tape
2 papers of needles
1 silk bonnet lining
3 yds. calico
3 artificials for Mrs. Bell [silk flowers]
39 skeins Zephir
1 ½ yds fine colored canvas
3 spools cotton thread
3 yds black silk velvet

Textile purchases from Brattonsville store by George W. Ladd, March, 1841 [121]

From Macon, Georgia, to a new residence in York County, South Carolina, one could imagine the Ladds transported a few belongings such as bedsteads and small furniture, and travelling trunks with books, art supplies, clothing, and personal objects that they accumulated over eleven years of marriage. Otherwise household articles were sold or left behind to avoid transporting them. Whether they travelled by boat, wagon, stagecoach, or a combination of modes, the journey was rough and long, with delays expected due to inclement weather and the unknown. As George bought items for their new home and school, Catharine penned academy advertisements for the local paper.

Brattonsville Female Seminary
Mrs. C. Ladd, Principal

This institution is situated midway between the Villages of Yorkville and Chesterville, on the main stage road.
As an instructress Mrs. Ladd is well known; therefore it will be useless, again to enumerate the high testimonials of her qualifications.
Arrangements have also been made by Dr. Jno. S. Bratton whose residence is nearly opposite the Seminary to accommodate with board, all young ladies who may wish to become pupils of this

institution. Board can also be had at the residence of Mr. Samuel
Moore, situated about half a mile from the Seminary.[122]

It was a new chapter and a definite advancement socially and
professionally for Catharine Ladd.

Brattonsville Female Seminary, c. 1839, remodeled Colonel William Bratton home.
Photography by Windy Cole. Culture and Heritage Museums,
York County, South Carolina.

Catharine Ladd began preparations for the opening of her
school. She wrote an advertisement for *The Compiler* (Yorkville,
South Carolina)[123] for Brattonsville Female Seminary to begin in
January of 1840 with a course of study in the English Department
to comprise all branches: orthography [spelling], reading and
writing, arithmetic, grammar, geography, and history.

Schoolroom furnished with reproductions, Brattonsville Female Seminary.
Photography by Windy Cole, Culture and Heritage Museums,
York County, South Carolina.

The Brattonsville Female Seminary advertisement listed fine arts' subjects of music on the pianoforte and guitar; drawing, oil, and miniature painting; and ornamental and fancy needlework. School supplies purchased by George Ladd were some textbooks: *Days Measurator, Roberts Expeditious Measurator, Days Mathematics,* two spelling books, and quires[124] of paper as well as six portrait brushes.

In advertising for the Brattonsville Female Seminary, Catharine Ladd stated her philosophy on discipline that demonstrated her enlightenment:

> No corporeal punishment will be allowed; and pupils over the age of twelve, who cannot be managed by the force of reason, will be expelled. [125]

She departed from the current trend in female academies by requiring a minimum attendance of five months and defining a strict adherence to plainness in dress in her pupils.

No superfluous expense will be allowed in dress; and pupils will
be required to be neat but plain. No pupil will be admitted for a
less time than a half term of five months. . . . N. B. No pupil
who is a boarder will be allowed to go in debt for articles of
clothing, beyond the sum of $25 per term without orders from
their parents or Guardians. [126]

This was a time when female academies were accused of paying
more attention to social refinement than academics. Take, for
example, an excerpt from Miss Mary Bates'[127] report on female
education given before the female seminary in Pendleton, South
Carolina, in 1842:

In this section of the country, we have some difficulties of a
peculiar nature, with which to contend. While we rejoice that we
have been enabled to accomplish so much, yet we regret, in
many cases, the disappointment of our hopes. The early age at
which many scholars are taken from school, ere the mind has
reached maturity, is a source of deep regret to those who feel the
value of a systematic course of education. In regard to this,
public sentiment has, at the North, within a few years, effected a
favorable change; and the daughters of New England are now
reaping its benefits, while the equally gifted children of the South
are too often interrupted in the early stages of education, and
thrust into society, long before they are qualified to adorn it.[128]

Enrollment in Brattonsville Female Seminary included the seven
Bratton girls, some cousins, and neighboring girls. An estimate of
the number of pupils during the Ladds' term was twenty-five girls,
counting the seven Bratton daughters.[129] As students progressed
through the levels of instruction, they followed a prescribed course
of study in the English Department listed in the seminary
advertisement. This meant a girl's parent could not randomly
choose courses in fine arts without the academic course of study. If
a student entered for the full term, the tuition was reduced,

including all electives, to one hundred dollars, for a total of two hundred dollars for a year of ten months.

"Life's Young Angels" Girls of school age with guitar, and younger girls, 1841.[130]

Managed by district commissioners under the Free School Act, indigent students' fees were paid by the district to the teacher. In 1840 York District paid forty-eight dollars for four students, indicating they took the entrance level of instruction in spelling (orthography), reading, and writing.[131] Yearly examinations and promotions of pupils were based on the student's progress. Girls both purchased their own textbooks and copied passages from the instructor's collection of books and from text written on a chalkboard. Replicating passages of text by quill pen into copy books was a common teaching method with memorization and recitation as a regular practice.

The varying roles of the Ladd family members played out in traditional fashion and in non-traditional fashion. The enslaved females, adult and child, were essential to the operation of a female academy, performing daily tasks such as fire starting and maintenance, fetching water from the spring, gardening, cooking, cleaning, candle making, sewing, caring for the two Ladd toddlers, washing and ironing for the family and students, and attending to the personal needs of family and students. Undoubtedly they lived in the outbuilding that existed on the north side of the Colonel Bratton home, "a little cabin in the yard."[132] Archaeological evidence of a well-worn path from the slave outbuilding to the back entrance of the house into the kitchen facilitated domestic chores like cooking.[133] How the two enslaved females interacted with the enslaved Bratton community of over one hundred individuals is unknown. In one of Martha Bratton's letters to her brother John, she described the Ladd's enslaved female, Vina, by name:

> . . . I should like very much if Miss Poulton would stay so that you could see when you come home, she looks, talks, & walks as much like Vina (that is Mrs. Ladd's Vina,) as any two I ever saw, she allways [sic] has her mouth open and shows all her teeth when she laughs, a fault to which I am subject to myself, But why should I thus spend my opinion as she has never done me no harm. . . [134]

The use of enslaved labor allowed Catharine and her mother to concentrate their efforts on academy and family matters. Catharine served as principal and instructress of Brattonsville Female Seminary. Based on store purchases only, her mother engaged in plain sewing and fancy needlework.

As principal, Catharine filled a non-traditional role for independent female academies, where women were rarely in charge.[135] To many, it was considered undesirable for a woman to contribute to the income of a family; [136] in fact, husbands could forbid it. In the Ladd household there was no evidence that George objected to his wife's employment in the public sphere as a principal and teacher earning income. George Ladd assisted with the physical set-up of a school and household and served a managerial role of maintaining store accounts. On occasion he served the Brattons in the store by signing as a witness to debt payment.

As an itinerant artist, George was well qualified to apply his skills in instruction. In female academies, artists were hired to draw patterns on canvas, preserve completed needlework with varnish, and frame the girls' painting and needlework. [137] In Miss Lambert's *Handbook of Needlework*, she advised about drawing patterns on canvas.

> Landscapes, figure pieces, still life, and animals, even when properly drawn on the material, require the talent of an artist to execute. [138]

Evidence of George's independent work as an itinerant artist during this time is absent. No portraits of the Dr. John Bratton family were attributed to George Ladd. [139]

A collection of surviving letters written by the oldest Bratton daughter, Martha, revealed details of the girls' experience as students in Brattonsville Female Seminary. [140] Martha's three oldest brothers, John, Rufus, and Samuel Edward, attended South Carolina College in Columbia during the time she attended school. She wrote regularly to John about the news and gossip of home. The letters provide insight into the relationships of the teachers, students, and Bratton family.

In January 1840, when Martha Bratton was fifteen, she wrote to her brother John, confirming that under Catharine Ladd's leadership academic studies were rigorous:

> . . . the school is still going on usual and we expect two more scholars in the course of this week I have to study very hard these days and my studies are Geography Grammar History Rhetoric Reading and writing and I can play three pieces in music . . .[141]

Three years later, on February 16, 1843, Martha wrote about taking harp instruction and Latin under the McWhorters, who were teachers after Catharine Ladd:

> Dear Brother Jack[142]
> I promised in Rufus's letter to write by the next mail, but as your favorite was coming here Monday, I thought it best to wait, until today, Uncle Steele[143] was here for dinner on his way home, he says Mat[144] looks as well as ever, John it is getting dark and you must wait until I eat my supper,
> I have just returned from supper and when I went in I found a Northern Gentleman he is quite handsome indeed, I understand that the new Harp [is] in Columbia which I am sorry to hear, I regret now that I ever had seen a Harp, or old Puck eye [Pucci][145] either I am just as busy as a Bee in [a] bucket-studying for life I find Latin very difficult but I do not wish (as you said I would) that I had ever commenced. tell Mat she may think she is studying very hard, but if she was to see me she would not say so...[146]

Catharine Ladd used newspaper advertisements and printed circulars for advertising her academies and curriculum. In December 1840 she publicized a poem written by fifteen-year-old Martha Bratton. Catharine introduced the poem with an

endorsement of her student, and quoted the Biblical verse that was
the religious theme of the poem.

> To The Editor: Sir, I have sent you the following lines for
> publication, they are the first productions of a young pupil of
> mine; they do credit for one so young, and I deemed them
> worthy of meeting the public eye:

> "And I heard a voice from heaven, saying unto me, Write,
> Blessed are the dead which die in the Lord." - [Rev. 14 chape.
> 13 v.]

> Lines on the Death of M.R.[147]
> By Miss Martha Bratton

> Farewell! Loved one farewell!
> Here we will meet no more;
> The voice of God hath call'd the[sic] hence
> To heaven's happy shore!
> No cloud was on thy summer's sky
> Bright was thy young heart's youthful dream;
> Bright as the sparkling dew drop when,
> Touch'd by the sun's radiant beam.
> Tho' all that made life dear was thine,
> Calmly thy spirit pass'd away;
> The christians[sic] hope was thine to light
> Death's path to worlds of endless day.
> Why mourn we then, that thou art gone;
> Before us to that world of rest;
> That world prepared by Jesus' love;
> Where all who die in him are blest.[148]

Martha's poem mourned the death of a youth whose identity
has not been ascertained. In a time when death was ever-present,
the sentiment expressed an attitude of faith toward life and death
that was taught at an early age. As a published poet herself,
Catharine Ladd recognized Martha Bratton's creative gifts and

sought to bring attention to them. Publishing a student's poem encouraged others, while promoting the success of students under Catharine's instruction.

The paintings, poetry, and letters of Martha Bratton enriched the interpretation of the advertised curriculum at Brattonsville Female Seminary. From the two paintings and one poem that survived, it is obvious that Catharine Ladd encouraged the talents displayed by Martha Bratton. It is also indicative of how Catharine paid attention to her students' individual abilities and remained flexible within the curriculum to focus her teaching on those assets that held the attention of her students.

An announcement of a public examination of the pupils of Brattonsville Female Seminary appeared at the end of August in *The Compiler (Yorkville)* with the results published October 10, 1840:

> The examination of the pupils of the Brattonsville Female Seminary under the direction of Mrs. C. Ladd took place on the 1st and 2nd of October.
> We the undersigned . . . are persuaded that the exercises gave general satisfaction, to the crowded audience; no person could behold but with pleasure the industry and rapid improvements that each class had made in their respective studies. We consider the qualifications of the Tutoress to be equal to any in the state, and recommend the Institution to the public as worthy of patronage.

It was signed by seven men on the Committee of Examination. The school term ended the first of November and resumed on the first of January 1841.

Dr. John Bratton secured a teacher, a Mrs. Bassett, for music instruction on the pianoforte, but her abilities were limited as mentioned in the following letter after the departure of the Ladds at the end of term in December 1841. Dr. John Bratton wrote to his son John, asking him to help find a more versatile music instructor:

> Dear John,
> We are not altogether pleased with our music teacher. I want you to see the German if he can be got to come to Brattonsville, his name I believe is Mayer for three months or more and at what price. Our school is growing fast upwards of thirty scholars. Don't send the seed potatoes and candles until I send for them. We are all well. Mrs. Bassett can only play on the piano and we want one who can play on the piano and guitar. Let me hear from you by return mail if possible.
>
> Your father
> John S. Bratton[149]

. . . Miss Poulto°un [Poulton] speaks of staying and taking music lessons, Mrs. Bassette is going to New York where she has two children going to school,[150]

Homestead house from the back with detached dining room. Photography by Mike Watts, Culture and Heritage Museums, York County, South Carolina.

Dr. John Bratton's plantation home had a detached dining hall with a full basement connected to the rear of the main house by a covered breezeway.

The large windows in the dining hall made an ideal setting for teaching music, art, and needlework, and space for musical performances. After the music teacher Mrs Bassett departed, her replacement was a Mr. Pucci.[151] Daughter and student Martha Bratton commented on a concert held at Brattonsville in March 1842:

> I shall now tell you something about our concert but I suppose the old Lady[152] has given you a full description of it before this time, well there was but few hearers old Pucci was a little displeased but he had to take it out in displeasing,[153]

In order to appeal to popular trends, a female academy in the 1840s offered polite subjects that appealed to the parental point of view, along with music. Of the ornamental subjects, evidence indicated that drawing and painting took precedence over embroidery for Mrs. Ladd.[154] That fact made sense, knowing the talents of George and Catharine in drawing and painting. At their previous residence in Macon, Georgia, George Ladd publicized his occupation as a portrait painter, and Catharine was the art instructress for Macon Female Academy. She published an advertisement of classes that included oil and miniature painting:

> Mrs. Ladd from her experience in the various branches she proposes to teach feels confident in saying she can give satisfaction to those who may wish to acquire a scientific knowledge of Drawing and Painting. &c.
> The different branches that will be attended to, are as follows:
> Oil, Miniature, and Crayon[155] Painting, and Pencil Drawing, Watercolor Painting of landscapes

Fruit, Flowers, &c., on paper, silk, satin and velvet.
Shell and Wax Work[156]
Rug Work and Embroidery of scripture and historical pieces.
Music on the Piano and Guitar. Lessons will also be given in
thorough bass.[157]

This being the position Catharine held just prior to her Brattonsville employment, the curriculum detailed above revealed the breadth of experience she brought to South Carolina. Surviving examples of these techniques from her academies in York and Fairfield Districts include landscapes, paintings of fruit and flowers on paper and silk, wax work, and a Berlin embroidery work of scripture. Surviving works of art by Mrs. Ladd's pupils at Brattonsville were a theorem painting, an Italianate landscape, a landscape of Brattonsville, and a piece of Berlin needlework. An examination of the surviving works offers details on what and how fine arts were instructed at female academies. [158]

Two pieces of student art have been attributed to Dr. Bratton's oldest daughter Martha.[159] One is a theorem painting, a still life of fruit painted in oil on silk satin. The technique called for the use of stencils for each object in the composition. After the whole picture was planned and drawn on silk satin or velvet, paint was applied through the stencil in circular motions to achieve a variety of colors in each piece of fruit.

Theorem painting supplies, exhibit case, "Virtue Leads and Grace Reveals,"
2003 Exhibit, Culture and Heritage Museums, York County, South Carolina.

Martha painted a watermelon sliced open, with a knife inserted in the melon placed on a marble slab and surrounded by other fruits. This genre of schoolgirl art was meant to be displayed in the home as an emblem of achievement, like a diploma.[160]

Theorem painting of watermelon and fruit, reproduction by Marian
Manheim, oil on velvet. Collection of Culture and Heritage
Museums. Original by Martha Bratton, c. 1840 oil on silk,
Private Collection. "Image Courtesy of the Culture & Heritage
Museums, York County, SC"

The other surviving painting attributed to Martha Bratton is a landscape of Brattonsville with the Brattonsville Female Seminary building in the foreground, including the outbuilding beside the academy, the road, and the plantation home with its surrounding buildings across the roadway. Houses, particularly personal residences, in a landscape of trees with a river, blue sky, and clouds above, were popular compositions for schoolgirl painting and needlework. In fact, a student's father could request a particular house or building with a preferred style of architecture for his daughter's painting or piece of needlework. Its purpose was to feature the family's identity or status, not necessarily to depict an accurate image of the family dwelling. The trees that framed the composition and were placed in the Brattonsville landscape resemble the stylized foliage seen in other paintings of the period, even the more famous examples of schoolgirl paintings of Mount Vernon that were copied from printed lithographs.[161]

A painting inspired by Martha Bratton's Brattonsville landscape,
c. 1840. Collection of Culture and Heritage Museums
"Image Courtesy of the Culture & Heritage Museums, York
County, SC"

In Martha's instance her originality brought authenticity to the piece. She painted the scene of Brattonsville from the perspective of facing south down the road toward Chesterville. As the painter, Martha gained an elevated point of view, possibly by sitting north of the academy on a knoll in a cleared field shown in the foreground.[162] The practice of being outdoors for art class was a new technique in the mid-1800s and demonstrated an enlightened attitude about how students should be taught to paint, rather than the usual way of copying from a printed source. Or, Martha may have painted the scene by viewing it close at hand and then executing the whole from memory. However it was composed, she applied the principal of perspective as the road diminished in the distance. The extreme erosion in and along the road painted in the foreground presented a stark reality.

Brattonsville Female Seminary was in the foreground of the painting, with the Bratton plantation home and outbuildings across the road. The Bratton plantation buildings fronting the road presented a symmetrical design that was complimentary to the neoclassical architecture of their "hospitable mansion," as it was referred to by Mrs. Harriet Bratton.[163]

The structures flanking the plantation home on the north side, partially hidden by trees, were a brick kitchen, brick slave dwellings, and a log building close to the road. A detached brick dining hall to the back of the main residence could be seen in the painting. In the distance south of the plantation home is a "ghost" building that is either the Bratton store or carriage house.[164] Besides being an example of student art, this landscape painting of the Brattonsville plantation dated between 1840 and 1842 provided important documentation to the historical record.

Elizabeth Robinson, a day student from the nearby Fishing Creek community of Chester County, painted an Italianate landscape in tempera on paper.

Italianate painting by Elizabeth Robinson, reproduction of original, tempera on paper. Original and reproduction Collection of Culture and Heritage Museums. "Image Courtesy of the Culture & Heritage Museums, York County, SC"

It bears the inscription: *Elizabeth Robinson, Brattonsville Academy, Miss Ladd, Teacher.* During the mid-nineteenth century the Italianate fascination influenced architecture, decorative arts, art, music, literature, and fashion.

Mrs. Ladd lived during and was knowledgeable of the Romantic Movement and taste in the arts, and she had access to published materials like prints to use as inspiration. The specific source for this painting is unknown. There is an Italianate landscape mural painted on canvas that covers all four walls in a house parlor in Lowrys, south of Brattonsville. It is very reminiscent of the painting by Elizabeth Robinson.[165]

Catharine Ladd advertised embroidery as part of the fine arts curriculum. George Ladd purchased specialty textiles from the Bratton store, indicating that embroidery was taught.[166] Over the two-year period George Ladd purchased fifty-two skeins of zephur [zephyr] wool,[167] two skeins of silk thread, and three spools of cotton thread. Zephyr wool was the best German wool for stitching Berlin work, a type of needlework. This evidence, as well as the purchase of flower patterns, indicated that the girls learned a type of embroidery called Berlin work.[168] The result was a needle picture of flowers, an animal, or an historical or religious scene, as previously advertised by Mrs. Ladd in Macon, Georgia, "embroidery of scripture and historical pieces."[169]

There is one known piece of Berlin work that survived in the Bratton family, with a line of scripture from the Lord's Prayer, "Thy Will Be Done," stitched on perforated paper[170] by Dr. John Bratton's daughter Elizabeth.

Berlin needlework, Zephyr worsted (wool) on perforated paper,
stitched by Elizabeth Bratton, c. 1840s. Collection of Culture
and Heritage Museums, York County, South Carolina.
"Image Courtesy of the Culture & Heritage Museums,
York County, SC"

Whereas no school bills describing the exact courses for the Bratton children exist for the Ladd's tenure, a bill from Reverend McWhorter for instructing the Bratton children dated November 1843 was settled by the Dr. John Bratton estate in 1844.[171] Compared to the lowest fees for a full term under Catharine Ladd, it appeared that the academy continued under the McWhorters with a comparable curriculum with fees established by the Ladds.

The bill revealed the details of which courses each of the seven daughters undertook during an eight-and-a-half-month period, January through to mid-September 1843—the second year following the Ladds' departure. All seven Bratton daughters took the English Branches, as did the youngest son, Thomas, age six. [172] Eighteen-year-old Martha elected French, Italian, and Latin, but she complained to brother John about wishing she had not undertaken a study of Latin.[173] Mary, Sophia, and Elizabeth took electives in piano and guitar. The three youngest girls, Harriet, Jane, and Agnes were in the second class of English, and their youngest brother, Thomas, was in the fourth class (entry level). Their total tuition bill for five months' instruction for eight children was $385.

The number of indigent students increased at Brattonsville Female Seminary. There were fourteen girls who qualified under the Free School Act for 1842 and 1843, resulting in $140 in tuition paid by York District commissioners to the McWhorters.

Catharine Ladd's success did not go unnoticed. In January 1842 Catharine and George Ladd left the school they began at Brattonsville and moved to Fairfield County under sponsorship of the Woodward family from Winnsboro. Before the Ladds' departure the Brattons planned a two-story brick building with a basement, inferring that the upstairs rooms were spaces dedicated to a growing female academy that reached an enrollment of thirty scholars by February 1842.[174] The Ladds can be credited with this success for establishing a female academy of repute.[175] At Brattonsville Catharine Ladd solidified her ability to run a female academy of high quality, establishing a reputation that earned her an invitation from planter families in adjacent Fairfield County.

Following the departure of the Ladds, Brattonsville Female Seminary continued under the Reverend Hugh A. McWhorter and his wife, Mary. Reverend McWhorter was a Presbyterian minister,[176] a native of Yorkville, South Carolina, who married Mary Harper, a native of Ireland, in 1841. His wife was an instructress in music and art.[177]

While the McWhorters led the Brattonsville Female Seminary through 1842 and 1843, the Bratton family experienced tragedy in the sudden death of Dr. John Bratton in April 1843. The free and enslaved families on the Bratton plantation family were recovering from a measles epidemic, as documented by a letter from Dr. Bratton to his son John.

> Brattonsville Feb. 10th 1843
> Dear John,
> I am just getting through the measles and am better.[178] Your Mother has the measles, the fever has left her the measles has not yet left her. She is doing pretty well and I am in hopes will be well in a few days. No more of the white family have taken. The Negroes have almost all taken and getting better.
> I want another bolt of bagging & coils of rope get it as low as you can You will have to get it from Crawfords You had better stay as long as you find the weather will suit to a[nd] as you get subjects.
> > Your Father
> > John S. Bratton
> NB Try to send the bagging and rope by some waggon who is indebted to me[179]

Like the Ladds, the McWhorters remained for two years before leaving to teach in Chesterville in 1844. For the next two years Mary A. Poulton was principal/teacher. Mary [Ann] Poulton was enrolled in Brattonsville Female Seminary from its beginning as a student/assistant who stayed on after the Ladds departed; she was frequently named in Martha Bratton's letters to her brother John as a female of interest. A school at Brattonsville was not documented again in the Free School Reports until 1854.[180] Whether a school existed in the interim period of 1845 to 1854 is questioned, but possible. The later academy in 1854 had both male and female pupils.

The Ladds in Winnsboro
and Feasterville, South Carolina
1843–1848

Catharine Ladd reached a phase of teaching where her success generated opportunities for new positions. As an example, in Virginia in the first half of the nineteenth century, a teacher's profile included many duties already descriptive of Catharine:

> Teaching was a business. . . . Teachers were therefore entrepreneurs, competing for students on the open market, and they were understandably preoccupied with the number of students they managed to sign on. . . . Teachers fought for patronage, bought or rented classroom space, charged what they thought the market would bear, kept accounts, dunned debtors, and took out ads in the papers.[181]

Two offers presented to Catharine Ladd led to new academies in Fairfield District, adjacent to York District. Around the time the Ladds began Brattonsville Female Seminary, the Osmond Woodward family from Winnsboro sent an ailing five-year-old daughter, Rebecca, to live with the Dr. Bratton family.[182] Osmond Woodward was a planter from Fairfield County who had five daughters and an adopted niece to educate. The Woodwards subsequently sent their two oldest daughters to Brattonsville.[183]

According to the reminiscences of Mrs. David de Verill Walker, Sr., a Woodward granddaughter, Mrs. Ladd approached Mr.

Woodward when he visited his daughters at Brattonsville, with the desire to open an academy in Winnsboro.

Afterwards the Woodwards sent their wagons and carriage to move the Ladds to Winnsboro. In November 1843 an ad appeared in the *South Carolinian* for Winnsborough Female Seminary stating the exercises "would be resumed on the first Day of January, 1844" and that it was "worthy of the liberal patronage it has received . . . C. Ladd, Principal."

Catharine conducted the "resumed" academy the previous year as documented by the 1843 Free School report. Mrs. C. Ladd was listed as teacher in Fairfield District for the year 1843, receiving sixty dollars for five pupils.[184] Other details of that seminary were lacking. Apparently not all went as planned, as another Fairfield County family attracted the attention of Catharine Ladd.

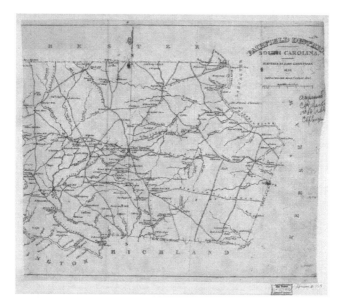

Fairfield District, South Carolina, Robert Mills Atlas, 1820.[185]

The arrangement at her next school was sponsored by a family who founded a Universalist community named Feasterville. The

Feaster (Pfister) family, of Swiss origin, moved south in the late 1700s from Lancaster County, Pennsylvania, to the northwest section of Fairfield County, South Carolina.

In 1836 John Feaster built the Liberty Church.[186] The Feasters were interested in agriculture, and they were also interested in the education of their children. This was the only academy with religious affiliation at which Catharine taught, and the second time her academy was located on a plantation.[187]

Feaster family history claimed that while Mr. Feaster attended a Christmas party in Winnsboro, he was impressed by Catharine Ladd's organization of the event. Later, when George painted a portrait of John Feaster (1844), Mr. Feaster remarked to Mrs. Ladd that she should be teaching in a school.

Her reply was that if she had a school she would teach; John Feaster proposed to build one.[188] Catharine received an offer in 1844 from John Feaster to teach at his newly built school, Feasterville Female Seminary. It opened in January 1845 "under the direction of Mrs. C. LADD, a lady generally known throughout the State as a teacher of high qualifications."[189]

Catharine Ladd served as principal of the academy from January 1845 until January 1849, under a board of trustees who set the terms of payment to be received at the end of the season or by note. The phrase "funds of the institution will be appropriated to the purchase of apparatus" taken from the advertisement indicated a possible trust endowment.

The Feasters built the school and a separate two-story frame teacherage/boarding house with a raised basement situated on five and a half acres, charging the Ladds rent for use of the facilities. Financial records documented that the Ladds received tuition directly from the Feasters for their daughters over four years from 1845 through 1848.[190]

The Commissioners of Free Schools for Fairfield District reported that Catharine Ladd received a tuition contribution of seventy dollars for seven indigent scholars in 1847 and thirty-six dollars for three indigent scholars in 1848 for the school at Feasterville, confirming the attendance of students other than the Feasters. Etta Rosson, a Feaster descendant, wrote a reminiscence about Feasterville stating that Mrs. Juliana Stevenson Coleman went to school there in 1848 and boarded with Mrs. Ladd in the "Boarding House." Other girls (day students) rode horseback from home.[191]

Feasterville Female Seminary, as it looked in c. 1844,
Fairfield County, South Carolina. Photography by Pat Veasey.

In addition to tuition there were fees announced for boarding, washing, fuel (firewood), and lights (candles).[192] The Ladds paid yearly rent on use of the academy building and the boarding house or teacherage. Students were required to "board at the Seminary with the Principal or with a nearby relative."[193]

George Ladd's roles at Feasterville were revealed in the Feaster family accounts. Given the account information about his activities, including the correspondence with Matthews Ripley & C of Charleston, it can be inferred that George Ladd was involved in the Feaster store operations, perhaps as a clerk or partner. Although no daily store ledgers were discovered, one correspondence in 1846 regarding the store at Feasterville was addressed to Feaster & Ladd.[194]

According to the financial accounts, George Ladd made improvements to the academy and teacherage, charging the materials and labor to their account:

> $107.41 Twelve months after date I promise to pay Andrew
> Feaster one hundred and seven dollars and 41/100 for work
> done and materials found on the academy at Feasterville.[195]

This and other receipts revealed that the Ladds paid for improvements they made to the buildings and grounds, including hiring of laborers, some of them enslaved, from the Feasters. On the Ladds' 1847 account with the Feasters, they owed $133 in rent [for living space in the boarding school and use of the academy]; advertising fees for the *Temperance Advocate* and the *South Carolinian* for printing a circular;[196] for nails, buckles and screw; for [enslaved] labor[197] of hauling and three days' work; plus interest on the total. In 1846 George Ladd owed the Feasters for splitting 950 fence railings and making a large gate; in 1848 he was charged for mauling 225 rails.[198]

The Feaster girls who are documented as students at Feasterville were children of Andrew Feaster: Caroline, Chaney, Julia, Sally, Narcissa, and Sophia, with ages ranging from eight to fifteen; and Drucy, John Mobley Feaster's daughter.[199]

Mrs. Ladd advertised academics to include: spelling, reading, writing, arithmetic, grammar and geography, ancient geography, astronomy and history for the entry levels; algebra, geometry, natural (physics) and moral philosophy, rhetoric, botany, Latin, French, and chemistry with use of apparatus for upper levels. Also offered were music courses in piano and guitar and ornamental subjects of landscape and flower painting in water colors; oil, mezzotint and poonah painting; and filigree, shell, wax, grotto work, and embroidery. [200]

According to a record kept by Mr. Jennie I. Coleman, Catharine taught music as well. "Mrs. Ladd, a fine musician, gave lessons to a number of girls, taught music, various kinds of fancywork, beautiful quilting, painting, and needlework of many kinds."[201]

At her former position with Brattonsville Female Seminary, Catharine Ladd illuminated her method of teaching art in the seminary advertisement:

> In the Painting Department, the pupils will be required not only to be good drawers, but to understand the principals of the art well before being put to colouring; will then receive instruction in both Oil and Water Colours.[202]

There are several surviving examples of schoolgirl art from the students at Feasterville Female Seminary. An entry of interest was "Wax work for Drucy . . . $8.00," substantiating that she produced a shade. (A shade was a composition of flowers or fruit of wax or silk supported by a wooden base and placed under a bell-shaped glass cover, meant for display in the home.) [203]

Wax work fruit arrangement under inverted glass bell on wooden stand. [204]

Mary A. Feaster painted an arrangement of flowers in 1848 using watercolors on paper. If she were the daughter of Andrew Feaster, she was twenty years of age at the time.[205]

Painting by Mary A. Feaster, 1848, watercolor on paper.
Collection of Culture and Heritage Museums.
"Image Courtesy of the Culture & Heritage Museums, York County, SC"

The painting is a balanced composition of flowers in a vase, roses in the center surrounded by blue tulips and asters, cherries dangling from one side and a bunch of grapes and strawberries at the base. She included bluebells, rose buds, and other small flowers to fill the vase. The penciled outline of the drawing can be seen at the edges. Details of the vase were drawn in ink and a wreath cartouche on the body of the vase enclosed the written word, *Hope*. According to the inscription on the wooden backing of the frame, Mary's painting was a gift to her sister Chaney, giving personal meaning to the word *Hope* inscribed on the vase. Borders of the painting were defined by double inked lines that crossed at the corners with embellished flourishes. The fine, finishing outline edge of the painting, the composition with its penciled lines, and the water colored flowers and urn demonstrated evidence of how drawing and painting were taught at Feasterville Female Seminary.

For the year 1846 Andrew Feaster paid ten months' fees for his daughters in the amount of $237.25.

Andrew Feaster to Catharine Ladd account for daughters, 1846

> 10 months tuition for Caroline and Chaney at $30. each
> 10 months tuition for Julia and Sally at $20. each
> 10 months tuition for Narcissa at $10.
> 10 months music for Caroline at $50.
> 10 months music for Chaney at $15.
> Drucy, no charge inpainting
> Wax work for Drucy at $8.
> 6 ½ months tuition for S. Norris at $13.
> Fuel for Sophia at $.25
> Use of piano for 2 pupils at $1.
> Painting for Caroline at $20.
> Painting for Chaney at $20.
> Total due and paid March 1847$237.25

1846 Account Bill for Feasterville Female Seminary for the Feaster girls: Caroline, Chaney, Julia, Sally, Narcissa, Drucy and Sophia[206]

It is unknown how many girls comprised the total enrollment; however, with a two-story boarding house and considering that nearly thirty girls attended Brattonsville Female Seminary in 1842 without a separate boarding house, [207] Feasterville's accommodations were ample.

Before George and Catharine Ladd left Feasterville, they settled accounts. Andrew Feaster paid "the amount of his tuition in full of all demands for the years 1845, 1846, 1847, 1848," signed by C. Ladd and G. W. Ladd.

The income from this enterprise appeared to exceed their expenses with the Feasters,[208] but most importantly opened new opportunities for Catharine to develop her academic pursuits. During their years in Feasterville Catharine gave birth to two more children, her first daughter, Josephine (Joe), in December 1844, and her third son, George Douglas, in 1845. From all evidence the Ladds were satisfied with life at Feasterville and the seminary; however, Catharine had an opportunity in 1849 to open her own female institution in Winnsboro. Feaster girls, Caroline, Julia, Sarah, and Mary, followed Catharine Ladd to enroll as students at Winnsboro Female Institute in 1850.

The Ladds' Achievement:
Winnsboro Female Seminary
and Winnsboro Female Institute
1849–1861

With twenty years of experience teaching, organizing, and leading female schools, Catharine Ladd entered the last and most successful phase of her educational ventures, made possible by her childhood privilege of an education in Richmond, Virginia. She achieved success by maximizing her talents, seeking the most advantageous positions, being flexible to change, not being afraid to advance her own causes, and negotiating with her husband and family as to how they might work with her ambitions for the future.

In January 1849, with the support of her family, Catharine Ladd left Feasterville to return to Winnsboro to head Winnsboro Female Seminary. Six years earlier patrons Osmund and Martha Woodward convinced her to move to Winnsboro as head of that academy, but in the interim she led Feasterville Female Seminary for four years.

Now Catharine was setting her own terms. She became the proprietor and principal of Winnsboro Female Institute. Her husband purchased the buildings and served as a teacher and administrator, and, as soon as they were qualified, their older children served as teachers. This advanced academy for girls lasted a decade and then reopened after the Civil War.

The advertisement in the Columbia newspaper in the fall of 1848 read:

> The duties of this Institution will be resumed on the first of January, 1849, under its former Principal, MRS. C. LADD, who has purchased the buildings[209] for the purpose of establishing a permanent school in that place. Mrs. L. will endeavor to make the Institution worthy the liberal patronage that has always been bestowed upon her exertions. The scholastic year will be divided into two sessions of five months each. The terms, including Tuition, Boarding, Washing, Lights, Fuel, &c., will be made known by circulars.[210]

The following year, 1850, there were forty-one girls boarding at the school, and additional potential day students enrolled.[211] The three oldest girls, age nineteen, were: Jane White and Margaret Lunfeson from Chester; and Mary Hammond from Lancaster. The average age of all enrollees was fifteen. The three youngest students were twelve. By 1850, girls twelve to fifteen were enrolled "in academies, seminaries, and institutes of a secondary grade; and twelve to eighteen in female colleges and higher level seminaries and institutes."[212] At female academies, pupils in a preparatory department could be enrolled by age ten with advancement dependent on her own pace through the book or material, so age did not necessarily determine class level.[213]

©Fairfield County Museum

Gold-plated medal awarded for achievement in Latin
to Priscilla Ketchin Ross, 1850. [214]

The Feaster girls, Julia, Sarah, Mary, and Caroline were among
the students. Most students lived in Fairfield County; however,
three were from Chester County, two from Richland County, two
from Lancaster County, one from Union County, one from
Columbia, and one from North Carolina.

The boarding students were listed in the 1850 United States
Federal Census under George as head of household, with George
and Catharine's occupations listed as teachers. Others listed at the
George Ladd residence were two teachers from Fairfield County;
Martha Holmes, age 18, and Isabella Coleman, age 18; and teacher
Louisa F. DaCosta, age 25, from Virginia.

The Feaster, Coleman, and McConnell families lived in the
Feasterville community, where Catharine Ladd had operated the
Feasterville Female Seminary. Isabella Coleman may have attended
school there as well.

Although George Ladd actively painted portraits during this
decade,[215] he also assumed a teaching role. Their school became a
full-time operation employing the Ladd children in the coming
decade. In 1850, Catharine and George had a family of five
children, three boys and two girls, aged three to fourteen, with their

last child, Annie, born the next year. The three oldest, Wash, Charles, and Josephine, attended school in 1850.[216] It is unknown where the Ladd children attended school, except for Dr. Charles Ladd, who was a student at Mr. Zion Academy/College in Winnsboro, then a graduate in medicine at the University of New York in 1859 at age twenty-one. It seemed likely the other two boys attended Mt. Zion Academy, a male academy of high reputation, and for Josephine, the advantage of attending her parents' school seemed logical and frugal.

In the ten years from 1840 to 1850 George Ladd increased his ownership of enslaved persons from two to seven: six females, aged forty-one to twenty-two, and one male child, aged six. As discussed in the chapter on Brattonsville Female Seminary and in the previous chapter on Feasterville Female Seminary, enslaved females completed domestic tasks essential to running an academy. With Winnsboro Female Institute being in a town near shops, enslaved persons might have been entrusted to run errands, shop, or make deliveries. Cheryl Junk's study of the Burwell School (female) in Hillsborough, North Carolina, asserted that female academies depended on enslaved labor.[217]

Katharine Obear, daughter of Reverend and Mrs. Obear, who operated another female academy in Winnsboro, recalled the "servants" who provided necessary labor for their school in 1859.

> We depended on candles for light. Our water came from a pump out in the yard not very near the house. Therefore many servants became necessary. It was Daddy Jason's job to cut the wood, bring in the vegetables from the garden, and cut up on the long pantry table the quarters of beef and whole hogs needed to furnish all the food for these young people. I can see him still with his long butcher's knife carving away and saying to me, if I came in, "I am the man that butt the bull off of the bridge" and all that rig-ma-rol, the rest of which I have forgotten. Then there

was Maum Beck, his wife, the grandest of cooks; two
housemaids, Maum Charlotte and Big Hester; then little Hester,
a girl of twelve who waited on everybody, and Mauma, nurse
and maid for Mother and Fin.
The servants' house was in the yard, a two-story house, with six
rooms, the center one being the kitchen.[218]

Catharine Ladd's mother, Mrs. Ann Stratton, who reached the
age of sixty-seven in 1850, if her physical condition required it,
could have had an enslaved adult or child dedicated to her personal
care like "Mauma" or "little Hester" in the above passage. Ann
Stratton died in 1856 at age seventy-three and was buried in the old
First United Methodist churchyard cemetery in Winnsboro.

Catharine Ladd, age forty-two at this time, continued to
contribute her poems and essays to periodicals and newspapers as
she conducted the duties of proprietor and principal of her school.
Farnham's extensive research on Southern antebellum female
education found principals had to be committed to long hours and
detail-oriented tasks.

The position of principal or president required long hours and
infinite attention to detail. Schools were operated in a personal
and patriarchal style in which all major decisions were made by
the head.[219]

This was the year Mrs. Ladd changed the name of her school to
Winnsboro Female Institute, like the renowned Mr. Marks' South
Carolina Female Collegiate Institute at Barhamville.[220] Girls could
graduate from such an institution like Mrs. Ladd's and subsequently
graduate from a college with two additional years.

Catharine assembled an impressive roster of faculty for the
announcement that the activities of the institution would resume
January 1, 1851. Her staff could offer a course to "embrace every
study calculated to give a thorough and finished education." [221]

With herself as principal, she named the following staff: Rev. G.W. Boggs; Miss M. B. Holmes, Assistant; Miss Jane Ferguson; Miss Jane B. Hall and Miss Mary Hill, Musical Department; Mr. J. R. Schorb, Professor of Chemistry and Philosophy; Mr. Henry Harris, Professor of French; Mr. G. W. Ladd, Painting and Writing Department.

This is the first instance where George Ladd's teaching duties were listed, indicating his specific subjects. Miss Holmes was retained from the previous year. Rev. G. W. Boggs was a Presbyterian minister from Pickens County, South Carolina. Perhaps he was an additional principal like those named in 1859. He and his wife, Fairfield native Isabella Adger Boggs, traveled to India as missionaries in 1832. After this, he migrated west to Arkansas, Tennessee, and Mississippi as a home missionary.[222] The music teachers came with credentials. Miss Hall had recommendations from Professors Hewitt and Seroburg, while Miss Mary L. Hill "comes from one of the first Institutes in the District of Columbia and with the best testimonials from Mr. N. Carusic, Prof. in Music in Washington City."[223]

Mrs. Ladd secured the talents of two distinguished men of letters on the faculty. Each became nationally and internationally known: a German, J. R. Schorb, one of the first photographers in America; and Frenchman Henry Harrisse, a noted scholar of early American explorers and exploration.

Mr. J. R. Schorb (1818–1908) studied at Hamilton College in New York where he "came under the tutelage of Dr. Charles Avery," who had studied the daguerreotype process in France under Louis Daguerre. In turn Dr. Avery tutored Schorb in the photographic process. Schorb began to travel and take photographs.[224] He came to Winnsboro as a professor of astronomy, chemistry, and "belle letters" at Mt. Zion Academy between 1850 and 1853. At this time, he also taught chemistry and philosophy at Winnsboro Female Institute. As the first photographer in the region, he may have influenced or instructed Albert W. Ladd in photography. Most interesting was that "Schorb had time to get involved in community affairs and was a member of a drama troupe known as the Winnsboro Thespian Corp."[225] This thespian troupe was founded and directed by Catharine Ladd. Professor Schorb left Winnsboro in 1853 for York County, South Carolina, where he taught at Yorkville Female Academy and Kings Mountain Military Academy. By 1869 he set up a studio in Yorkville and devoted himself photography.

The other gentleman of note was Mr. Henry Harris [sic] (1829–1910), professor of French, whose correct name was Henri Harrisse. Henri Harrisse lived in a Winnsboro hotel belonging to J. F. Gamble in 1850, listed under the Anglicized name Henry Harris.[226] He was born in Paris in 1829 and immigrated to America in 1840. Henry became an American citizen, graduating from the University of South Carolina with a Master of Arts degree. Between 1850 and 1853 he lived and taught in Winnsboro at Catharine Ladd's female institute. In 1853 he moved to Chapel Hill, North Carolina, where he taught at the University of North Carolina and studied law. As a lawyer, bibliographer, and historian, Henri Harrisse studied early American exploration and published many books on the topic. He returned to Paris in 1866, continued to write and publish, and served as an advisor on the Panama Canal project.[227]

Catharine Ladd's ability to attract and hire teachers on the collegiate level like Mr. Schorb and Mr. Harrisse gave her students an opportunity to engage in a higher level of thinking and scholarship, equivalent to or even above the level of curriculum and faculty in a male academy. It was an advantage to have Mt. Zion Academy in town, with its established reputation as a male academy of high repute, whereby Catharine could hire professors like Mr.

Schorb. Catharine's drive to locate and hire competent faculty alongside her husband and children served several purposes. She freed up funds to employ experienced faculty with a national reputation by using her (unpaid) family as teachers. She elevated the reputation of her institution, exposed her students to current ideas, educated her family by association with teaching scholars, and demonstrated her talents as a leader in female education. All of this supports the premise that Catharine Ladd owned her ambitions.

Tuition at Catharine Ladd's school was calculated according to class level and subjects. As a student rose from first to senior class, the tuition cost doubled to twenty dollars per session or forty dollars for two sessions of ten months. Languages were extra, with an added charge for use of the library. According to the 1851 advertisement, boarding, light, and fuel were seven dollars and fifty cents per month and washing one dollar per month. A boarding student's fees for ten months averaged $140 per year, up to $187, depending on her class and how many electives she took. Music was the most expensive course in the ornamental department at twenty dollars per instrument —pianoforte or guitar—per session. In addition to music remaining popular in the curriculum, other ornamentals were drawing and painting, and fancy [needle]work of different kinds. Their boarding school with forty girls plus some day students brought the Ladds a potential income of over $9,000 a year. Christie Ann Farnham found in her extensive research about antebellum education in the South that tuition from the primary and preparatory departments provided the most income and carried the ability of an academy to offer more advanced subjects.[228] The Commissioners of Free Schools awarded her school forty-eight dollars for four [indigent] scholars in 1849 and eighty-four dollars for seven scholars in 1850 and 1858.[229] The Ladds brought in additional income by charging rent for vacant rooms to parents or other visitors in town.[230]

In 1852, George and Catharine Ladd purchased the Ketchin house, a three-story brick home, for the Winnsboro Female Institute.[231]

According to a reminiscence by a Woodward descendant, next door to the Ketchin house were frame buildings used for dining and recitation.[232]

The Ketchin Building is a Federal style, three-story brick building, built by Richard Cathcart about 1830 in Winnsboro, South Carolina. The building was purchased in 1852 by George W. Ladd and used as the academy building for the Winnsboro Female Institute until 1862 when George Ladd sold it to Philip E. Porcher. The building currently houses the Fairfield County Museum.

Instruction in the primary or rudimental branches was added in 1854, at ten dollars a session. The first class subjects were writing, arithmetic, grammar, geography, history, and composition, at twelve dollars a session. The second class, in addition to the first class subjects, included philosophy, astronomy, rhetoric, and composition at fifteen dollars a session. Junior and senior classes "comprise all these branches that complete a thorough English Education," at twenty dollars a session. Fuel, with the use of maps, globes, and library, added three dollars.

The musical and ornamental department and modern languages ranged from ten to fifteen dollars per session for each instrument or subject, with a fee for the use of piano for practice. The advertisement suggested that an average fee for everything for five months would be from sixty to seventy dollars, depending on the student's class, and that a reduction in the fee would be offered for those enrolled for ten months.

The sessions of 1858 and 1859 marked the peak of success for Winnsboro Female Institute. Advertisements in the fall edition of the neighboring town newspaper, *The Yorkville Enquirer,* described a thorough English Education. "Board and Tuition in the English Department, including Music, Painting and Fancy Work, will not exceed $200.00 for the two sessions."[233] Then, prior to the beginning of the 1858 session, was the following endorsement in the Yorkville paper:

Mrs. Ladd's School

This accomplished lady announces the next session of her school in Winnsboro'. Many of our people remember Mrs. Ladd pleasantly, both as a lady and a teacher, and with them she needs no recommendation; but we would ask those who have not enjoyed this privilege, to turn to her advertisement and consult the large and respectable list of references appended. Mrs. Ladd has devoted her life to the business of teaching, and in all the departments of a young lady's tuition, she is thoroughly accomplished and faithful to her charge.[234]

In the spring, *The Yorkville Enquirer* printed an article about May Day, acknowledging an invitation from Mr. and Mrs. Ladd to attend the celebrations in Winnsboro, but admonishing the local town teachers and officials for not presenting a May Day celebration of flowers and female pupils in Yorkville.

The next year, in June 1859, the Yorkville paper published a glowing account of May Day at Winnsboro' Female Institute in detail. All the speeches and songs were written by Catharine Ladd. There was the usual May Queen and her court, with costumed heralds, canopy-bearers, scepter-bearer, and crowner. Two little boys visited the court as Robin Hood and his Merrie Men, marching about. Then came a personification of characters from classical mythology, the flowers of spring and Flora, and the queen of the fairies in an "air-borne" car. The evening ended with a grand National *tableau vivant*[235] "in which our national prides, as well as some other feelings, were particularly gratified to observe that Victoria held a prominent place attended, as she usually is, by Liberty, Peace and Justice." A national song was then sung by the school in chorus with accompaniment. Following the exhibition was a frolic and dance, promenades, and talks.[236] The first-hand report pronounced it the best of innocent entertainment available.

Winnsboro' Female Institute closed for the holidays in November 1858 and resumed in January 1859 with three principals, Mrs. C. Ladd, Rev. C. B. Betts, and Rev. J. Douglass. This was a once and only tri-administrative team for the school, indicating an increased enrollment and the burdens of managerial decisions for a large student population.

This year's advertisement mentioned discipline and moral guidance of pupils:

> The discipline of the School will be mild but positive. The aim
> of the Principal will be to instil [sic] a high sense of moral
> rectitude. Pupils will be allowed to attend any Church preferred
> by the Parents or Guardians of the pupils.[237]

Both men in principalship with Catharine were ministers. Reverend Betts was an Associate Reformed Presbyterian minister and Reverend Douglass's denomination was unknown.

Pupils were urged to board at the institute, although not required, but preferred, "under the immediate charge of Mrs. C. Ladd."[238]

Under new curriculum organization, the literary department consisted of the three principals and son A. W. Ladd as assistant. A French teacher was yet to be named, but the music and fancy work were taught by the Misses E. and S. Crossitt. Music instruction was in piano, guitar, and an additional new instrument for the institute, melodeon.

In the junior and senior class level, students now studied language electives Latin or Greek. George W. Ladd took applications and offered a new service: he would procure a piano, guitar, or melodeon for a student, fully guaranteed by him, with a ten percent discount for cash.[239]

As mentioned in the notice "Mrs. Ladd's School," the advertisement had an impressive list of over twenty references, beginning with Gen. J. H. Means, ex-governor of South Carolina, encompassing state representatives, and clergy from varied protestant denominations.

During the ten years from 1850 to 1860, Catharine's school flourished. From all appearances, the Winnsboro Female Institute was a permanent fixture with an established reputation. Applications were taken by George Ladd.

Winnsboro Female Institute continued operation until the Civil War, with a last advertisement in December 1860 for the 1861 session. Catharine Ladd, principal, listed her family members among the teachers: A.W. Ladd, G. W. Ladd; Miss J. N. Ladd, Oriental, Grecian, or Indus Painting.[240] Miss P. Baker instructed Music, French, Composition, &c.

The scholastic year remained the same since 1857; that is, two sessions of twenty-one weeks. Vacation began the third week in July. The fees varied little in the institute's ten years of continuous operation. The academic department provided a reward and recognition by a silver medal upon graduation.

Silver medal, Winnsboro Female Institute, awarded to student Priscilla Boyd, 1851. Collection of Fairfield County Museum.

Although George Ladd's occupation in the 1860 United States Federal Census was teacher and painter, no known portraits by him from the 1860s exist.[241] Catharine's occupation was teacher and the occupation of her son, A. W. Ladd, was artist (this designation included photographer).

Living in the household at the time the Civil War broke out were sons A. W. and George D. Ladd and daughters Josephine, Kate, and Anna Ladd. Their other son, Dr. Charles D. Ladd, was now a twenty-two-year-old physician living in Bossier, Louisiana. There were four others within the household this year as well: a music teacher from Massachusetts, Elizabeth Crossett;[242] and three students from South Carolina, Mattie William, 14, Emma Hunt, 15, and Laura Gibbs, 17. Unfortunately, it is not possible to use the census data in 1860 to determine the total number of pupils since they are not listed in one location. Mary T. Tardy's biographical entry of Catharine Ladd claimed that her school had up to one hundred students but did not specify the year. After eight years, the Ketchin house, their three-story brick school building, was still in use. The Ladds' reported real estate value was $10,500.[243]

There were no equivalent female academies in Winnsboro to compete with the staff, curriculum, and enrollment at Catharine Ladd's schools from 1844 to 1860. However, there were at least two other female academies in the 1840s: Winnsboro Boarding and Day School for Young Ladies, operated by Rev. and Mrs. Samuel E. Norton,[244] and a School for Young Ladies operated by the Obears—Reverend Josiah Obear and his wife Julia Saffery Obear.

The Obears were contemporaries of Catharine, Josiah being an Episcopal minister from Vermont and Julia being from London. They came to Winnsboro in 1841 to serve the Episcopal church and teach, but Josiah's respiratory problems caused them to return to Vermont in 1849, serving a church that could support them without having to teach.[245] They returned to Winnsboro in 1855 and advertised a "Boarding and Day School for Young Ladies." Tuition fees for the school were comparable to the Winnsboro Female Institute, but they conducted classes and boarded students in their residence, not in a separate academy building. In the 1860 United Stated Federal Census their property was valued at $3,100.

Josiah Obear's occupation was preacher and teacher with a household numbering eleven: wife, Julia; four children aged thirteen to three; three female boarding (students), Elizabeth Robertson, Francis Robertson, and Martha Harper, ages 20, 19, and 17; and two female teachers from Vermont, Susan A. Phinney [sic], age 38, and Bissie [sic] A. K. Parish, age 22, a music teacher.[246] Like the Ladd household, the Obears owned less than ten enslaved individuals.

Their daughter Katharine wrote a reminiscence of their lives in Winnsboro, describing the school in their home, with boarding students and teachers also living on the premises. Her account confirmed what Catharine Ladd experienced in 1858 and 1859, years of prosperity for Winnsboro schools:

> The next year, 1859, was a prosperous one. Schools were not graded then. Pupils from fourteen years to twenty sat in Father's room. Besides all English branches he had classes in Latin and Greek. Miss Finney taught the children from six years to fourteen. Miss Mackey taught music. She did not live in the home, but she and Bruce, her devoted poodle, came each morning. Mother also taught music,[247] both piano and guitar. Then she taught penmanship in both rooms, and had besides three or four classes in French. There was another teacher this year who lived with us—Miss Bessie Parish from Randolph, Vermont. She was young and very pretty, but unfortunately too tall, six feet. Dressed in the crinolines and flounces then in fashion, she spread over much ground. She was stupendous! She taught painting, drawing and different kinds of fancy work.[248]

It was no coincidence that the Ladds' success peaked in Winnsboro. In 1860, Fairfield County, South Carolina, ranked third in the state in free per capita wealth ($72,817 in 1996 dollars) and third in per capita wealth.[249]

The enslaved population statistics shed light on this prosperity—having enslaved labor made thriving possible. In 1860, Fairfield County ranked fifth in the state in percentage of blacks at 71.2 per cent of the population.[250] These facts support the presence of a wealthy planter class whose use of enslaved labor in producing a marketable crop enabled them to afford an education for their daughters.

The Ladds prospered in this heyday of Southern culture from 1850 to 1860, and Catharine participated beyond the gender boundaries set for women. Tuition from school enrollment enabled them to purchase a building and a full teaching staff. It is easy to infer by the evidence available that Catharine's reputation as a teacher and her leadership as a principal proved financially lucrative for the Ladds.

Catharine Ladd's name was synonymous with distinction in female instruction for nearly fifty years from the Carolinas to Georgia. The number of her students over those years reached into the thousands,[251] with her influence extending through the nineteenth century. Her impact reached beyond the boundaries of class in that some indigent white female students were included in her academy enrollment through the South Carolina Free School Act. It is unknown whether, or how many, enslaved women employed in her academies also absorbed an education, but it seems likely that, at least for some, vicarious learning would have taken place and that some of these women were literate as a result of association.

Catharine set her goals of excellence and pursued positions that furthered her ideas of a classical education with an emphasis on academics, grade completion, and graduation. All the while, she paid attention to the practical business matter of catering to the preferences of her students' parents, as they were the ones who chose their daughters' schools and financed their education. Catharine also shared her talents in drama, inspiring confidence in her students by their participation in plays and productions at Winnsboro's Thespian Hall. Her community involvement in the social life and entertainment for the students, like her elaborate May Day celebrations, added to her academies' success and popularity.

Long after she retired from teaching and moved to live with her daughter in the Monticello area west of Winnsboro, Catharine's community continued to acknowledge her contributions and generosity.

Resumption of Female Education
in Winnsboro after the Civil War
1865–1870

In the December 14, 1865, edition of the *Tri-weekly News* (Winnsboro, South Carolina), Mrs. C. Ladd published *A Card* announcing:

> I will commence the duties of my school on Monday 8 January 1866. I have procured the large building known as the Fairfield Hotel,—but decline for the ensuring year opening my school on the scale that I first intended. I will not admit more pupils than I can personally attend to. Provisions will be taken for either Board or Tuition.
> The Musical Department will be under the charge of Mrs. Mackey.
> Families wishing to procure competent English and Music Teachers can apply to Mrs. C. Ladd, former Principal of the Winnsboro' Female Seminary.

In January 1866 Catharine Ladd purchased the lot in Winnsboro "formerly known as the Fairfield Hotel property with all the buildings" from the heirs of David R. Aiken for five thousand dollars; the deed was recorded in March.[252] This was one of two major property acquisitions by Catharine Ladd after the war.

Catharine Ladd no longer had a monopoly on the female student market in Fairfield County. Beginning in December 1865, others, eager to escape the devastation of war elsewhere in the state,

appeared in Winnsboro to open female schools. One was Rev.
Aron G. Stacy, a Methodist minister who lived in Chester, South
Carolina, with his wife and two children before the war. He
established himself as principal of Winnsboro' Female Seminary,
advertising December 2, 1865, the first session to begin January
1866 with "the plan of our best Female Colleges," a certificate upon
graduation, and a primary department. Beneath Catharine Ladd's
published announcement of a card was the Reverend Stacy's full
advertisement with a fee schedule and an intention to pay particular
attention to the primary department. His fees ranged from twenty-
two dollars per session for the collegiate course to sixteen dollars
for the primary department, with twenty dollars for ornamental
branches, no charge for vocal music, and a contingent fee of two
dollars:

> These charges will be reckoned in specie, but payment may be
> made in paper currency at the rate which is customary at the
> time of settlement.[253]

In this last statement lay the entanglement for most residents in
1866: how to pay for goods and services after the war. No other
academy advertisements included a statement like this one,
specifying acceptable methods of payment, not even Catharine
Ladd, although her fees advertised in December 1866 for the 1867
school year were comparable to those of Reverend Stacy.

In March 1866, Reverend Stacy published the names of his
staff: Miss C. J. Whitaker, Instructress; Miss I. J. Whitaker,
Assistant; Miss M.S. Porcher, Ornamental Dept. That same month,
"A Patron" who observed the pupils' examinations, endorsed
Reverend Stacy's institution as "flourishing," and, in May 1866,
Reverend Stacy announced in *The Tri-weekly News* the outcome of
examinations:

> The examination covered a good deal of ground, was quite
> varied, and discovered an encouraging proficiency in the pupils,
> not simply in book knowledge, but in the principles underlying
> the several branches of study. Examinations are not appreciated
> as they should be by those mostly interested.

Reverend Stacy remained in Winnsboro one year. In December 1866, the house and farm rented by Rev. A.G. Stacy from Mr. G. H. McMaster was available, and on Christmas Day 1866, an advertisement for Mecklenburg Female College at Charlotte, North Carolina, posted Rev. A.G. Stacy as president.[254]

Four years later, in 1870, Reverend Stacy and his growing family of six children resided in Jefferson, Missouri.[255]

Other independent teachers offering instruction in Winnsboro were a Miss S. A. Finney at the residence of Miss Porcher; a Miss Peronneau with music by Miss Gaillard; Rev. J. Taylor Zealey, principal of Monticello Female Institute in Fairfield District; and Mr. Stewart at Salem Academy in Fairfield District. Twelve miles south of Winnsboro, Fairmount High School opened under Rev. James Douglas[256] and Rev. T. W. Erwin. The brief advertisement mentioned only the English course of study with no electives or student gender specified.

In December of 1866, the Winnsboro Female Institute resumed its advertisement with Mrs. C. Ladd as principal, jointly with Rev. Josiah Obear, former principal of the Winnsboro Ladies Academy.[257] This was the announcement of Winnsboro Female Institute's 43rd session:

> Having purchased the large and commodious building known as
> Bank Range, [258] I will resume the duties of this Institute on the
> charge of Mrs. C. Ladd, Principal of the Winnsboro Female
> Institute and Rev. J. OBear former Principal of the Winnsboro
> Ladies Academy.

> Tuition will vary according to classes from $15, to $18 and $22
> per session of twenty weeks.
> Languages, Ancient or Modern, Music, Drawing and Painting in
> Oil or Water Colors, a separate charge.
> The Musical and French Department will be under the control
> of Mrs. OBear.
> Board may be obtained at the Institute or with Mr. J. S. Stewart,
> Mrs. Rosborough or Mr. J. M. Elliott. [259]

Rev. Josiah Obear[260] had commenced his School for Young
Ladies in January 1866, but apparently Catharine persuaded him to
collaborate with her in 1867. From 1866 to 1867, Catharine Ladd
taught a limited number of girls, organized her new space, decided
to partner with the Obears, and located boarding for resident
students. As she clearly stated the prior year, despite pressure from
other competitors, her principles of excellence for her students
would not be comprised by accepting too many pupils.

Advertisements for academies in the ensuing years were
infrequent until August 1869, when a School for Young Ladies (the
former academy name used by the Obears) resumed under
Benjamin R. Stuart as principal. Mrs. Obear's School operated in
1869 and 1870.

In January 1870, the year that she was sixty-two, several
endorsements for Catharine Ladd as an instructress appeared in the
newspaper along with her advertisement:

> We direct the attention of our readers to the card in today's issue
> of Mrs. C. Ladd. She is an old, true and tried teacher, and
> deserves the patronage of the public.[261]

> Mr. Editor:
> The numerous former patrons of Mr. C. Ladd, cannot fail to
> notice with pleasure her reappearance as teacher of young ladies
> at Winnsboro. There is probably no other teacher who has
> educated more of the daughters and sisters of old Fairfield, than

this gifted and indefatigable woman, and we confidently bespeak
for her a full share of the patronage of the District, to whose
reputation for hospitality and learning she has contributed so
much.
Auld Lang Syne [262]

Boarding and Day School
On Monday, January 10, 1870 I will re-open a Boarding and Day
School. The scholastic year will be divided into two sessions of
20 weeks each. The English department will embrace every
branch that constitute [sic] a thorough education. Languages,
Music, Painting and Fancy Work, a separate charge. Musical
department under the charge of Miss M.L. Gaillard. The
Ornamental branches will embrace Painting in Oil and Water
Colors, Grecian Painting, Wax and Shell Work.
Boarding including washing $75 per session
C. Ladd[263]

Catharine continued to "embrace every branch" of "a thorough
education," which in her definition included electives in languages
and fine arts; however, this was her last advertisement. Despite
advancing age, she was making every effort to provide a quality
education for the female students in Fairfield County, but female
education as she knew it was passing by the wayside.

For forty-two years, from Charleston, South Carolina, to North
Carolina, Georgia, and back to South Carolina, Catharine had been
teacher, principal, and founder of academies to institutions for
female pupils. She diversified the curriculum to suit the times and
the tastes of parents, eventually evolving as an upper-level
institution of academics.

A public school system was yet a long way off for the South,
whose residents generally mistrusted government-run schools, but
formerly wealthy citizens no longer had the financial means to
sponsor private academies. An anonymous group of ladies
attempted to organize and offer a free school in Winnsboro, but, in

December 1866, had to admit failure. In June 1869, County Treasurer John W. Clarke published a notice that subsidies under the Free School Act would be paid to all teachers who provided services for the year beginning in 1867 for those presenting claims.[264] Under a Reconstruction government, one positive outcome was the creation of a national public school system under the Constitution of 1868; J. K. Jillson was the first state superintendent of education.

Unfortunately, political events of the second Reconstruction in South Carolina prevented progress in educational opportunities. In 1878 the former prestigious Mt. Zion Institute (male-only) in Winnsboro announced a school for boys and girls.

> A graded school in the English Branches and Arithmetic, for white children between the ages of six and sixteen years will be opened at Mount Zion College, . . . [265]

Those over sixteen years of age were to make a special application to Mr. Davis.[266]

The next year, in January, a notice to citizens "who return real or personal property" in School District No. 14 (a four-mile square with the Winnsboro courthouse in center) was posted to convene property owners to consider levying a district school tax. With this small step began a movement toward public-funded education. Given Catharine's relentless commitment to education, one could make a strong case that Catharine would have been a staunch supporter.

Part Two

Catharine Ladd as Entrepreneur

Letters of War: A National Flag, Confederate Volunteers, and "Our Irrefusable Loss"

Catharine Ladd followed national events leading to civil strife, including South Carolina's decision to secede from the Union on December 20, 1860, and the firing on Fort Sumter, on April 12, 1861. Catharine, born in Virginia, lived and taught in the South her entire life. She and her New England-born husband, George, lived and raised their family in the South for thirty-three years. She found herself embracing the formation of the Confederacy, a source of pride that refocused her fervor of dedication to a new Confederate Republic. As noted in the prologue, according to Devereaux D. Cannon, Jr. at least by January 1861, Catharine and George worked together to design a national flag for the Confederacy, and George's drawing included elements of the flag chosen by the committee. [267]

Catharine's letter of application accompanying the flag design expressed strong emotion. She added her patriotic sentiments about the flag design:

> I am vain enough if you please to term it so, (but I term
> it patriotism) to feel that I would wish no greater honor
> than to see the slightest ^thing I had a hand in, adopted
> by the Southern Confederacy.

She also composed a few celebratory lines:

> May it yet be unfurled,
> Floating proudly and free,
> O'er the bright sunny South
> And the dark rolling sea

Catharine then paid tribute to the legacy of Washington's Republic:

> Our great Washington fought for the principles we are now
> contending for, and thought he had secured them; may our
> young republic honor his memory with the name of Washington
> Republic, dating from the 22 of February, the day would then be
> kept to celebrate two great events. [268]

In presenting her letter to the committee, delegate William W. Boyce established Catharine's place in the female sphere in language that confirmed it:

> She is a lady of remarkable intelligence, whose path through life
> has been illustrated by all those virtues which adorn the female
> character.[269]

In other words, the letter was penned by a woman who adhered to the precepts of republican motherhood, embodying virtue in her actions and holding ideas that were within the expected boundaries of her sex.

Catharine's letter in its entirety revealed aspects of the Ladds' commitment to the American Republic and their willingness to adapt and embrace changing times in light of the coming civil war. In the letter itself, Catharine used language that reinforced her belief in a noble Republic, which is how she referred to the Confederate states.[270] Besides submitting a design for the Confederate national flag, her letter included other ideas and commitments.

Catharine suggested a name for the new Confederate Republic—Washington Republic in honor of George Washington.

She commended their three sons to the Confederate cause, an expected act of sacrifice for all mothers of her time. In the early years of the American nation, virtue was synonymous with a willingness to forgo private interests in pursuit of the public good.[271] During this period, women were recognized as the special progenitors of moral conduct in the family and community. That Catharine Stratton Ladd's life did demonstrate a high regard for public service and moral leadership was evident in the story of her life.

Catharine Ladd, as a founder of female academies and an art instructress, was particularly well-situated to carry out public acts of patriotism. On at least two occasions, she assisted her pupils in the painting of militia flags and arranged for her pupils to present them to military volunteer corps.

The first opportunity for a flag presentation was in Macon, Georgia, in 1838.[272] An article in the *Macon Georgia Messenger* described this flag presentation in May of this year:

Presentation of a Standard

The Macon Volunteers under the command of Lt. James A. Nisbet, received a Standard on Tuesday afternoon from the young Ladies of Mrs. Ladd's school. The colors were presented by two young ladies of the school, and a very beautiful address delivered by E.A. Nisbet, Esq. which was appropriately replied to by Lt. Nisbet. The Standard as a work of art, is highly creditable to Mrs. Ladd: the design is felicitous, and the execution excellent. The fair donor has [secured] the gratitude of the corps, for her patriotism in conferring this splendid present, and their admiration of her skill for the beautiful manner in which the work was designed and executed.[273]

Catharine Ladd's second known flag event was in conjunction with the adoption of the Confederate national flag in the winter of 1861. A new flag was presented to the "Boyce Guards," Company D of the 6th South Carolina Infantry in Winnsboro, as formerly mentioned in the diary entry of Mrs. W. W. Boyce for March 8, 1861:

> At the appointed hour the Boyce Guards, escorted by the Fairfield Fencibles, proceeded to Mrs. Ladd's Female Institute, in front of which the presentation was to take place. They were received on their arrival by Miss Minnie Boyce and her six attendants-Misses Sallie, Sue and S.W. Lyles, Pearson, Alston and Fannie Boyce-representatives of the seven States each of whom wore a breastplate, so to speak, bearing upon it in golden letters the name of the State they represented, surrounded by seven golden stars.
> Miss Boyce in presenting the flag to the company said,. . .
> The flag was received by Capt. J. N. Shedd, a veteran of the Mexican war, in some remarks eloquent with the spirit and patriotism that belong to the true volunteer soldier. [274]

And Mrs. W. W. Boyce's diary stated:

> March 15- All of us went to Winnsboro to witness the flag presentations. Minnie presented one to the Boyce Guards and acquitted herself admirably. Her address was simple but to the point, was responded to by Capt. Shedd who then handed it over to the color bearer, Mr. Jenkins an old Mexican war veteran. Our flag function took place at 12 o'clock in front of Mrs. Ladd's, and at 3 o'clock just opposite, Mr. Osmund Woodward presented one to the other company, I think named for him.[275]

In addition to having experience with flag design and presentation, Catharine was confident in her written expression. George expressed himself visually regarding his opinions by creating a flag design. Catharine wrote out her thoughts in a letter, giving credit to her husband for the design and pointing out what she added to his idea: a crescent moon surrounded by stars in a wreath.

Ultimately, the committee used an adaptation of what was largely George Ladd's design, excluding, as mentioned in the prologue, Catharine's suggested crescent moon. In the extant records of the Committee on Flag and Seal there were no acknowledgements to individuals as to credit for the adopted design. However, the *Weekly Chronicle & Sentinel* (Augusta, Georgia) printed a copy of Catharine Ladd's letter in its edition from February 16, 1861, six days after the letter was presented to the committee, and prior to the announcement of the chosen design. The Augusta newspaper printed the same letter as part of the published proceedings of the Provisional Congress of the Confederate States of America. There is nothing to indicate Catharine and George Ladd thought their design contributed to the final decision. Attribution for the flag design was not an issue at that time and place, but became a controversial discussion more than fifty years later.[276]

With eighteen years of residence in Fairfield County, Catharine and George were well-known educators and artists in the community. A New Englander by birth, George Ladd at age fifty-nine had lived and worked in the South for over thirty years, painting portraits and teaching in female academies. Their four youngest children were born in Fairfield County. In 1861 they were Josephine, age seventeen; George D., age sixteen; Kate, age fourteen; and Annie, age ten. Their two oldest boys were by this time living elsewhere.

All three of Catharine and George's sons served in Company G, 6th South Carolina Infantry, in the Confederate army. In May 1862, their eldest son, Dr. Charles H. Ladd, was appointed surgeon and assigned to a military hospital near Farmville, Virginia. He was transferred to Company K, 56th Regiment North Carolina Troops, in May 1863 and served through August 1864, although he was absent sick during that time. In December 1864, he was relieved from duty with the 56th Regiment.[277]

Their second son, A.W. Ladd, served in Companies D and G, 6th Regiment South Carolina Infantry. Their youngest son, George D. Ladd, served in Company G, 6th Regiment South Carolina Infantry, but later was transferred to Stuart's Company, Beaufort Volunteer Artillery. With only one surviving letter from any of them during the war years, that from A. W. Ladd to his sister Josephine, the particulars of the sons' personal war experience are unknown.

Another Fairfield resident, William Floyd Jackson, also served in Company G, 6th Regiment South Carolina Infantry with the Ladd brothers, and his letters home gave a few glimpses of the Ladd family during the war. Returning to camp from furloughs, Wash (A.W.) Ladd carried packages and letters from Winnsboro to Floyd Jackson. The letters identify the type of items sent from home and those collected by the Ladies' Relief Association, for which Catharine Ladd served as president. The constant and unpredictable movement of troops sometimes meant that boxes of food and clothing were stolen or lost, as Floyd Jackson's letters also make note of:

> Camp Taylor
> Near Orange C.H. Va.
> March 23rd 1862
>
> Dear Mother:
> I received yours sent by Wash Ladd [A.W. Ladd] last night also the box sent by Chas. Robinson. We have stopped here for the purpose of going into camp, reorganize & c. We are at this time laying out in the woods, the weather is spring-like. Genl.

Anderson thinks that there is no doubt about our getting furloughs. But will have to organize first.

Col. Winder has been appointed Brigadier General. he leaves us to-day.

This is the first opportunity that have had of writing we have been sixteen days on the road. I spent my birthday on the road with little or nothing to eat But will have my " birth-day party-" with the cakes that you sent.

I am quite well, and all of the boys the same.

In writing direct to Orange C.H. [Courthouse] Va.

My love to all hands [278]

Dear Mother:

I received your letters sent by Wash Ladd & Charly Robinson but as is too often the case the ham & hominy were lost. Wash's box was stolen from him at Gordonsville. Hereafter do not send anything of the kind unless you are <u>sure</u> that I will get them, for I would rather that you should enjoy them than the public. I have written to Father for summer clothes. All of my clothing that were at Manassas were lost. Please send me two coarse towels, also some thread needles & c.[279]

In 1862 Floyd Jackson's letters home complained about Catharine Ladd's aggressive campaign to get men to re-enlist:

Centerville Va Feby 25th 1862

Dear Father:

I write to inform you that I have re-enlisted "for the war" We have got our company safe. Thirty five men. All of my mess except Wm Cambell have gone in. Leut. McCombs I think will go home as recruiting officer. Shedd has not volunteered. I have written to you several times and told you I would not, but after a careful consideration I thought it would be best. Calls are a coming in every day urging us to re-enlist. (I do not mean from Mrs. Ladd of [sic] any of that kind) but from President Davis, Gov. Pickens, Genl. Beauregard, Johnston & Longstreet.

Phinney will be our Captain, for the Leut. I can not say. If things
continue as they are, we will be home by the 25th of March.
The news from Tennessee is still bad but I hope the accounts we
get are exaggerated. This now is the main point, and we need
every man we can get. I hear that a call has been made in S.C. for
ten thousand more men. It will very near clean her out, don't
you think?
We are all getting along finely.
Your affectionate Son Floyd [280]

. . . Capt. Shedd received a letter from Winnsboro, from one
who represents herself as a "Quiet Little Woman", the other day
urging us to re-enlist, we can all guess who it is from. She has
done more harm than good. Our men think that "a quiet little
woman" had better be quiet, and leave us to ourselves.[281]

George D. Ladd visited the 6th Infantry Company G encamped
in Virginia in July 1862, but was sent home for being under
eighteen.[282]

Besides using her pen to support re-enlistment and her
dedication to the Confederacy, Catharine joined the war effort by
serving as community organizer in support of the soldiers. She was
elected permanent president when the Ladies' Relief Association of
Fairfield County organized in 1861. Throughout the war the ladies
assisted "the sick and wounded soldiers of South Carolina"
wherever they served.

The women collected money and sent food, cordials and wine,
herbs, clothing, dressings, blankets and bed linens, candles, soap,
and personal items to hospitals and regiments. A list of
contributions by Mrs. Ladd included barley, five shirts, one bundle
sheets, three bottles blackberry cordial, one bundle of sage, and two
dollars in cash.

Despite their unsuccessful request to locate a wayside hospital in Winnsboro, in July 1864, the Winnsboro ladies sent one hundred shirts to the Central Association and one hundred dollars to each of the following: Wayside Hospital, the hospital in Columbia; Wayside Home in Charleston; and to the Reverend Mr. Yates for sailors.[283]

Catharine's daughter Kate Ladd Cureton, honorary member of the Pickens Chapter of the United Daughters of the Confederacy, credited her mother with keeping the soldiers supplied with clothing. Catharine donated her German tableware to be melted into bullets and her "fine telescope to the officers. . .with which you could see thirty miles."[284]

Catharine Ladd kept her school open at least to July 1862, and perhaps longer. Letters home from William Floyd Jackson asked if his sister Emma, age 12, liked going to Mrs. Ladd's school.[285]

In 1862, George Ladd sold the Ketchin house, the three-story brick building that housed the Winnsboro Female Institute.[286] By 1864, Floyd Jackson's letters indicated his brother Warny may be attending a field school,[287] and he advised his mother to delay their schooling until they could get a better quality of instruction.[288]

Through a surviving business correspondence after the war, it was known that Catharine boarded students other than her own during the war. She may or may not have been teaching at the time.

It is known that she corresponded with a lawyer named Mr. Daniel Horlback of Simons and Simons in Charleston from 1867 to 1868 to collect a debt.

She sent a financial statement to Robert Fishburne for the boarding of his sons Francis and Julius Fishburne[289] in 1864 at eighteen dollars per month, plus an extra charge of one dollar for wood. The boys in 1864 were age fourteen and thirteen. The bill of seventy-six dollars was partially satisfied with a payment of thirty-six dollars for two months, leaving a balance of forty dollars for nearly two months' board plus interest from January 1, 1865. She attempted to recover the balance through the lawyer, but did not want to pursue a lawsuit, as she wrote:

> Winnsboro Oct. 8
> Messers Simons & Simons
>
> Gentlemen
> I [sic] would be no use to sue a man who would not pay his sons
> board unless forced by law to do so;
> The sum is small but would have been something to me. Mr.
> Fishburn and his sons knew I was burned out, and lost every
> thing I had.
> Please accept my thanks, and my kindest regards to Mr.
> Horlback when you see him.
> Yours With Esteem,
>   Mrs. C. Ladd
>   Simons & Simons
>   Charleston [290]

Like his wife, Catharine, George Ladd navigated numerous jobs using his skills as an educated man. By 1850, as a literate male who owned real estate and enslaved workers, George Ladd was among the privileged class. George Ladd functioned in various paralegal capacities, from attesting to debt payments to acting as a court-appointed legal assistant or petitioner on behalf of clients.

When the Ladds lived at Brattonsville, he served the Brattons by signing as a witness to several debt payments.[291] At Feasterville, a letter addressed to "Ladd and Feaster" from a business in Charleston concerned a bill payment, indicating a role such as clerk in the Feaster store. He "served for the benefit of another" to sue or collect debts from 1844 to 1861 in the Fairfield District Court of Common Pleas. In this capacity, he would have been paid for his services, but a record of such was not found. He was also involved in a personal lawsuit in March 1861 when he succeeded in collecting fifty-two dollars and forty-nine cents from R. C. Woodward for a balance and interest due on a note.[292]

From 1849 to 1863, George Ladd engaged in several real estate deals in the town of Winnsboro. It is unknown whether he had bank accounts, so that source of tracking other conveyances was unavailable.

George Ladd's first real estate exchange in Winnsboro on record was in 1849, when he purchased two lots, 19 and 20, for which he paid $400. The deed was recorded within the year meaning he owned the property.

In 1852, George Ladd purchased the three-story brick Ketchin house, which served as the Winnsboro Female Institute building from 1852 to 1862, along with lot #53, for $3,500—paid and recorded within a month, the same year.

In 1855, George purchased lot #54, one-half acre, for $300, paid and recorded the same year.

In early December 1862, George sold the Ketchin house, the four lots he'd purchased, 53, 54, 19, and 20, and "outbuildings thereon situate[d]" for $6,000 "paid in hand to me." [293] In December 1862, George also paid a gentleman named Francis Elder $1,800 for a 58- by 109-foot lot, part in cash, with the balance recorded in February 1863.

His last conveyance, in June 1863, was the purchase from his son A.W. Ladd and Thomas H. Christmas of one-fourth acre with a house and a wooden building for $1,600.[294]

After the death of George Ladd in July 1864, the facts reveal that Catharine and her sons A. W. and Charles, as well as her daughter Josephine, separately bought and sold property in Winnsboro and Fairfield District at least through the 1880s.

George W. Ladd, who had remained at home while his three sons went to war, died from an unspecified infirmity in 1864 at age sixty-three.

His oldest son, A. W. Ladd, wrote about his father's death in a letter from Charleston to his oldest sister, Josephine, then age twenty, who was staying in Florida due to ill health:[295]

> Charleston, S.C.
> July 24, 1864
> Dear Sister,
> You mentioned in your last letter to mother that I had not written to you in some time. This is true, but it occurred not from a non-desire to spend a short time in corresponding with my wandering Sis, but on account of the many days that I have lost during the last six weeks; which loss has so far thrown me behind hand with my papers, that I have very little time to spend in the more pleasant relations of life.
> I suppose you have heard before this reaches you, of our irrefusable loss. Our dear old Father died on the 16th of this month. It came very sudden on us all; more so, I know on you, George and Charly, as you had no intimation of his illness and the first word you received of it was his death. This I know was very heavy on you and George, but, dear Sis, we should not complain at the wise dispensation that has called him hence. It is a debt that all must soon or later inevitably settle. Father had been with us a long time. We could not rationally expect to keep him allways[sic], and he had reached the ripe age of 63, not far distant from the "three score years ten," beyond which very few ever reach. It would have been greater satisfaction to the family could they have clustered around the bed of affliction, and shared each others grief; But a wiser power has willed it otherwise, and it is not well for us to criticise [sic] the justness of His acts. Kate and Anna were the only ones present. I did not arrive at home until 11 O'Clock at night; and he died about 12, M. It would not have been any more satisfaction, to him, to have had us there; as he was almost continually unconscious from the time he was taken until his death. His resting place is side by side

with grandmother, in the old Methodist church yard. Mother
wrote me not to persuade you to come home. This I certainly
will not attempt to do if you are contented in Florida, and your
health continues to improve. [296] Stay, by all means, and if you
ever want any money, I will send it to you. I came very nearly
sending you one hundred dollars some ten days since, but
Mother would not let me
I received a letter from George last evening. He was very well.
We have not heard from Charley in the last seven days. He was a
little unwell when we last heard. I am writing this at night after a
very heavy days work, and feel very tired; So goodnight dear Sis
try and be a brave girl under your affliction
With Love Your Bro Wash [297]

This letter from Wash to his sister revealed that, in this
instance, he acted as the spokesman between home and the
scattered siblings during the war. It also confirmed that Catharine,
now head of household, was the decision-maker whose wishes were
respected. Catharine had much to consider with her husband
deceased, her three sons away at war, her oldest daughter away in
Florida, and her two younger daughters, sixteen-year-old Kate and
fourteen-year-old Annie, still at home.

George Ladd's will of September 13, 1859, was recorded five
years prior to his death; it was executed August 22, 1864.[298] A
reading of his will, along with others either written or proved in
1859 and 1864 in Fairfield District, disclosed that his was unique for
its time in its simplicity and departure from the usual language of
antebellum wills.

The language of antebellum wills typically conformed to the
common law of the state, which denied married women the right to
own property. In George's case, the implications for his wife,
Catharine, were contrary to the norm and confirmed some unusual
conditions for her as a woman.

His will was among twenty-four wills[299] total on record in Fairfield District for the years 1859 and 1864.

Leaving a will was not considered essential for most people in 1864; it was reserved for those who owned substantial property to disperse to heirs. George and Catharine were not wealthy, but they were part of the rising middle class. George Ladd's estate could not be compared to the others with wills in Fairfield District whose wealth was calculated in the tens of thousands, but the fact that he owned enslaved persons elevated his status. Historian Walter Edgar stated: "Most of the accumulated wealth of white South Carolinians was in human property."[300] George was no exception, with four-fifths of his estate value invested in five enslaved individuals.

George Ladd was the only husband in the group whose wills were examined who left decisions regarding the estate division to his wife rather than dictating exactly how and what he wanted to be left to his heirs after his death. His children were not named, nor given real property in his will. He did not appoint his sons, daughters, or other individuals as executors. Instead, Catharine was named the sole executor of the will, eliminating others from the decision-making process. There was no evidence of a legal marriage settlement contract, a premarital agreement about property, between George and Catharine.

This was remarkable, as in most states, in the time up to the Civil War, under common and equity law, a woman's legal obligations and rights were, upon marriage, taken over by her husband. Upon marriage her legal status changed from "feme sole" to "feme covert," so that she was no longer allowed to own property. Any property a woman brought to the marriage belonged to her husband.

Consider a will by a gentleman named Richard Watson, in which he states that his wife was to have use of the enslaved persons and the plantation that she brought to the marriage, for her lifetime.[301] It was customary that one-third of the real and personal estate be left to the wife for use "during her lifetime" and the remaining two-thirds be equally divided among the children and/or their descendants. Wives did not have any decision-making ability about inheritance beyond their lifetimes.

Of the Fairfield County wills examined, there were a total of eight recorded in 1859, including that of George W. Ladd, and two more were recorded in 1860. (The fact that wills were normally left by only wealthy citizens accounts for the small number of examples.) Of the ten, none were recorded by women. Nine of them—all but George Ladd's—had large estates of land, plantation houses, and enslaved workers.

All had in common the use of traditional language. Take, for example, John Campbell, who desired his wife and daughter "be allowed the use and occupation of the house wherein they and myself at present reside." John Campbell specified that the yards and gardens be included to their use if either chose to occupy the house, likewise that the house furniture and certain contents be enjoyed by them. To his son, John Campbell left eight hundred acres of land and his gold watch, and to his daughter, money.[302]

In all the wills, executors were named other than family, except in the case of a gentleman named Thomas C. Means, who named his wife and brothers to serve jointly in that capacity. Executors were to act in the best interest of the deceased in settling debts, however that was accomplished, and several wills expressed the desire that property and family stay together. After that, the interests of the wife and children were to be foremost, the wife to have use of property and monetary support "during her lifetime," even if that meant selling land and enslaved workers.

Several wills specified that unmarried daughters could live on the plantation with the wife if they remained unmarried. Two men who did not have surviving wives, as well as one who had no wife nor heirs, left the executors to sell the estate in the best way to settle debts. A reading of these nine wills confirmed that most decisions were made by the husband and his named executors. If a wife remarried, she might lose her privilege to live in the house, and other inheritance would automatically be divided among the children.

What we can surmise of what Catharine Ladd owned at the time of her husband's death comes from the probate record, which held an inventory of the estate.

We know that, in 1862, George Ladd sold the three-story brick building housing the Winnsboro Female Institute and three adjacent lots for $6,000 "in hand." It is logical to think that, at this time, their academy—and the business of teaching girls—shifted to their residence. George Ladd's estate inventory of 1864 contained a school-related list of itemized property that inferred teaching in the residence, including: one dozen stools, one dozen chairs, school benches, books, a writing desk, ten tables, a chess table, and a pianoforte. Outstanding for their high value were a lot (an undetermined quantity taken as a group) of books at $100, and a pianoforte valued at $250.

Also, of high value were a painting of a ship in a storm valued at ten dollars, a bureau valued at ten dollars, and an extension table valued at fifteen dollars. Other categories of personal property were: personal furniture, such as bedsteads and bed furniture (linens); household goods; kitchen furnishings, such as fireplace items, a stove, and pots and pans; livestock of a cow and calf and three pigs and a sow; and five enslaved persons named Lucy, Henry, Anderson, Alex, and Ailsey.

From the probate there was no record of a sale, indicating that George Ladd died without debt. For widow Catharine Ladd, having no debt would have been liberating and meant she could continue with her present status.

The entire estate appraisal was $3,825, including five enslaved individuals valued at $3,000. The appraised value of the enslaved persons was nearly four-fifths of the estate.

A comparison of the gender and ages of the seven enslaved persons owned by George Ladd in 1850 to those eight listed in 1860 led to a conclusion that few were the same individuals.

There is only one known document that records a sale of George Ladd's enslaved property. It was discovered adjacent to the deed of sale in 1862 for the Winnsboro Female Institute building and four lots. The deed of sale, dated November 1862, stated that he sold two enslaved persons named as August and his wife, Lisette, both aged around sixty years, to Maria L. Porcher of Winnsboro for $600. In the 1860 United States Federal Census Slave Schedules (listing the number, age, and gender of enslaved persons by the owner's name), the ages and gender of the two oldest enslaved persons correspond to August and Lisette, but in 1850, August, according to age and gender, was not on the list.[303]

At George Ladd's death in 1864, he owned five enslaved persons, two females and three males. The ages of the five enslaved were not listed, so it is difficult to determine whether some were part of the Ladd household in 1860. As formerly stated, George Ladd sold a male and female couple named August and Lisette in 1862, accounting for the absence of two out of eight from 1860 to 1864. Another explanation for the discrepancy in number between 1860 and 1864 is that perhaps some of the Ladd children inherited enslaved individuals. One may have accompanied son Charles to Louisiana where he was a physician before the war; one may have gone to war with one or more of the Ladd sons; another may have traveled with Josephine to Florida as she recovered from illness. Others may have escaped or deserted the Ladd household before or after news of the Emancipation Proclamation by President Lincoln on January 1, 1863.

A clue to identifying one of the five named in 1864 might be the 1870 United States Federal Census in which domestic servants Lucy Hopkins, age forty, Harriet Hopkins, age fifty-five, and Edward Hopkins, age 5, were a part of the Ladd household, and, in the inventory of George's estate in 1864, one of the enslaved females was named Lucy. It is unknown if Lucy [Hopkins] was the same individual with the name Lucy in George Ladd's estate of 1864.

While there is little evidence, it does appear that George Ladd bought and sold enslaved laborers between 1850 and 1860. Because it was illegal by this time to engage in importation of enslaved persons, purchases were usually made through sheriff's sales for debt collection on mortgages, personal property, or through estate sales.

The Ladds' accumulated real estate and personal property at the time of George's death attested to a middle-class existence, but it would prove short-lived, due to the events of the next year. After burning Columbia, Sherman's troops came through Winnsboro in February 1865 and burned the business section of the town, as well as some residential areas, destroying Catharine's home and its contents.[304]

An account of the Union army in Winnsboro was written by W. W. Lord, Jr. as a reminiscence in 1910, published in *Harper's Monthly Magazine*. W. W. Lord, Jr. was the son of the Episcopal church rector who arrived at his assignment in Winnsboro in March 1864; his family were war refugees. Reverend Lord previously served churches in Vicksburg, Mississippi, and Mobile, Alabama, where he and his family suffered the depravations of war: near starvation and lack of necessities. On arriving in Winnsboro, he was greeted with a rectory supplied richly with basic foodstuffs and what seemed like luxuries to his family. "The bin was full of corn, the wood-shed full of wood, and the pantry well supplied with bacon, rice, and meal."[305] However, just a year later, Sherman's troops were headed toward Winnsboro after burning Columbia in February 1865. Reverend Lord and a small delegation traveled to the Union lines and asked for the troops not to burn and pillage their town of civilians, mostly women and children. They were met with disdain and warnings to return to their town quickly. The foragers and bummers arrived in advance of the army but moved on because the main body of the army was just behind them. Ten-year-old W. W. Lord, Jr.'s remembrance of the time was:

> Down-town, however, the torch was soon applied by the main body of the army, which had entered the village by another road, and the business portion of Winnsborough was at once wrapped in flames. Like truants out of school, these overgrown "Boys in Blue" played snowball along the fire-lit streets with precious flour; made bonfires of hams and sides of bacon that were worth almost fabulous sums in a time of such dearth; set boxes and barrels of crackers afloat on streams of vinegar and molasses that were sent flowing down the gutters from headless barrels; and fed their horses from hats filled with sugar, throwing what remained into the flames or the mud. In this wanton horse-play enough foodstuff was destroyed to have nourished the community abundantly for at least a year. [306]

By encamping in the Episcopal rectory, Brigadier-General Slocum of New York prevented further destruction of the town:

> Claiming that an extension of the fire line might endanger the headquarters residence, he organized a bucket brigade of bluecoats and saw to it that "Uncle Billy's" [nickname for William Sherman] house and the public buildings escaped the flames. [307]

Catharine was said to have saved her school building by securing a Union sentry to guard the girls.[308] She also instigated action that saved the Masonic jewels as well as a Masonic insignia painted by her husband.[309] That the Masonic Order was a sacred, secret organization throughout the United States that would provide a degree of respect and protection for its members, regardless of circumstances, was valuable information to know. Catharine was obviously savvy enough to understand this and use this knowledge to her advantage with the Union officers.

Always looking forward, widowed Catharine did not curtail her community involvement after the war, but rather increased it. Her positive attitude of moving ahead and not looking back was amazing considering her losses. In the next chapter, her considerable activities in Winnsboro are revealed as chronicled in the local newspaper.

"Mrs. Ladd Is in Charge:" [310]
Renewing a Life-Vision
in Reconstruction and Beyond

Catharine Ladd's early life experiences in the capital of Virginia, Richmond City, impressed her with visions of a promising future for the new American nation. She had held the hand of the Marquis de Lafayette as he challenged his audience of school children and adults to take pride in the future of the New Republic of America. It was, after all, the 1820s: the end of the Revolutionary era and its generation, and the beginning of a national expansion West, with new leaders who embraced exploration and development of seemingly unlimited natural resources.

Those years set her on a determined course of public service, aiming to inspire citizens to self-improvement as responsible members of society. She apparently was not deterred by her gender, but chose a profession dedicated to educating females. It was an acceptable career choice for a woman, although earning money outside the home sphere was not so favorable in Southern society. She apparently was not deterred by this fact either, and her husband, George, was willing to accept her determination.

As a teacher, Catharine promoted herself through advertising her skills in newspapers, circulars, and word of mouth or networking. According to the curriculum she offered, Catharine was educated in the English course, in fine arts, modern languages and Latin, mathematics, and the sciences.[311] Although she hired teachers in specialty areas, every principal had to be prepared for the likelihood that she would teach every subject as advertised, if necessary. Except for surviving examples of ornamental pieces, family letters (Martha Bratton), and receipts for tuition (Feasterville and Brattonsville), it was uncertain which of the advertised electives were taught by Catharine. Teachers were essentially entrepreneurs who competed for clients who were female students, as evidenced in these advertisements:

> Rolesville Academy, 1832
>
> Mrs. L. will use every exertion on her part to forward her pupils in the branches she intends to teach, and hopes, by the advancements held out, to merit a share of public patronage.[312]

And after the examination of pupils at Rolesville Academy, the trustees endorsed her abilities:

> Praise Mrs. Ladd
> Rolesville Academy
>
> The undersigned, Trustees of this institution, convened at the Academy on Monday, the 17th day of June, 1833, and, after patient and diligent attention to the examination of the pupils . . . think it no exaggeration to say, . . . that Mistress LADD, the preceptress of the above institution, may, with impunity, compare the progress of her scholars with that of the pupils of any other English institution in this section of the State . . .[313]

The parents had money available and the motivation to educate their daughters, because an educated daughter was refined, able to entertain guests in the parlor with music and intelligent conversation in several languages, and, therefore, would be eligible for a good marriage.

In Catharine Ladd's plan, girls should be as informed and proficient as their male counterparts, partly in order that they would be able to educate their own children in the skills of good citizenship. Catharine was also religious and promoted a high moral ground.

Parents wanted an endorsement of an instructor's intention to guide their daughter's moral behavior, desired a healthy location for the school, and were especially encouraged when a rural school located on a plantation was owned by a physician like Dr. John Bratton, who could care for their daughter in case of illness.[314]

Clockwise, top, left to right: Brattonsville Female Seminary, Feasterville Female Seminary, Winnsboro Female Institute.

Catharine's awareness of the importance of location was evidenced by the location of the schools at Feasterville, Brattonsville, and Winnsboro:

> The ideal female college or seminary[315] was built on the edge of town.

> The preferred setting for female schools was high ground within
> a grove of oak trees on which to build a two- to four-story main
> structure. [316]
> Indeed, the local female school was often the most imposing
> structure in the vicinity and a point of pride amongst its
> citizens.[317]

> This Institution (Feasterville Female Seminary) is situated in the North-
> west section of Fairfield District about 4 miles from Buckhead, in a
> high, healthy situation. Large and commodious buildings have been
> erected for the accommodation of boarders, and the funds of the
> Institution will be appropriated to the purchase of Apparatus, and every
> thing necessary to render the Seminary worthy of patronage.[318]

Within the academy environment, Catharine promoted her
students in various ways, at the same time bringing attention to her
school and to herself as instructress and principal. As mentioned,
her students participated in May Day celebrations by presenting
flags to military officers and their regiments. The girls, who were
part of the pageantry, received recognition in the local newspapers.
Catharine attended to the special talents of pupils, such as the time
she submitted Martha Bratton's poem about the death of a young
girl to the local paper in Yorkville, where it was published. In this
action, both the writer and teacher were recognized, and the pious
theme of the poem, accompanied by scripture from Revelation
14:13—"And I heard a voice from heaven, saying unto me, Write,
Blessed are the dead which die in the Lord"—established the
instructor's moral ground.

By the numerous surviving examples, it was evident that
Catharine and George's art education in the academy ornamental
department favored painting, as opposed to needlework. In several
advertisements, prospective clients were invited to view the
specimens of student art:

Specimens can be seen, and terms made known, by applying at
No. 101 Broad-street, opposite St. Andrews Hall.[319]

Mrs. L. invites all who can make it convenient to call at the
Academy and view the progress of the pupils.[320]

Catharine was aware of the importance of opportunities for
parents and the public to enjoy student progress. In a letter written
by Martha Bratton to her brother John, Martha describes a concert
for the public held at Brattonsville, no doubt to display the musical
abilities of pupils at Brattonsville Female Seminary.[321]

The reputation of Catharine and her Winnsboro Female
Institute were well known by the 1850s. She offered incentives of
certificates, medals, and diplomas to students at their various levels
of academic achievement. Several medals survived, attesting to their
importance. One was for achievement in Latin for Priscilla Ketchin
Ross, and the other for Junior Class Premium Reading for Priscilla
Boyd. (See images on pages 101 and 111.)

Attuned to changing trends in education, Catharine emphasized
academics, yet she continued to offer ornamentals to please and
attract parents.

As a successful business woman, Catharine had other methods
of attracting students. She knew how to attract pupils by offering a
discount: she advertised a lower tuition for students who attended a
full term of ten months.[322] By 1860 she relaxed the enrollment
period formerly allowed at the beginning of each session. Now
students could enroll at any time in the year, and those traveling to
school by train were met at the depot.[323]

In her role of principal, Catharine Ladd hired the faculty for
her school. She persuaded her family to be teachers. Her husband,
George, son A. W. Ladd, and daughter Josephine Ladd, who taught
Oriental and Indus Painting, were all instructors in 1860. This
saved the cost of paying those salaries to outside faculty and

enabled her to hire qualified others. She brought in extra money when there were vacant rooms in the academy building by renting them to parents, visiting family, and refugees during the war.[324]

One conclusion that can be made about the implications for Catharine Ladd in her husband's will was that she had more experience, and more latitude, in making decisions than other women of her time and place. As George stated in his will, Catharine could do as she saw necessary, using the real estate or money generated from the sale thereof to do as she thought best.

> I will bequeath and devise the whole of my estate both real and personal to my beloved wife for life with full power during her life by will or otherwise to dispose of any or all of my estate among our children according to their necessities to be judged of by her.
>
> Should it become necessary in the life time my wife to sell or exchange any part of my property she is hereby fully authorized and empowered to make such sale or exchange the proceeds of such or the property acquired by such sale or exchange to be held by her for life with the power during her life to dispose of the same as provided for in the first clause of this will.[325]

It must have been an amazing experience for Catharine to own control of property when it had previously been beyond her reach. As Joyce Warren stated in her study of women, money, and the law:

> Under common law, the wife's labors and the fruits of her labor were the property of the husband as head of the household.[326]

What choices Catharine, as a widow, made regarding her monetary inheritance may be revealed in the evidence of two deeds of purchase in Winnsboro in her name in 1866 and 1867. Catharine intended to continue her female school after the war, and, in 1866, she made a purchase of a town lot in Winnsboro that contained Dr. David Aiken's former Fairfield Hotel and all outbuildings.[327]

She paid $5,000 for the purchase in January and proved the deed in March. The next year she "secured to be paid" $10,000 for a large lot—one hundred by two hundred feet—adjacent to and south of the Court House on Congress Street.[328] Her advertisement for Winnsboro Female Institute began:

> Having purchased the large and commodious building known as Bank Range, I will resume the duties of this Institute on Monday, 14th of January.[329]

The deed was recorded in 1875 indicating that it was paid in full at that time. It is unknown how Catharine had money to make large purchases so soon after the war, unless she was able to secure inherited and saved money in the form of specie (coin). Ambiguities about the Ladds' financial life persist. For example, did the Ladds have cash saved from the academy business? Did they have a bank account? Did George make money through real estate transactions before the war? Did Catharine successfully secure specie (silver and gold coin) during the war? [330] Despite what those answers were, the facts of Catharine's life in the next three decades proved that she moved through those years as a self-assured and energetic woman.

By the 1840s, when Catharine and George Ladd made Fairfield District, South Carolina, their permanent home, she established a reputation as the social organizer in the community. Family history held that Catharine impressed John Feaster with the way she managed a Christmas party in Winnsboro,[331] a factor that led to her leadership of Feasterville Female Seminary.

The Winnsboro newspaper frequently promoted her role as one responsible for societal gatherings, especially for young people, even during her later years.

> The young people are looking forward to the entertainment at Buena Vista on New Year's Eve. To say that Mrs. Ladd is in charge is sufficient to insure success.
> Wishing you a pleasant and prosperous New Year, I will close, N'Importe [332]

It is worth speculating that Catharine could have been very influential if she had circulated in a more prestigious and political society like that in Washington, D. C., before and during the Civil War. Cokie Roberts discovered women of distinction from the North and South in Washington, D. C., functioning very like Catharine Ladd in Winnsboro:

> The sleepy little prewar Capital City went from being a social center for self-described belles to a place where purposeful women assembled to effect change. And it was not just the city that was transformed; it was also the women themselves. The antebellum belles spent their days calling on Cabinet and congressional wives or listening to debates in the Capitol galleries, and their nights at dinners and dances. Deeply political, they promoted their husbands' and fathers' careers and competed with each other for preeminent position in the Capital City's close-knit social circles.[333]

Catharine used a pen to voice her opinions and create poems, plays, and prose for inspiration and entertainment throughout her life. [334]

She was a proven organizer and director of not only social functions, but of dramatic productions at Winnsboro's Thespian

Hall. It was her action after the war that publicized Thespian Hall as a community gathering place:

The Thespian Hall

We learn that this Hall is now offered free for meetings of Clubs, the Town Council, and all public Town meetings also for the use of Fairs given by the ladies of any denomination, as well as for Histrionic exhibitions.

As we understand the matter the rent will not fall on any particular organization. It has been generally settled that a Concert shall be given, the proceeds of which shall be turned over to Mrs. C. Ladd, to defray the rent and erect suitable tables for the Fairs. It is to be hoped that when the Concert comes, the public will not fail to give it a crowded house, that Mrs. Ladd may be no loser by her generous exertions to secure a Hall for public use.

The Hall will always be lighted up and made ready for any of the above uses, upon notifying Mrs. L.[335]

She focused her attention on restoring the town of Winnsboro after sections were burned in 1865 by, for example, raising funds for rebuilding the Episcopal church. In March 1866 there was a call for a meeting:

Notice

We are authorized to state that a meeting of the ladies interested in the Fair to be given for the benefit of the Episcopal Church of this town, will be held at Mrs. Ladd's residence, at 10 ½ o'clock on Thursday morning. This notification, we are informed, is designated to embrace all the ladies of the town who may be disposed to lend their cooperation in the matter.[336]

In May, the above-mentioned Ladies Fair was held in Thespian Hall with Mrs. C. Ladd as one member of the committee to direct the event. Contributions in money, food, fancy needlework, or other goods were encouraged as donations.

The month prior to the fair, the Aid Association for rebuilding St. John's Episcopal Church gave a concert under the management of Mrs. C. Ladd. The *Tri-Weekly News* detailed an account of two-and-a-half hours of entertainment that was "a complete success":

> The first thing attracting attention was the new and beautiful scenery just finished previous to this Concert. The stage presents an appearance entirely in keeping with the well-known taste of Mrs. Ladd, who executed the paintings of the scenery which is henceforth to be an "institution" in the Thespian Hall.[337]

The entertainment included dances, vocal duets, solo piano instrumental music, and dramas. The main drama reviewed was *The Grand Scheme*, written by Catharine Ladd, which was declared "a charade that occupied one hour in the performance." The plot wound three schemes and several sub-schemes unwittingly carried on by the characters to accomplish a grand one. There was also "a comico-sentimental courtship" titled "Mr. and Mrs. Poe" that caused much laughter.[338] These fund-raising events for the Episcopal Church and a new church organ continued through 1869.

It is known that Catharine Ladd organized a drama troupe known as the Winnsboro Thespian Corp before the war, because between 1850 and 1853, Professor Schorb, who taught at Winnsboro Female Institute, was a member. Some of her plays, like *The Grand Scheme*, were performed by the troupe's actors. Visiting drama companies advertised in the local paper and engaged some local actors: Johnny Reb Minstrels, the Baily Troupe, and the amusing "Jedediah Bobbins' Singing Skule." [339]

After the war, there were balls and tournaments held, the latter supposedly to give an opportunity for men to remain fit in horsemanship at a time when membership in military organizations was forbidden. These physical events mimicked jousting with knights who vied for prizes and presented maidens with crowns. In October 1866, George D. Ladd participated as a knight.

Rentals and entertainments at Thespian Hall must have been very successful because in July 1870, the Town of Winnsboro enacted an ordinance "that it shall not be lawful for any person to represent publicly for gain or reward any play, comedy, tragedy, interlude or farce, or exhibit, wax figures, or show, or entertainment of any kind whatsoever, without first obtaining a license from the Town Council. " The license fee was five dollars "for all exhibitions other than those under canvass, and fifty dollars for all circus companies." The fine for any violation was fifty dollars "for each and every offense."[340] The town saw an opportunity to make money from the Thespian Hall enterprise.

A circus-type entertainment, called a Great Combination Show, visited Winnsboro in March 1867 and performed under one immense pavilion, or as the town defined it, "under canvass." It included circus and trained animals from New Orleans, with Mons. William Cobb's wonderful trained dogs and goats, trained bears, acrobats, gymnasts, and other curious acts.

There were other causes that attracted Catharine's skills and made use of Thespian Hall in the 1870s. An Agricultural Fair held in the fall of 1870 listed Mrs. C. Ladd as a member of the committee on domestic fabrics. *The News and Herald* referred to evening theatricals in June 1877 to benefit The Gordon Light Infantry for new uniforms as ". . . perhaps the largest gathering of the season." The program consisted of tableau,[341] plays, and a comic duet, "Polly Hopkins." Catharine was praised for her contributions:

> We are pleased to note the great improvement in the stage
> arrangements of the hall. New curtains have been added, and the
> stage has been made in every way better fitted for the rendition
> of plays of different kinds. This scenery was all painted and
> arranged by Mrs. C. Ladd, to whose enterprise the public are
> indebted for the pleasant theatrical entertainments already
> given.[342]

In October 1877, dramatic performances, with "a sumptuous collation" of refreshments for sale, followed by a dance, were held to benefit Mt. Zion Institute. The two-part program offered tableau, a poetry reading, songs, and a string band, mixing in comedy with more serious themes.[343]

With her eyesight failing, Catharine Ladd moved her residence west of town in the 1880s to live with her daughter Josephine Ladd at Buena Vista. The newspaper noted her presence back in town in 1883 when she was seventy-five years of age:

> Mrs. C. Ladd is now in town and will be for some days for the
> purpose of rendering assistance in the management and conduct
> of the entertainment to be given in the Thespian Hall on the 18th
> Ins. Mrs. Ladd was for a number of years a resident of this place,
> and her familiar face will be welcomed by her many friends in
> Winnsboro.[344]

When Catharine purchased town lots and property in 1866 and 1867, it appeared that she had purposes besides establishing her residence, a school, and as discussed previously, a community center. For example, she resided in a building large enough to accommodate a dental office. J. D. Cureton, Surgeon Dentist, announced that having returned to Winnsboro to resume his practice of dentistry, he would welcome seeing his old friends and patrons "at Mrs. Ladd's, where I have opened my office."[345]

Coincidentally, this notice appeared just below Reverend Stacy's advertisement for Winnsboro Female Seminary. Catharine's original desire was to continue educating young women by setting up her school in a building on property she purchased, but as previously discussed, those plans never materialized.

Her family dynamics had changed. Josephine, the oldest, was unmarried at twenty-two. The two youngest girls, Annie and Kate, were fifteen and seventeen in 1866. That same year, Kate married dentist Dr. James D. Cureton. By 1867, Josephine made local real estate transactions and taught school. Catherine's sons A.W. and Charles Ladd partnered with various others in the dry goods business.

Four years later, in the 1870 United States Federal Census, sixty-one-year-old Catharine Ladd was head of household (census age recorded as fifty-seven), keeping house, with real estate valued at $8,000 and personal property valued at $500.[346] Of the nine members in her household, her five unmarried children were Josephine, Annie, A.W., Charles, and George. Their occupations corresponding to name were teacher, "at home," dry goods merchant, physician, and "works on farm." Twenty-one-year-old Kate Cureton lived with her own family.[347] Three of the nine household members were African-American domestic servants with the surname Hopkins—two females, and one five-year-old boy. It's possible that forty-year-old Lucy Hopkins may have been formerly enslaved in the Ladd household.

A. W., Charles, and George had a variety of jobs after the war. These activities were chronicled in the Winnsboro newspapers. Catharine provided building space and collateral for her sons' businesses at the same time she promoted and organized events in Thespian Hall. She continued her relentless efforts to share her resources and help her family make a living after the war, but, as for most in the South at this time, it was a hardscrabble life.

The next discussion is a summary of the known employments of the Ladd family and exemplifies how Catharine Ladd spent her time and assets in the two decades after the war. Despite many challenges, the Ladd Bros. mercantile store and drug store, run by Dr. Charles Ladd and A.W. Ladd, successfully competed as a dry goods and pharmacy business in the town of Winnsboro following the Civil War. After two decades of doing business on credit, they ran into financial difficulties, but managed to survive. Their mother Catharine provided collateral for their business ventures, even purchasing buildings in town to house the mercantile stores. In the 1870s they added a store in the country on their Flint Hill farm and concentrated on a rural trade that relied on business with new citizens, freedmen and women. [348]

A. W. Ladd began as a store clerk before the war, ran a furniture store, repaired furniture, operated a dry goods and drug store with his brother, made coffins, and was a photographer. After the war George D. Ladd was a store clerk, a baker, and operated a confectionary for several years.

Dr. Charles Ladd practiced as a physician, partnered with his brother and others in a drug store and dry goods store, and at the same time ran for and held local political offices. He was town warden, secretary and treasurer of the town council, secretary of the Fairfield County Medical Society, and served on committees for events like the Agricultural Fair. He was an entry in *The Physicians and Surgeons of the United States,* published in 1878. From that biography it was learned that he traveled to Europe in 1869. His specialty was surgery. He wrote papers on medical subjects such as 'Tetanus," "Phosphates in Urine," "Surgical Dressings," and "Causes of Miasmatic Fevers." He communicated several papers to the surgeon general's office of the U. S. Army. In 1877, Dr. C. H. Ladd was chosen by the Medical Association of South Carolina to be a delegate to the 1878 American Medical Association meeting in Chicago. [349]

Except for daughter Kate Ladd Cureton, Catharine's adult children postponed marriage until the 1870s. The youngest daughter, Annie James Ladd, married John J. Neil in 1874. The next year her brother A. W. Ladd married Mary Ann Owings. Catharine held a reception after their spring wedding, and confided to a guest the reason that Annie couldn't attend the party. She had been exposed to whooping cough and was sick. Annie Neil gave birth to a son in October who lived but a few days, and her death followed in December.[350] For Catharine to lose a grandson and her youngest child was, no doubt, devastating. Perhaps it cheered her that, around that same time, George D. Ladd married Louise Phillips. Catharine's other two children, Dr. Charles Henry Ladd and Josephine Ladd, never married.

The 1880 United States Federal Census reflected these family changes. Catharine Ladd, seventy-two, lived in the household of her son Dr. Charles Ladd outside Winnsboro in Fairfield County Township 1. Other family living with them were Josephine Ladd, thirty-seven, and seven-year-old Josephine Cureton, daughter of Kate Ladd Cureton. There were two non-family members in the household: Emma Kelly, an eighteen-year-old servant, and Edward Rawls, a twenty-seven-year-old boarder, both of whom were Caucasian. A. W. Ladd, forty-three, and his wife and three children lived in Township 13. George D. Ladd, thirty-five, and his wife lived in Township 5 with two children under age five. The census was recorded in June 1880. Dr. Charles Ladd died that year on October 12, at age forty-two; the cause of death was consumption (tuberculosis).

The 1890 United States Federal Census was destroyed, therefore statistics from that year are unavailable.

The medical career of Dr. Charles Ladd was a credit to
Catharine both during and after the war. He was an example of her
mission to promote an educated, informed citizenry with
productive lives. Her sons A. W. and George succeeded in
mercantile careers and farmed. Daughter Josephine demonstrated
her abilities in teaching, operating a farm, and buying and selling
real estate. Three of her children married after the war and
continued her family legacy. Catharine Ladd remained active, living
with her daughter Josephine in the Monticello community on
Josephine's farm, Buena Vista. She enjoyed tending a flower garden
and orchard in her later years before her sight diminished. She
continued to write poetry. When asked how she managed it despite
being blind, her reply was this: she composed the entire poem in
her head, memorized it, and then dictated it to her daughter who
wrote it down and sent it to the Winnsboro newspaper.

Part Three

Catharine Ladd as an Author

Unknown Flower:
Catharine Ladd Writes Against the Heart[351]

Throughout her life, Catharine Ladd shared her opinions, feelings, and emotions in the form of articles, essays, poems, stories, and plays. It is in her writing that Catharine's mind, heart, and spirit round out the fervent, relentless teacher and civic advocate that she was. To begin that examination, we trace back to the 1830s when her poetry first appeared.

Before 1834, Southern literary readers and writers relied on publications from the North and England. "In fact in all the South there were at that time no notable literary magazines."[352] A Southern-published journal, *The Southern Literary Messenger*, made its debut in Richmond, Virginia, in August 1834, published and owned by printer Thomas Willis White. The magazine published works of writers Edgar Allan Poe, William Gilmore Simms, and others who wrote under pseudonyms. Benjamin Blake Minor, who was editor of *The Southern Literary Messenger* in the 1840s, noted about the September 1836 issue that "Morna and Simms furnish most of the poetry."[353] Morna's real name was Catharine Stratton Ladd.

Catharine's literary works were never compiled in their entirety, since her life's writings of thirty years were destroyed in the "conflagrations" of the Union army in Winnsboro, South Carolina, on February 21, 1865.[354] However, enough original examples remained or were found in published sources to explore her development and style as a writer.

Catharine's poetry and prose were published in Southern and national magazines, although there were few attributed to her. The nature of these magazines was that many were short-lived, and the writer's name was often eliminated, making it hard to identify pieces written by Catharine Ladd. Jane Turner Censer commented about Tardy's *The Living Female Writers of the South*, that numerous women with biographical entries "published so little or in such obscure journals that the modern researcher can find almost none of their printed efforts." [355] For example, in the *Ladies Pearl* published in Nashville, Tennessee, there was an entire section titled "Tales" with no writers identified. Catharine was said to have contributed tales to periodicals.[356] As was the case for many women of her time, her pen was her voice, accomplished within the acceptable model of writing from the domestic sphere,[357] often with the anonymity of a pen name. No existing journal or diary of Catharine Ladd's has been found, nor did she write novels.

The name of Catharine Stratton Ladd was an entry in three contemporary biographies of the time, and also in a dictionary of nineteenth-century pseudonyms written between 1870 and 1898. There were seven twentieth-century published references that included an entry for her, and numerous autobiographical sketches published in newspapers.

Mary T. Tardy (pen name Ida Raymond) included a two-page entry on Catharine Ladd, dated 1869, in her collection of *The Living Female Writers of the South*. This text is frequently quoted, and misquoted, in biographies after that date.[358] Mary T. Tardy's article stated that Catharine Ladd wrote poetry for several years after her marriage for periodicals, including the Charleston magazine *The Floral Wreath,* published by Edwin Heriott.[359] She also contributed regularly to newspapers.

For three years she was a regular correspondent of several
newspapers, and published a series of articles on drawing,
painting, and education, which attracted considerable
attention.[360]

Literature flourished in Charleston during the period from
1825 to 1875. If one agreed with George Wauchope that magazines
accurately reflected the "intellectual activity of a people," then,

Judged by this standard the industry of writers of Charleston
down to about 1845 was as great as that of the litterateur[361] of
either Boston or New York.[362]

One noteworthy example is that Caroline Gilman began editing
the first children's paper in the country there, called *The Rose Bud, or
Youth's Gazette,* in 1832.[363] Unfortunately, no work in surviving
Charleston publications has been identified as Catharine's writing.
Editor Caroline Gilman wrote many of the poems in her magazine,
and other writers were not named.

Corresponding with editors of newspapers and periodicals was a
time-consuming business, particularly for a teacher. As Miss Mary
Bates of the seminary in Pendleton, South Carolina, laments in an
address after her pupils' examinations in 1851:

True, if devoted to the improvement of others, her [viz., the
teacher] own studies must in a measure be laid aside, and she
must leave unexplored the literature of the day.[364]

Counter to the opinion of Miss Bates, although busy, Catharine
demonstrated in her writing that she was well-read and subscribed
to current journals. During their first years of marriage, George
worked and lived away from home for periods of time, pursuing art
patrons. Since her mother, Ann Stratton, lived with them, and no
children of record were born until 1836, perhaps George's absence

and her mother's assistance in teaching and child care allowed time to write.[365] In the Mary T. Tardy biographical sketch, Catharine was remembered as being oblivious to distractions when she was writing:

> She has a powerful will and habit of centring [sic] every thought and feeling instantly on the occupation of the moment. The confusion of voices or passing objects never seemed to disturb her when writing.[366]

The Ladds lived in Chester, South Carolina, and Macon, Georgia, during the years 1835 to 1837, when Catharine's poetry appeared in *The Southern Literary Messenger* under the pseudonym Morna. In 1836, she bore her first son in Chester, and, in 1838, she bore her second son in Macon—at the same time she corresponded with magazine editors in Richmond and submitted her manuscripts. And, after moving to Macon, she was also teaching school.

One of the first editorial assistants at *The Southern Literary Messenger* was Mr. James E. Heath, who acknowledged that he might have been lenient as to the contents of the magazine's early editions. As reported by Norman Foerster in his 1957 book, *American Poetry and Prose*:

> But he [James Heath] maintains that its purpose was not only to furnish a vehicle for approved and practiced writers, but also to incite and call forth the slumbering and undeveloped talents of the Southern people. [367]

Edgar Allan Poe came to Richmond in August 1835 at William White's request to offer editorial assistance with the magazine; he remained editor until January 1837. David K. Jackson asserted that Poe looked to the *Messenger* as inspiration for subject matter prior to his arrival as editor in 1835, especially for Gothic themes.[368] Poe was known for his critical eye and opinions on literature.

Publishing poetry in a magazine with Poe as the editor may have rejuvenated Catharine's memories of him in her early years in Richmond. And perhaps Catharine did—while not being a friend of Poe's—encounter him. If she attended and boarded at Miss MacKenzie's (Jane) Seminary for young ladies[369] between the ages of twelve and sixteen, the typical age of school girls, she may have had contact with Poe at that time. He was known to sometimes entertain the girls at Miss MacKenzie's with his poetry readings. Poe's sister, Rosalie, resided at MacKenzie's and taught penmanship there.[370]

Catharine published a total of seven poems in the *Messenger* from 1835 to 1837. She wrote on romantic themes of mortality, love, friendship, nature, spirituality, betrayal, human frailty, happiness, hope, and loss. These themes supported a popular ideology of the time known as the cult of sensibility: that women had a greater capacity for being in touch with their emotions than men, which made them especially suited for writing poetry and prose.

Antebellum American poets, men and women alike, were influenced by their academic courses in literature that included the Greek and Latin classics. Writers also strove to mimic the style of successful writers, especially English poets like Thomas Gray and later Wordsworth, Byron, Shelley, and Scott of the Romantic Period. The Romantic Movement, subtitled Individualism in Feeling and Imagination,[371] spread to America and gave rise to poets like Edgar Allan Poe, John Greenleaf Whittier, and Henry W. Longfellow. The most popular poetic style was that of rhymed verse in alternating lines.

Catharine's poetry reflected her knowledge of classical mythology and the works of English poets like Thomas Gray. Her pieces were contemporary in her choice of a rhyming pattern and meter. For example, Thomas Gray's "Elegy Written in a Country Churchyard" (1751) exhibited the rhyming pattern a/b, a/b, and the frequently used meter, iambic pentameter.[372]

· · · · · · · · · · · · · · · · · · · ·

Full many a gem of purest ray serene,
　　The dark unfathomed caves of ocean bear:
Full many a flower is born to blush unseen,
　　And waste its sweetness on the desert air.

· · · · · · · · · · · · · · · · · · · ·

(Thomas Gray, "Elegy Written in a country Churchyard" 53-56)

Catharine directly quoted line 55 from Gray's poem as a subtitle to her poem "Unknown Flowers" (1836). Its twenty-four lines celebrated "unknown flowers" that thrived and blossomed unnoticed:

Unknown Flowers
"Full many a flower is born to blush unseen."

Oh! Many are the unknown flowers,
By human eyes unseen,
That bloom in nature's woodland bowers,
Of bright and changeless green.

· · · · · · · · · · · · · · · ·

The wood-bee revels on their sweets,
And 'neath their leaves the bright Fay sleeps;
And by them bounds the gentle deer
So full of life, so full of fear:
And lovely birds, who brilliant wings
Are bright with hues of brighter things
Make music in those woodland bowers,
Those Edens of the unknown flowers.

Did she regard herself as an "unknown flower"? Her poem shared the pages of the January 1836 edition of the *Messenger* with a writer who would become famous: across the page from her verse was "Metzengertstein," a tale by Edgar A. Poe.

In two poems Catharine explored a theme of death. A character from classical mythology, "Ianthe,"[373] was the title of Catharine's lengthy elegiac-style poem. She wove a story of the early loss of parents and compared it to Ianthe's story of loss. "Ianthe's" theme of a fearless death and future perfection were presented in this poem of Catharine's as a spiritual eternity.

"The Dove of my Bosom Lies Bleeding" (1835) mourned the loss of a child: "Earth's brightest is low with the dead." The eye is "clouded with silence and doom" and the locks [of hair] once gleaming with sunlight "are damp with the dews of the tomb." Identified as a girl in the line "and my heart is with her in the grave," the sentiments over her death are laden with grief and with tears that will not cease "till I greet her above." This poem may tell of a life experience for Catharine in the death of a first-born, an unconfirmed supposition.[374]

The tone of her poems was described by Mr. Edwin Heriott, publisher of *The Floral Wreath* in Charleston, who claimed Mrs. Ladd's poetical works among the literary talent in the South:

> They were sweet, smooth, and flowing, particularly so; but, like Scotch music, their gayest notes were sad.[375]

The remaining four poems of Catharine's published in *The Southern Literary Messenger* in 1835 and 1837 had a common theme. "To H. W. M." (July 1835) was about opposing circumstances of lost love and the comfort of friendship. Images of matrimony, hearth and home, absence, sadness, and gladness were evoked by the words. The use of initials instead of a name in the title was a literary device to hide identity and add mystery to the circumstances. This poem makes use of the fact that, since the beginning of time, lovers have cherished anonymous tokens of affection such as a painted miniature of a lover's eye or secret messages written in code. The meaning of the poem is clouded. Did disappointment in love lead to a forbidden relationship never realized? Or, was the desire for such only an idea vented in the poem, the feelings that arose from Catharine's loneliness? According to Angela Leighton, the act of writing creates another self, separate from the actual person, making biographical connections superfluous. This creates a split between the person displayed in public and the one who writes poetry—the public face and the private mask, writing "against the heart." [376]

During the years these poems were written and published, Catharine and George lived apart for long periods of time. They had, at this point, been married eight years with no surviving children, until a son was born in October 1836. Airing her feelings in poems published in Richmond, Virginia, under the pen name of Morna, offered her some freedom of expression. Whether this poem was a personal experience remains unknown, but that does not diminish the understanding of sentiments conveyed on a universal theme of love's disappointments.

To H. W. M.

When the cup is pledged, and the bright wine flowing,
At the festal board, in the halls of light;
And gentle eyes, like stars are glowing,
In the cloudless sky of a summer's night:
Oh! breathe but my name o'er the wine, for yet
I will dare to believe that all will not forget.

When the moon looks out on the leafy bowers,
Where the gladsome daughters of beauty are wreathing
The brightest and fairest of all the flowers,

To crown their altars with incense breathing,
Oh, name one flower for the absent one,
Who forgotten by thee is remembered by none.[377]

In that home, to thee brightest and best upon earth,
Where the spirits thou lovest are yearning to greet thee,
When round the light of the household hearth,
The smiles and the tears of affection greet thee,
Mid the beam of the smile and the glow of the tear,
Shall a thought ever whisper "I wish he were here?"

For if life were changed, and its beamings of gladness,
Were shrouded in gloom by the veil of sorrow,
And the pale cold shade of unaltered sadness,
Found no ray of hope in the coming morrow;
Each pang could but render more precious to me,
The friendship of M***, the beauty of B.
Morna [378]

In "Song" (August 1835), Catharine composed four-line
stanzas, with alternating rhyming lines within each stanza. Returning
to the theme of lost love, the speaker presented an attitude of
acceptance by "putting up a front" of denial. If the absent one
returned, then the pain would be suppressed by a smile. The
language and meaning of the poem are clear, as seen here in the
first and fourth stanzas:

Song
I will twine me a wreath of life's withering flowers,
    And bind with their brightness this aching heart,
And wear a smile through the long, long hours,
    As if in their gladness I bore a part.
. . . .
And if ever we meet upon earth again,
    He will not know it by word or by token:
For the eye shall still sparkle, though only with pain,
    And the lip wear a smile, while the heart may be broken.

The first lines are reminiscent of the first verse of Appalachian ballad tune "Wildwood Flower."

Wildwood Flower
Reese Witherspoon

I will twine mid my ringlets of raven black hair
The lilies so pale and the roses so fair
And the myrtle so bright with an emerald hue
The pale amaryllis and violets so blue
I will dance I will sing and my laugh will be gay
I'll cease this wild weeping drive sorrow away
Tho my heart is now breaking, he'll never know
His name made me tremble, my pale cheeks to glow[379]

The last two poems published in *The Southern Literary Messenger* were in the April 1837 edition. In "Lines" is a remembrance of young love's "sunny hours" that do not return, but "a tone hath lost its lightness" and "an eye hath lost its brightness." Comparing lost love to withered flowers, the last lines were direct: "Of the love thou hast forsaken, And the vow which thou hast broken."

In "To. . . ," Catharine addressed an unnamed person and imagined two lovers visiting "some sunny and sea-girt isle" where all would be reconciled and peaceful, ending in the lines:

. . . .
And the pure love of early years,
Ere we have known the false one's guile,
Or shed the heart's repentant tears,
Should win us to that lonely isle.

These seven poems from the 1830s were the only poems of Catharine Ladd's published in *The Southern Literary Messenger,* and the only poems published under the pen name Morna.

An interesting fact is that Catharine's first cousin, Rev. John Collins McCabe,[380] published poems in *The Southern Literary Messenger* at the same time as Catharine. Another connection through *The Southern Literary Messenger* was Matthew F. Maury, the "Pathfinder of the Seas," who published articles in the magazine at this time. In 1835 George W. Ladd painted a portrait in miniature of Lieutenant Matthew F. Maury.

For the next fifteen years, Catharine Ladd's main occupation, besides her family—husband George, mother Ann Stratton, and six children—was being a principal and teacher in female academies. As discussed in Part One, Catharine and George moved from Macon, Georgia, to York County, South Carolina, where she organized and ran Brattonsville Female Seminary, 1839–1841, and was then recruited by the Woodwards of Fairfield District, South Carolina, to be principal of a female academy in Winnsboro. The Ladds remained in Fairfield District the rest of their lives.

When Catharine accepted the assignment as principal of a new female academy on the plantation of Dr. John Bratton in 1839, she had to leave her teaching position at Macon Female Academy. The February 19, 1839 edition of the *Macon Telegraph* of Macon, Georgia, published a poem entitled "Lines" by Mrs. C. Ladd. "Lines" conveyed thoughts of leaving home, in this case by ship, recalling what was left behind—youth and family—to become memories.

Lines,
by Mrs. C. Ladd

> Farewell, farewell, my early home-
>   Home of my joyous hours-home of my youth,
> Where I have pass'd my happiest days
>   Of innocence and truth.
> And now for wealth to distant climes I roam,
>   And bid adieu to my loved native shore.

The sixth line was inspired by Lord Byron's verse published in 1812:

. . . .

> Oh! With what deep intensity we gaze,
> Till twilight shuts each object from our view;
> Then with the noble bard we say,
> "My home-my native land, adieu!"[381]

. . . .

(Lord Byron, "Childe Harold's Pilgrimage")

In 1841, another poem of heartbreak was written and published by Catharine Ladd. "Oh Do Not Say Again Love's Blind" was the only known poem by Catharine published by Sarah Hale, the editor of *Godey's Lady's Book*. It was signed Mrs. C. Ladd.

There is a critique and auditory reading of this poem on the Boston Public Library webpage. Catharine's poem was chosen as part of a project to read selections from nineteenth-century publications in the Boston Public Library's collections and post critiques of the choices on the website.[382] While the reviewer was critical of the writer's poetic technique, the review acknowledges heartbreak as a real inspiration for the verse.

Catharine Ladd enjoyed writing lines to fit a tune. In 1844, she composed an ode that was sung at the Celebration of the Anniversary of Lafayette Lodge [Masonic] in Winnsboro. It's not surprising, given her encounter with him when she was young, that her favorite patriot was the Frenchman Lafayette. She dedicated the first stanza to him:

> Ode
> A year, a fleeting year's roll'd round,
> Since first our little band
> Assembled, and together pledg'd,
> Their faith with heart and hand;
> Thus far we have each proved,
> Since the first hour we met—

Honor alone has been our chart—
Our model "LA FAYETTE."[383]

. . . .

Catharine's last known published poem until 1866 was also created to the rhythm of an "Air." It was published in September 1861, when Charleston was under a naval blockade and after the shot was fired on Fort Sumter. The words of this first stanza are as written in the *Weekly State Journal* (Raleigh, North Carolina):

Hurrah for Bethel
By Mrs. C. Ladd
Air "Run, Niggers, Run"

There comes old Rip, - he's wide awake,
And might good aim he's sure to take,
I've peddled out there, in days gone by,
And seen Rip shoot thro' a squirrel's eye; -
So - run boys, run; them gentlemen are coming;
Run boys, run; - for the Fort away! [384]

. . . .

Throughout all six stanzas that ended in the same two-line chorus as above, the meaning clearly has racist tones. The mood of the "Air" was clear, and its intent was to ridicule formerly enslaved people. With sarcasm couched in humor, she referred to farm or land grants for freedmen and how they took to fright and flight in their naivete to avoid the fight.

This work is pivotal to understanding the nature of Catharine's conflicting emotions. Without the poem, it would be conjecturing to surmise Catharine's stance about race. This, along with her essay "New Improvement," highlighted her complex opinions and feelings as a Southern, white, Christian woman.[385] She may have applied her high ideals of an educated, voting citizenry to women, who could not vote, and to blacks, who had the right to vote, but in her time and place both groups were "discouraged" from promoting or exercising their rights for years to come. Here, her feminine sensibility of compassion conflicted with a heart that was angry over a war beyond her control, that was about to erase all her years of accomplishments in her community and home.

The glimpses into her thinking on race remain incomplete, but true. This was the only known publication of "Hurrah for Bethel" and the only known piece by her published in the Raleigh newspapers.[386] Although Catharine Ladd's lifelong writings were destroyed, and although she published on an irregular basis, the singular examples that were discovered, by themselves, and in relationship to each other, provide invaluable pieces to solving her puzzle.

After the Civil War, Catharine's poetry and songs, published almost exclusively in the Fairfield newspapers, were sentimental and religious reflections of her late life from 1866 to the 1890s. The following titles suggest the topics: "I Am Growing Old" (1867), "Hurrah for the Christmas Tree"(1868), "I Love God's Beauteous World" (1868), The Village Where I Was Born" (1868), "The Great I Am" (1894), "The Old Grist Mill" (1894), "Never-More" (1896), and "Memories" (1897).

Here is an example, "The Old Grist Mill," written when Catharine was eighty-six and published in the *News and Herald* on January 10, 1894:

> The Old Grist Mill
>
> Mr. Editor: The Old Grist Mill is no fiction. That, and the dilapidated school-house stood about a mile and a half from Richmond. They both saw their best days about the close of the year 1799. From that time, it began to lose its custom. It stood too near the city where fine mills had been erected, but a more

picturesque or lovely spot you could hardly imagine. In the mills old garden many lilac and snowball bushes were still standing. The broken roof of the old cottage was covered in summer with hop vines. He had planted the running lay against a few of the trees, that had long ago reached their tops. Many of the other trees were festooned by the wild grape. The beautiful ivy bush and sweet briar rose were growing there in their greatest luxuriance while the smaller bushes were covered with the flower that well deserves its name—the morning glory. More than seventy years [c. 1824-Catharine would have been sixteen years old.] have passed away, with its smiles and tears, joys and griefs, sunshine and shadows, since I stood with one of my companions and said good bye to the

The Old Grist Mill

I am standing again by the Old Grist Mill,
The dam is broken, the wheel is still,
The sun streams in, far o'er the floor,
Through the shattered windows and broken door.

The miller's house, just over the way,
Has fallen in, all in decay;
The spring is choked with trash and leaves,
The mill-road blocked by fallen trees.

Two noble willows stood by the race,
Though much decayed, are still in place;
The weeping branches, now touch the ground,
Seeming to mourn for the loss around.

No birds are seen on bush or spray,
The mock-bird's song at break of day
That echoed around from hill to hill,
Is heard no more at the Old Grist Mill.

No longer loads stood at the door
No bags of corn lay on the floor,
Where busy life, so long had been,
No voices heard, no foot-prints seen.

Our school-house stood not far away,
The mill-road was our scene of play,
No longer comes the glad wild shout
To the mill boys, "our school is out."

If the grist was slack on Saturday,
The miller joined us in one play,
Or sat indoors, wild tales to tell,
Tales, we school-boys loved so well.

Tears have come, and years have gone,
Since I stood here on a bright morn,
With a sad heart, and smothered sigh
I've come to bid old friends good-bye.

My mother's kiss was on my brow,
Her low, sweet voice-I hear it now-
Why for love, my boy, why sever
The ties of home, perhaps forever?

My stately home I still can see,
Or what is home or lands to me.
I came not back to claim the place,
I am the last of all my race.

My mother's voice still I hear,
Her blessing ever, ever dear,
Then, with the kiss left on my brow,
Are all the wealth I covet now.

The winds were hushed, not a single sound.
Silence, but beauty reigned around;
Lovely as some enchanted dell
Wrought by the fairies' mystic spell.

One more look at the Old Grist Mill,
At the broken dam, and wheel so still;
One more look at the sunlit floor;
Before I turn to leave the door,
A tear-drop fell upon the broken sill,
Memory's gift to the Old Grist Mill.

Catharine's vision failed in 1891, but she continued to write and
publish her poems by a method she related in an interview in 1895.
She composed the lines in her head, memorizing them, and then
recited the complete poem to her daughter, who wrote it down and
sent it to the *News and Herald* in Winnsboro.

And, yes, there was another poem of heartbreak published in 1897, "I Cannot Love Again." Catharine Ladd had her share of heartache in her long life, long enough to work through all these heartaches, except one. The speaker of the verse never found a healing balm for lost love, love's promises broken, dreams shattered, false love.

The tone was hard, a closed door, resolved, yet forever broken. Again, her feminine sensibility for forgiveness conflicted with her heart, as she had the last word at age eighty-nine. She introduced this last published poem, set to a tune, with a tribute to a Miss Crossett who was a music teacher for Winnsboro Female Institute from 1856 to 1860:

> A favorite song with her, as well as myself, was one written by the Honorable Mrs. Norton, of England, many years before, called "Thy Name Was Once a Magic Spell;" the air was very sweet, and the song below runs smoothly to the same tune:

> My girlhood's dream of love is o'er,
> The wheels of time roll fast,
> All that made life so dear to me
> Lies buried in the past.
> In fancy still I sometimes hear
> The tones that whispered love's refrain;
> It brings a sigh for times gone by—
> I cannot love again. . . . .

> I'm standing 'neath the old oak tree;
> Where oft we lingered, often met;
> I heard a voice, I saw a form,
> I never can forget.
> Forgive, forgive me, darling;
> I heard again the love strain-
> They woke no throb within my heart,
> I cannot love again.

> Buckhead, S. C.[387]

In a family scrapbook about Catharine Ladd were some transcriptions of poems, newspaper copies of articles and poems by Mrs. C. Ladd, pieces of autobiographical information, and recollections. The writer of the hand-written copies included in this scrapbook remains unproven, but it is probable that Catharine penned unpublished verse.

Three of Catharine's prose writings were discovered in American journals published under her pen names Arcturus and Alida.

"Mother and Child" appeared in Volume 4 of the *Ladies' Garland,* published in Philadelphia in April 1841 under the pen name Arcturus. The non-fiction, single-column homily praised the love that bonded a mother and her child:

> We believe that no other relation in life, no other phase of
> human nature, presents so perfect a picture of unmixed,
> unselfish love and devotedness, as that of a mother for her child.

Catharine Ladd followed that sentence with examples of mothers in poverty, sickness, widowhood, desertion, fire, shipwreck, and all manner of depravity, each clutching her babe in desperate love.

> It is an article of our creed, that the American mother is the best
> mother in the world; and that the best elements of the American
> character, those which mark us a peculiar people, and have most
> contributed to make us a great nation, were fashioned and
> moulded by the plastic hands of American mothers.

It is in the last two sentences that follow this lofty oration that a twist of meaning occurs. After establishing the point that American mothers' hands molded the American character, and in that act, made the biggest contribution to forming a great nation, she challenged those who make "any disparaging distinctions between her and the other sex."

Going further, she ends:

> Any law that makes or sanctions such a distinction is founded in folly, and should be blotted out forever, as anti-American in principle, and a disgrace to the code of a humane and enlightened people.[388]

Without knowing if Catharine referred to a specific law, there were still numerous possible intents. Referring back to the discussion on women's property rights, in antebellum South Carolina, principles of common law forbade married women from owning real property, from owning the wages of their labor like writing and teaching, from divorcing, and, of course, on a national level, from voting.

As head of household, husbands owned the property; women could only own personal property granted by the husband (even if she entered the marriage with real or personal property).

Enslaved black women had no legal rights. A married woman could claim money as her own only "if she could prove that she needed control of her earnings for her own and her family's protection."[389] More important, even female writers who were economically independent did not risk advocating the same in their writing for fear of being labeled "promiscuous" or immoral:

> Although they had in their personal lives often adopted the role of principal bread winner for their families, in their fiction they continued to portray domesticity as the only acceptable goal for women.[390]

Catharine's earnings as an educator and writer were certainly counted as essential to the family's income, especially when compared to the irregular nature of George's portrait painting and miscellaneous jobs. There is a possibility that the few published examples of Catharine's prose were due to some opinion-pieces like this one that would have prevented its publication. Or, perhaps the meaning behind this one slipped past the editor's attention and was published despite its politics? The other reasons previously mentioned were that uncovering works attributed to her was difficult due to the lack of names published with pieces in the magazines and journals of the time, and that her collection of writings burned with her house in 1865, destroying the scope and titles of her writings.

Mary T. Tardy mentioned in her biographical notes on Catharine that she contributed tales to magazines or journals. One surviving story was under the heading "Tales" in the *Rural Repository,* published in Hudson, New York, in March 1850. Entitled "William Brown, Or, the Reward of Virtue." it was by Alida*,* another pen name of Catharine Ladd. Her story spread over the first four pages of the journal.

Here is a summary of the tale. In his youth, a slight lad named William Brown, age fifteen, experienced the death of his mother and a father who drank. William chose to become a seaman when a ship captain accepted his offer. He left his only love, Adele, behind for nine years. During William's time at sea, Adele's father died, leaving her and her mother alone and in poverty. They left their country home and eked out an existence in Boston. While a seaman, William clung to the leather Bible that was a gift from Adele. He studied the Word and tried to follow a moral path, read constantly, and once back in Boston, studied to be a lawyer. There, he coincidently encountered Adele as a charity case. They renewed their friendship, married, and lived happily. The story fit perfectly in the category of an uplifting story with a moral ending. Catharine provided what publishers and readers sought.

The third prose piece was also written under the pen name Alida. In 1852, "Our Cousin Ellie" was published in *The Ladies' Repository* by the Methodist Episcopal Church in Cincinnati. The discourse was a memory of one who died as a sweet, young girl. The memory was one of hope and "the ushering of heavenly bliss" or "enough to rob death of its terror and the grave of its fearful gloom?"[391] Her theme of death as a freeing experience returned in this prose.

The sense of humor and delight in fun that Catharine Ladd displayed in her Thespian Hall productions after the war were documented by reporters in the Winnsboro newspaper. Not only did Catharine write plays, she produced her plays, and designed and painted the scenery. [392]

Other titles of plays not written by Catharine but found in her scrapbook were: *The Honeymoon* by John Tobin, published in 1879, and a printed fragment of *The Last Loaf, a Temperance Drama in 2 Acts* by George Baker, published in 1868. According to former students' stories, another popular play was *H. M. S. Pinafore, or The Lass Who Loved a Sailor*, a comic opera by Gilbert and Sullivan that debuted in London in 1878. Her own Winnsboro Thespian Corp began performing as early as the 1850s.

The most popularized play attributed to Catharine Ladd was *The Grand Scheme*, a play in four acts written in 1853 for the Thespian Corp. An account of its performance in 1866 in Thespian Hall was recorded by the *Tri Weekly News*. The plot recalled elements of Shakespeare's dramas like *A Comedy of Errors* in its simultaneous schemes of crossed loves and hidden identity.

On a surviving hand-written script, next to the twelve characters' names, were the names of the actors, including members of the Ladd family. With daughter Annie Ladd playing a waiting maid in this version, it must have been performed after 1860 and before 1875, considering that she was born in 1851 and died in 1875.

The Irish and Yorkshire servants' lines were written in a brogue, although Tom, as a Yorkshire servant to the main character Old Chester, spoke in a vernacular with Southern Negro expressions mixed in.

> *Chester.* Well I am looking for the young men every moment.
> *Tom.* They be cumed too
> *Chester.* Stupid Dolt! Why did you not tell me?
> *Tom:* I noa nowed it my own self till I went to go down and I seed two fine looking folks like Lords a cuming sir, Lordy-Mercy that bees them a cuming up.[393]

Additional plays with hand-written scripts that have been attributed to Catharine Ladd were *Ruth, Naoma & Orpah* and *Mrs. J's Wax Works*. The plot and characters of the former closely followed the Biblical text, whereas the latter drew on randomly chosen historical and folk references written in an irreverent and comical manner.

Mrs. J's Wax Works was set in a wax museum with the character Nell taking a tour conducted by the owner, Mrs. J.

Here is a passage about Pocahontas:

> This is Pocahontus [sic] she was the favorite daughter of the King of the Cannibal Isles. When Alexander the Great went out and discovered America he carried with him in that expedition a famous General called Julius Caesar he fell in love with Pocahontus married her but had to kill the King of the Cannibal Isles. He would eat nothing but baby soup he eat Caesar's first

> baby So if Caesar had not killed him Pocahontus would not have
> left to Virginia one of her first families, all the first families in
> Virginia came from Pocahontus and Julius Caesar.[394]

This selection about Pocahontas was humorous, like a bragging-nonsensical folk song. Take, for example, one sung by North Carolina bluegrass guitarist Doc Watson that began, "I was born about six thousand years ago. They ain't nothin' in this world that I don't know."

Here is a passage about the Ku Klux Klan:

> This is Ku Klux can't hurt you, you have heard of Goliath that
> was his Grand Father now that Ku Klux was the fellow that
> slayed his thousands and his tens of thousands he done it with
> the jaw bone of an ass, he has it still in his hand also the head,
> you see he is on wires I can pull this wire (see)
> [Ku Klux strikes the jaw bone on the skull then drops to his
> natural position]There Sampson was not a caution to him he is a
> great specimen, . . .

It was in the selection on the Ku Klux that the reader got another glimpse of Catharine's political thinking. The fact that she included the Ku Klux Klan dated the piece to the first Reconstruction, after 1868 in Fairfield District, South Carolina; that was also when she wrote the editorial essay "New Improvement." This Catharine was obviously not fearful of the vigilante group and was not afraid of poking fun at their activities. In that respect, Catharine shared an unadvisable camaraderie with black residents about the futility of mindless violence as a means of solving differences.

Catharine was an example of an educated, middle-class, working female whose writing income helped her family prosper financially.

Catharine never achieved professional status or notoriety as a writer; however, those who did were often born into the upper class, with fathers who enjoyed professions like physicians, university professors, publishers and printers, lawyers and clergymen. Their writing careers were assisted by financial support, access to publishers and printers, social connections, and encouragement. Jane Turner Censer noted in a review of Mary T. Tardy's biographies of Southern female writers that many came from "well-to-do" Southern families and often published one piece or one novel with a local printer.[395]

Northern author Emma Manley Embury (1806–1863) was, by age twenty, a renowned composer of poems and prose who wrote under the pseudonym Ianthe. She was for a time co-editor of *Graham's Magazine*. A New Yorker, her father was a physician. Her husband was a banker and mathematician who supported her literary efforts. Emma Manley Embury enjoyed a circle of literary friends. As a writer, she wrote under the appropriate umbrella for women, domestic industry.

Other well-known nineteenth-century American female writers who published under their given names were Louisa McCord, Mrs. Lydia Sigourney, Elizabeth Ellet, the Grimke sisters, and Harriet Beecher Stowe, to mention a few. Their works were published in collections and literary magazines as well as in school textbooks. Popular English authors Mrs. Hemans and Hannah More wrote poetry and essays within the household sphere. They wrote on acceptable themes of the time: domestic tranquility, obedience to God, piety, temperance, duty, and a high moral ground— appropriate themes for the aforementioned cult of female sensibility. The Grimke sisters of Charleston, South Carolina, and Harriet Beecher Stowe of New England delved further into abolitionist pamphlets and novels.

Where did Catharine Ladd fit into this picture? As a writer Catharine expressed herself in clever, satiric dramas, and in melancholy and sanguine poetry. She ventured into political opinions in her essay "New Improvement," although its publication was questionable. Comparatively few of her writings survived, but she displayed in them that she dared to inject personal feelings on race, heartbreak, and women's rights in her work. A study of her writings uncovers a woman of high intelligence who had a capacity to recall a wide berth of literary and musical sources that were part of her poems, plays, stories, and essays. When her career as an educator ended, Catharine channeled her energy and imagination, along with her great sense of humor and fun, into writing, producing, and designing scenery for dramatic performances.

Catharine's gifts were overlooked by modern studies of female nineteenth-century journalists and writers of poetry and prose not due to lack of merit, but more due to the difficulty of extracting her story from the hidden evidence. Her surviving quantity of published writings was not enough to classify Catharine Ladd as a professional writer, although her newspaper correspondence was regular. Her writings were a significant example of a Southern woman who provided leadership, entertainment, and information for her community throughout the decades of the nineteenth century. She is one example of a Southern woman in the nineteenth century who dared to speak out on issues of women's equality and stood for female education and community activism.

Catharine Ladd as a Journalist

Catharine Ladd held political opinions that she expressed through her actions, but also in her writing. Mary T. Tardy included the subject matter of Catharine's writing in *Southland Writers: Biographical and Critical Sketches of the Living Female Writers of the South.*[396]

> For three years she was a regular correspondent of several newspapers, and published a series of articles on drawing, painting, and education, which attracted considerable attention.[397]

According to Tardy, Catharine began writing in earnest in 1851 on "education, home manufactories, and encouragement of white labor,"[398] believing that the future prosperity of the South depended on it.

There were opinions published in the Winnsboro newspapers on these subjects. In December 1866, an article on "The Supply of Labor" pointed out the migration of labor from Fairfield District to Florida, Louisiana, and Mississippi was "deleterious to her [South Carolina's] own industrial interests."[399]

Catharine held strong opinions about yet another New Republic emerging from the ashes of war, that of a united America, girded by strong local communities with citizens who participated in government. In August 1868, *The Fairfield Herald* published a notice of a local industrious citizen, F. Elder, who engaged in home manufactory. This notice was likely written by Catharine, as it contains the same praises she used in an editorial, "New Improvement."

New Advertisements

> Special attention is directed to the advertisement of F. Elder. Home Enterprise. If any man in the community deserves patronage and success it is certainly our enterprising fellow-citizen Mr. F. Elder. All unite in praising his labor-saving machines. The bed he patented before the war was universally pronounced an excellent thing, and the same is now said of his Clothes Washer, Dough machine and Churn. All success to him.[400]

Similar opinions were voiced by Southern orators like Benjamin Hill (1823-1882), Georgia state legislator and later United States Senator from Georgia (1877), and a generation later by Henry W. Grady (1850-1889), journalist from Georgia, who followed Hill's example and coined the phrase "The New South." Hill opposed secession but endorsed it in the end. Catharine made it clear in her editorial "New Improvement" (1868) that she opposed secession and recognized the early causes of division, but she also embraced the South's separation from the union when war became eminent. Hill and Grady favored moderation regarding Reconstruction and making peace after the war. Neither were Southern apologists but held a strong line toward post-war rebuilding and praised the Southern manufacturing efforts as successful. Grady supported prohibition; Catharine expressed sympathy with temperance.[401] Catharine Ladd undoubtedly was acquainted with the published opinions of Hill and later in the 1880s read the speeches of Grady in the Atlanta *Constitution*.

Winnsboro newspapers published opinions after the war that promoted manufacturing, such as "A Call upon 'True Reconstructionists'" in January 1869.

The Chairman of the Democratic Clubs of this District, has not
thought it worth while, or perhaps, has forgotten, (and it
indicates the general indifference) to respond, . . . to devise
means for furthering the manufacturing and other industrial
pursuits of South Carolina.[402]

Other examples of her opinions arise within the pages of *The
Fairfield Herald.* In 1869 an opinion piece entitled "Ladies Should
Read Newspapers," summarized a belief that Catharine embraced
on females, education, and civic affairs. She was always concerned
with improvement:

It is a great mistake in female education to keep a young lady's
time and attention devoted to the fashionable literature of the
day. If you would qualify her for conversation, you must give her
something to talk about-give her education with the actual
world, with the outer world, and its transpiring events. Urge her
to read newspapers and become familiar with the present
character and improvement of our race. History is of some
importance, but our thoughts and our concerns should be
mainly for the present time-to know what it is and improve the
condition of it. . . . Let the whole family men, women and
children read newspapers.[403]

The difficulty of Catharine's situation was that only one
example of her political opinions can be attributed to her. It is a
hand-written editorial entitled "New Improvement" that remained
in her family. The unsigned editorial ends with initials in a cipher
that appear to be CL. There is no published example that survived.
Because she wrote for newspapers without a by-line, her signature
was not attached to articles. There are multiple facts that
corroborate Catharine Ladd's authorship of the editorial. The piece
remained in the Ladd family, and it was initialed with stylized letters
CL. Mary T. Tardy enumerated Catharine's writings about
education, home manufactories, and white labor. All these subjects

were included as part of her editorial. With this background Tardy maintained that Catharine was a newspaper correspondent.

The Winnsboro *Tri Weekly News* posted a story in June 1866 of a new staff writer. "We welcome 'Petite' to our columns and hope the pen wielded in a manner so facile will continue to grace our paper." [404] It is likely that "Petite" was Catharine becoming a correspondent. The newspaper office was in the former Fairfield Hotel building owned by Catharine, and she lived in the building. (An advertisement also stated that the office would soon be separated from Mrs. Ladd's residence by the addition of a dividing wall.)

If, as the evidence suggests, Catharine is the writer of "New Improvement," it reflects the working of her mind and reveals her political thoughts. As an example of her non-fiction writing, it is full of insight about her convictions.

"New Improvement" was written after the war, just prior to the presidential election of 1868. For South Carolinians, these were turbulent times. Catharine Ladd, the likely writer, had foresight and was conversant with causes and consequences of political topics of the day. Some historical context is needed to understand the meaning and intent.

The piece includes references made to South Carolina's history back to 1832. That year, John C. Calhoun resigned as Vice President to President Andrew Jackson over the tariff and nullification controversies. Low export tariffs were desired by cotton growers in the South who sent raw cotton to England and imported cheap ready-made goods. Low tariffs were opposed in the North by those whose business owners desired high import tariffs to protect their cotton textile industry from English-made imported cloth.

Radical South Carolinians wanted to nullify the high tariffs. President Jackson defended the Union, warning South Carolina of treason if the state nullified the tariff acts of 1828 and 1832. Calhoun, who had ambitions for the presidency, tried to avoid embracing the radical Nullifiers, but in 1832, he allied with them and resigned as Vice President under Jackson in December 1832. South Carolina and the Union were tied up in "divisions and animosities" lasting ten years[405] that led to the Civil War.

Her editorial of 1868 echoed past predictions about the demise of the slave labor system as it existed and the promotion of white labor in the South—not a popular viewpoint in South Carolina at the time.[406] Before the war, the opportunities for white labor in South Carolina were scarce and mill wages were low, second only to North Carolina as the lowest in the South. "The concept of a white working class in a slave society made some people uneasy."[407]

There were some, like William Gregg of Graniteville (Edgefield District), who began the first cotton mills in the Upstate in the 1840s and fought the antibusiness climate. However, John C. Calhoun used his considerable influence to promote an anti-labor climate during his time as Vice President, and then as senator from 1824 until his death in 1850.[408]

Following the war, South Carolina sought to re-establish the old political order. Several significant actions that began in the summer of 1865 delayed South Carolina rejoining the Union. First, the provisional government refused to ratify a new state constitution but did ratify the Thirteenth Amendment that freed slaves and forbade slavery.

Second, South Carolina proceeded to enact the "Black Codes." These codes, in three statutes, stated that persons of color did not have "social and political equality with white persons," but did have certain rights of property, contracts, and protection of person and property. A person of color was defined as being seven-eighths black. Travel was limited, participation in trades was encumbered by high license fees, and a system of district courts was created where only blacks were tried. The codes were an effort by white South Carolinians to offer a plan for Reconstruction.[409] A national backlash to the "Black Codes" resulted in Radicals controlling the majority in the South Carolina Congress. To make matters worse, in December 1866, the South Carolina General Assembly refused to ratify the Fourteenth Amendment guaranteeing equal protection under the law to blacks.

Elections in 1868 sent a black majority to the South Carolina General Assembly, who in turn ratified a state constitution in 1868. However, the white population never accepted the new government. In 1868, Republican Governor Scott (a native of Ohio) sent Federal troops to the upstate to oppose the Ku Klux Klan and armed black militia units to ensure enforcement of the Fourteenth Amendment.

"New Improvement"[410] written by Catharine Ladd was aimed at admonishing the white male voting population of Winnsboro District, South Carolina.

New Improvement[411]

> We would call the attention of the public to the new churn
> invented by Mr. F. Elder, It is simple convenient and in our
> opinion cannot fail to answer the purpose for which it was
> invented, The Spring Bedstead invented some years ago by Mr.
> Elder was not only a convenience but a positive luxury, Mr.
> Elder has alway shown considerable Mechanical ingenuity, I
> would that our district had a few hundred more of such citizens,
> with such men in our villages and with white agricultural labor in
> the country, we would soon be again a prosporous[sic] people.
> The call seems to be altogether for white labor on the plantation
> this cannot make us prosporous unless our towns keep pace and
> call in white mechanic, It is our duty now to call in white labor
> of any kind, our existence as a people depends on it, The south
> was and has always been deaf to her own interest, For years past,

slave labor on so large a system realized no profit, your waste old fields has been the result of it, and the cotton made went to buy mules, horses, and hogs, you could find but very few of our large planters who were not in debt, what they had, came by inheritance or the matured increase of the negro, in no instance can you point out a wealthy man who purchased lands and negros[sic] and paid for them by making cotton.

Frequent and urgent were the calls made within the last 15 years to arouse you [missing section]   true situation of the [country] to every call, blind to y[ ] [missing section] would neither [missing section]   with Nigros[sic] and cotton. For three year past have we been verging towards the vortex we have now fully entered how many of our people put forth their strenght [sic] to steer clear of it, How many used their influence in the past elections, How many in fact not only totally indifferent as to how their hands employed voted, but absented themselves from the poles[polls], let the white men of Fairfield District answers My vote can make but little difference was the answer of many have the citizens [of] our district any Idea how many made the same remark, if you have not come and examine the book of registration, A negro thought nothing of walking twenty or thirty miles to vote, it was [a] hardship for some white men to ride five. It was also a [co]mmon remark I don't care who is elected it is a matter of indifference to me, who fills the various offices, Since in the past elections you have been so indifferent as to who represented you, [or] by whom the helm of state was guided, don't arouse now and grumble at the acts of our talented Legislature,

If the yoke preparing for you, if the chains that your apathy has helped to forge, if the situation of the country generally cannot arouse you from your lethergetic[sic] slumbers, then sleep on and hand to your posterity the prints of your indifference. To them you are accountable. the [ques]tion is will you leave to your children a white man's government, The presidential election will in a great measure de[cide] the fate of the South. The few with all [ ]tions can accomplish but little   [missing section] the many are like thumps [missing section] [ ]ise, but nobody hurt. The first popping breeze bares away the thundering sound into space or perhaps into the lands of the K.K.K.

The old adage says, words are leaves, Deeds are fruits, Every generation is accountable to the coming one, we are reaping the fruits of the acts of the past thirty-five or forty ye[ars] Secession was the fruit of those acts,

The cold calculating policy of England knew well upon what point our country [missing] could be made to split, English influence, English gold was not spaired [sic], the apple of discord was thrown by her agents (Abolitionists), The North and South both eagerly seized it, [t]here followed acts, recriminations, abusive language anything that could build a wall of bitter hatred between the North and South was used as [mat]erial, Secession them[then] originated in the acts of more than thirty-five years ago, [th]e present poking of the North arises not as every man knows from any love for the negro, but from bitter hatred engendered past acts. The South despised the North the term Yankee that was in the days of the revolution an honor, was considered by us the lowest term of reproach, Farthers [sic] handed down their hatred as a legacy to their children, it was taught in the schools and preached in many instances from the pulpit both North & South. Nullification was the corner stone upon which Secession was built, the fabric has fallen and thousands have perished [missing section]   A different policy years   [missing section]   have found us a [missing section] rival not onl[y] in everything that makes a country's greatness, Remember the coming generation like yourselves must reap the fruits of the acts of those who preceeded [sic] them, Awake if you do not wish to leave to your prosperity [posterity] a country ruled by renegade white men, and an illiterate colored population who are merely [missing] in their hands.

[Signed with a script cipher CL intertwined][412]

Catharine introduced "New Improvement" by citing a local citizen, Mr. F. Elder, who had new inventions to his credit: a labor-saving new churn and a spring bedstead.[413] He was her example of a person with ingenuity who engaged in home manufactories. She argued that with a hundred more men with talents in "mechanical ingenuity" in towns and with white agricultural labor on plantations, the South could return to prosperity. An important point was that Elder was an Irish immigrant, and not a native citizen.[414]

In 1860, ninety-five percent of the white population of South Carolina was native born, and many of the black population, although likely a lower percentage, were also native born.[415] As a contrast, in 1860, out of a total population of twenty-seven million in the United States, four million, or approximately one-seventh, were foreign born.[416] According to Walter Edgar, South Carolina became a closed society after 1835,[417] and the native-born male population likely resented the editorial's reference to an industrious citizen who was an Irish immigrant, regardless of the truth of its argument.

Catharine's supporting points were a strong indictment of the status quo in 1868, claiming that South Carolina never looked after its own interests but repeated its earlier mistakes of over-planting cotton, investing in slave labor, and ignoring the benefits of manufacturing in the South. She believed that no real profit was realized from slave labor in producing cotton: "In no instance can you point out a wealthy man who purchased lands and negroes and paid for them by making cotton."[418] In this statement, she tackled a subject that was still debated in the twentieth century proving that she was conversant with controversial political topics.[419] She pointed to the last fifteen years as clear indicators of the present situation, and to the events of 1865–1868 as the final blows to a successful solution for South Carolinians. These were politically charged statements in a climate hostile to such allegations.

Catharine's indictments focused on the indifference of "the white men of Fairfield District" who said, "My vote can make but little difference," and challenged these citizens to "examine the book of registration" for the facts she subsequently shared:

A negro thought nothing of walking twenty or thirty miles to
vote it was a hardship for some white men to ride five.
Since in the past elections you have been so indifferent as to
who represented you, [or] by whom the helm of state was guided
don't arouse now and grumble at the act of our talented
Legislature, ...[420]

From 1865 to 1868 in the South Carolina Upstate, the
Republican Party and the Union Leagues organized freedmen and
taught them to be politically assertive. Blacks turned out in large
numbers at the polls, whereas "whites took a walk," a strategy that
backfired for whites and created a black majority in the legislature.

Catharine also tried appealing to the reader's sense of
responsibility by predicting that future generations would bear the
fruits of the present lethargy, and that the upcoming 1868
presidential election would determine the future of the South. Her
warnings had the urgency of frustration in seeing a population
chained by inaction and apathy. She vented this frustration by
charging as useless the deeds of those who voiced dissension into
the wind without action and those who resorted to threats and
violence: "The first popping breeze bears away the thundering
sound into space or perhaps into the lands of the KKK."

Repeating that "every generation is accountable to the coming
one," Catharine held answerable those who contributed to political
discord: South Carolina citizens and English abolitionists. She
believed that "English influence, English gold" promoted a
calculated division between the North and the South, building a
wall of hatred and distrust that led to Secession; and that the North
and the South were both to blame for embracing the conflict out of
historical differences that handed down a legacy of hatred to their
children. "It was taught in the schools and preached in many
instances from the pulpit both North & South."

In her final remarks, she urged her readers to, "Awake if you do not wish to leave to your prosperity [sic] a country ruled by renegade white men, and an illiterate colored population who are merely [missing] in their hands."

For Catharine to acknowledge ownership of these opinions locally was a personal risk,[421] though her understanding of where the South was heading was sound and accurate. With black militia units parading in the streets and freedmen asserting their voting rights at the polls, the white citizenry was ripe for the Ku Klux Klan's appeal to their paranoia about the threat against their personal safety. In many ways the KKK was an extension of the old patrol system from slavery.[422] Klan activity was so widespread in Upstate South Carolina that President Grant suspended the *writ of habeas corpus* in 1871 in ten counties, including Fairfield, Chester, and York, the only area in the country ever put under martial law due to Klan activity.

Fairfield, Chester, and York counties had strong familial, political, and economic ties.[423] Daughters of prominent families in all three of these counties during the antebellum period were students of Catharine Ladd, and several plantation owners had their portraits painted by George Ladd. Therefore, Catharine Ladd was not anonymous to those involved in Klan activity. If local periodicals published her essay under her name, both the writer and the editors would be suspect and possibly under attack.

The fact that Catharine was a white female would be no protection; the Klan showed no deference to women, whether black or white.[424] Her anonymity, while essential to her safety and to encourage publication and protection by the editor, could possibly have been betrayed by the subject, since promotion of white manufacturing was an ongoing theme of hers. If her essay themes were known to contemporary biographers, then others were also privy to this information. It is more than curious how this editorial

might have been circulated in a small community and remain
anonymous, especially when the literacy rate in the South for white
men and women in 1850 was over sixty percent.[425]

These facts may support the possibility that her essay was
printed as a pamphlet or circular and could explain why it was not
found in Fairfield County newspaper archives. Yet it remains
puzzling that she would have addressed a very specific, local
audience in an impassioned plea if she did not intend it to be
distributed to this audience. Her objective was, most certainly, to
arouse white voting citizens to the polls. The possibility remained
that she chose, or her family advised her, to withhold publication,
even as a circular, and that it was never read by its intended
audience. Victoria E. Bynum summed up what acceptable opinions
from women were during this time period in *Unruly Women*:

> Southern women were not to question or seek to influence
> public policy but only to encourage the wisdom and leadership
> of their men.[426]

Catharine was so impassioned about the privilege of voting
denied to her that she defied caution in expressing her views. She
fought ignorance on all levels and personally experienced a lifetime
of opportunities taken as a well-educated woman, pressing the
gender limits of her time and society. As a champion of education,
dedicated to over forty years of organizing and teaching females,
Catharine regarded education as the antidote for ignorance. To her,
ignorance was the enemy of informed, responsible citizens.

Catharine named causes of the societal ailments of the South:
Nullification that begat Secession, English influence and money
spread by her agents the abolitionists, and people of the North and
South who embraced the seeds of discord and spread hatred from
the schoolroom and pulpit. Her attitude about division extended

beyond regional and political boundaries and reached toward a peaceful solution, beginning with a first step by the white male voters of Fairfield. She ended the essay on the same theme that began her remarkable life—the importance of a citizenry's participation in democracy for the country to realize its greatness. Catharine agreed with the voice of Henry Grady, calling the "New South" in his speech in 1889. Perhaps she read his speech in the Atlanta *Constitution* twenty years after she wrote "New Improvement."

> *Henry Grady to the Bay State Club of Boston, 1889*
> I attended a funeral once in Pickens county in my State. . . . This funeral was peculiarly sad. It was a poor "one gallus" fellow, whose breeches struck him under the armpits and hit him at the other end about the knee—he didn't believe in *decollete* clothes. They buried him in the midst of a marble quarry: they cut through solid marble to make his grave; and yet a little tombstone they put above him was from Vermont. They buried him in the heart of a pine forest, and yet the pine coffin was imported from Cincinnati. They buried him within touch of an iron mine, and yet the nails in his coffin and the iron in the shovel that dug his grave were imported from Pittsburg. They buried him by the side of the best sheep-grazing country on the earth, and yet the wool in the coffin bands and the coffin bands themselves were brought from the North. The South didn't furnish a thing on earth for that funeral but the corpse and the hole in the ground. There they put him away and the clods rattled down on his coffin, and they buried him in a New York coat and a Boston pair of shoes and a pair of breeches from Chicago and a shirt from Cincinnati, leaving him nothing to carry into the next world with him to remind him of the country in which he lived, and for which he fought for four years, but the chill of blood in his veins and the marrow in his bones. Now we have improved on that. We have got the biggest marble-cutting establishment on earth within a hundred yards of that grave. We have got a half-dozen woolen mills right around

it, and iron mines, and iron furnaces, and iron factories. We are coming to meet you. We are going to take a noble revenge, as my friend, Mr. Carnegie, said last night, by invading every inch of your territory with iron, as you invaded ours twenty-nine years ago.[427]

Catharine Stratton Ladd, photography by Crosby Studio, c. 1891,
Crosbyville, Fairfield District, South Carolina.
Fitz Hugh McMaster Photograph Collection, Caroliniana Library,
University of South Carolina, Columbia.

Epilogue

The Legacy of Catharine Ladd

A life that spanned the nineteenth century from a woman's point of view would be remarkable. Catharine Stratton Ladd's experiences revealed in this biography offer insight into the many phases of her life. Her individual example increases our understanding of the "depth and nuance" "of gender, work, and region." [428]

A Relentless Spirit is the story of a young woman growing up in Richmond, Virginia, who became a confident school teacher and principal and established her own female academies. Within that environment, Catharine had relationships with men, personal and professional. She married an itinerant portrait artist and included her mother in her new family of six children. As a wife, a daughter, and a mother, Catharine managed her professional and personal lives in harmony, within and without the spheres defined by men for women in her time.

Living through the Civil War and the death of her husband, Catharine began again, with vigor, to rebuild her town and her children's opportunities, as well as provide a place for entertainment to boost morale in her community.

She succeeded in these areas, smoothing the path for the future of a new South. This new South would include women who wrote opinions boldly under their own names, who were able to vote, who owned property and claimed wages, who married and divorced, and whose race was not a barrier to education or equality under the law.

As a writer, Catharine joined Southerners who contributed to new Southern publications that appeared in the 1830s. She contributed poetry and prose to national women's magazines. Writing both under pen names and her own name, Catharine proved that she was conversant with classical literature and her contemporary literature in culture and politics. After leaving Winnsboro to live with her daughter in the country west of town, Catharine became blind. However, she continued to compose and publish poetry in the local newspaper up to her death in 1899.

The Winnsboro community expressed appreciation and respect for Catharine's legacy through announcements such as this one:

Tribute to Mrs. Ladd
One of Her old Pupils Suggests a Donation to Her

The friends and pupils of Mrs. Catharine Ladd are desirous of making some sort of testimonial of their affections and esteem in this the ninetieth year of her age. There is scarcely an old citizen in Fairfield and adjoining counties to whom this noble and talented woman is unknown, and many of them have been recipients of her kindness in various ways. A nature peculiarly unselfish, with lofty ideals, an untiring energy, and great faculty for organization, she instituted many plans for the public benefit, and was ever foremost in advancing social and charitable schemes.

When the war came none were more active and ardent in home-work for the soldiers; and it is not strange that at a recent meeting of veterans her name spoken in a passing tribute was greeted with a storm of applause. Every Confederate soldier was

a son to her, and they will not forget her earnest efforts for the
amelioration of their needs. Her strength, her purse, were freely
given to all who needed, and now in the hour of darkness it is
but meet that those who shared her bounty as teacher-and there
are few who have not, directly or indirectly, in one or the other
of these,-should have the opportunity of adding their names to
the list which will be sent with the testimonial

There is no need of entering into details of her present and
circumstances- total blindness, entire helplessness, and a lack of
those things which are essential to the suffering invalid. Friends,
let us rally and give the dear and aged lady our hearts' warm
greetings with this gift to cheer and comfort her last days!
Subscriptions will be received by Dr. G. B. McMaster at the drug
store, and packages also left there. It is hoped that this list will be
full and generous donations of various kinds by July 4th, at which
time they will be forwarded to her. Don't delay this good work,
but come at once. It may soon be *too late*!

An Old Pupil
The Fairfield News and Herald June 29, 1898

Obituary of Catharine Ladd

And then, at her death a year later, this obituary and memorial
poem was published in her honor:

Mrs. C. Ladd Dead
A Remarkable Woman Passes Away
Buckhead Jan 30 [1899]
 Mrs. C. Ladd died this evening at Buena Vista about five
o'clock. For the last week she has been quite sick and the end
was not unexpected. Mrs. R. L. Wilks and Dr. J. D. Cureton of
her immediate family were with her. Miss Josephine is yet quite
ill with pneumonia, but hope of her recovery is now entertained.
I suppose Mrs. Ladd will be laid to rest beside her son Dr. C. H.
Ladd in Salem Presbyterian Cemetery.

BEYOND THE NIGHT

"The lark-like voice that sang so true,
Through bitter days or bright,
Has found the source of deathless song
Beyond the night.
The loyal heart that beat so true,
Unchanged by earthly ills,
Has reached the everlasting blue
Of God's own hills.
The poet soul that clearly saw
In every noctral [sic] thing,
Twin miracles of love and law.
The eyes by stress of time made dim,
Death's myrtle border passed
Beyond the far horizon's rim
See light at last."

This beautiful poem was written by W. J. Hayne, Esq. and as it is
so applicable to our friend Mr. C. Ladd I have copied it as a
tribute in her memory and hope that you will give it space in
your columns.
N'importe The Fairfield News and Herald

Acknowledgements

I start with sincere thankfulness to Wade Fairey, former director of Historic Brattonsville when I joined the staff there in 1990. Wade shared what he knew about Catharine Ladd and Brattonsville Female Seminary, and George Ladd, her portraitist husband. Based on what was known I planned programs for elementary students about attending school in 1840. In the mid-1990s, Wade instigated a partnership with Rock Hill School District to replicate an extant building where Catharine Ladd had been principal, Feasterville Female Seminary. The reproduction of that school was built at Brattonsville by students in the Applied Technology program, and still operates for elementary students as a popular immersion program called *Historic Brattonsville Academy: Schooldays of 1840*. Wade supported my interest in Catharine Ladd by encouraging me to do more research and share it through lectures in the community. He helped me with research trips, including locating and copying Catharine Ladd's scrapbook. Without Wade's encouragement and support I would not have continued my interest in Catharine Ladd. I want to thank the current manager at Brattonsville, Kevin Lynch, who suggested the title for Catharine's biography and shared insights as a reader of the draft. Kevin felt the story of Catharine Ladd was an important one in the history of women's rights.

Interns in the education department at Historic Brattonsville in the 1990s were research assistants for the Brattonsville Academy

1840 project; eventually their findings contributed to the book. Ms. S. Sturgis-Workman tirelessly inventoried and transcribed the contents of Catharine Ladd's scrapbook, and also located more of her writings. Karen Timmons Ellison investigated antebellum female education, including arcane schoolgirl arts and crafts. Jaime Robinson Fawcett explored Mecklenburg genealogy and sampler makers for the exhibit and catalog (2003), "Virtue Leads and Grace Reveals: Embroideries and Education in Antebellum South Carolina." Jaime is now Executive Director of the Edgar Allan Poe Museum in Richmond, Virginia. Thank you each one for your positive attitude and excellent studies.

Early in my research Alex Moore, now retired from South Carolina Press, was very helpful to meet with me and suggest sources for Catharine Ladd's writings. Most of these leads were productive. He also directed me to the R.G. Dun & Co. Collection of credit insurance records in Historical Collections at the Baker Library, Bloomburg Center, Harvard Business School. I found the Dun Collection most helpful in learning about the Ladd Bros.' (sons of Catharine and George) mercantile businesses in Winnsboro and Fairfield County after the Civil War. Another retired editor from South Carolina Press, Linda Fogle, made a workable suggestion to separate the story of George Ladd, the portrait artist, from Catharine Ladd's biography.

In the years before internet search engines expanded the possibilities of research to digitized collections, Columbia was my second home. The search for information began with exploring the South Carolina Department of Archives and History for public records. Former Director Roger Stroup and the staff have continued, for over twenty years, to tirelessly search for requested records, some of which were hidden within other files. They always amazed me by managing to ferret out yet another possibility!

Repositories like Caroliniana Library at the University of South Carolina yielded papers of Southern families, mercantile accounts, letters, collections of historical newspapers, and journals. I owe appreciation to Henry Fulmer and the staff there who graciously retrieved collections of interest. York County Historical Center in York, South Carolina, part of the Culture and Heritage Museums, is an invaluable source of York County genealogical records and material culture. The staff always show patience and eagerness to assist, including Director of Archives Nancy Sambets, Director of Collections Jillian Matthews (and formerly, Latasha Richards), Historian Michael Scoggins, Research Assistant Wanda Fowler, and additional staff. Jillian Matthews and her assistant, Sarah Breaux, traveled to Fairfield County Museum to photograph their collections for the biography and for the Catharine Ladd web page.

Pelham Lyles, Director of the Fairfield County Museum in Winnsboro, South Carolina, continues to be a faithful colleague in researching evidence of Catharine's life. A native-born daughter, she is the go-to person on Fairfield County history. The museum houses important collections on George and Catharine Ladd, including original portraits by George Ladd, schoolgirl art by Catharine's students, family history, and original documents and photographs.

Friends whose interest in history is a hobby were especially helpful. Angela Purcell, interpreter at the Museum of York County, whose specialties are Edwardian clothing and needlework, is an apt online researcher who found the Boston Public Library site that included a critique of one of Catharine Ladd's poems. A former student, junior docent, and adult volunteer interpreter at Historic Brattonsville, Angie Alexander, located and sent a needed newspaper article from the archives at the University of Georgia, where she is currently a doctoral candidate in history. Nancy Craig kept me going with timely reminders of her investment in my ideas.

She and Pam Schmidt were always willing to travel to conferences on antebellum needlework and education. Merry traveling companions are, like the Moravian saying, "music on a journey."

Carey Tilley, director of the Culture and Heritage Museums, and the Culture and Heritage Museums commissioners agreed to sponsor my research and the biography as part of the museum's mission to share local history with York county residents and beyond. Carey also read the manuscript and offered his comments. Stephen Crotts designed the webpage on Catharine Ladd and Brattonsville Female Seminary.

Dr. Melissa Walker, Heyday Coaching, offered me nourishment and encouragement along the way, helping me stay focused and *relentless,* saying, "Way to go!" Dr. Walker was a reader along with Sam Thomas, Curator, T.R.R. Cobb House, Athens, Georgia; Charles LeCount, Deputy Director, North Carolina Division of State Historic Sites and Properties, Department of Natural and Cultural Resources, Raleigh, North Carolina; and friends and colleagues Pam Schmidt and Marsha Hanna. I am deeply grateful for their diverse research specialties, careful reviews, and suggestions with which I edited the manuscript.

My editor, Maureen Ryan Griffin of Floating Leaf Press in Charlotte, North Carolina, led the way to completion. She taught me the craft of writing. Her enthusiasm, imagination, and positive force gave me the energy and belief to envision this biography. Maureen especially motivated me to consider the audience and readability factors in the manuscript. Mary Charles Nash, a local artist, created the cover, using an image of Catharine Ladd that interpreted her life.

My husband, Ed, was a stay-by-me companion, sometimes suffering through the disappointments, but shall I say, ecstatically relieved to see the project to its conclusion. Thank you for loving me that much!

Postscript

Ladd Brothers' Mercantile, 1865-1880

The following is a narrative of a small Southern town in the post-war years and how the Ladds and its other residents attempt to learn a new way of doing business by regrouping, partnering, and being "jacks of all trades." It is an intimate glimpse of how business owners competed for and attracted customers, including freedmen and women whose business would become vital.

Dr. Charles H. Ladd was relieved from military duty in the 56th Regiment, North Carolina Troops, Confederate Army, in December 1864 after several bouts with illness. In a letter written by his brother A. W. Ladd from Charleston on July 24, 1865, quoted in the section on George W. Ladd's death, A.W. said that he had not heard from Charley in seven days, and that Charley had been unwell. It is unknown if Charles Ladd was at home in Winnsboro at the time when his father died. What is known is that an advertisement appeared in the Winnsboro *Tri Weekly News* on May 30, 1865:

> Dr. C.H. Ladd (LATE ASS'T MEDICAL DIRECTOR, CSA)
> Will give his attention to the practice of MEDICINE and
> SURGERY in Fairfield District.

A full supply of Medicines on hand.
Office No. 2, Law Range, in rear of Court House.

In August 1865, the *Tri Weekly News* advertised:

Furniture, &C, A small lot of Furniture, Mattresses, &c. on hand
yet. AMBROTYPES At the solicitation of several persons, I
have opened my Gallery for a short time. Call soon if you want
pictures. A.W. Ladd Court House, Up Stairs.

Besides selling and repairing furniture, A.W. Ladd was one of
eight photographers who were in operation in South Carolina in
1865.[429]

The partnership of Dr. Charles Ladd and A. W. Ladd in the dry
goods business appeared the following month:

Messrs. LADD BROS. (Leventritt building) calls[sic] attention
to their establishment.
Mr. JAS. M. DALY has opened a stock of watches, jewelry, &c.,
at Ladd Bro's. Drug Store.
Dr. C. H. LADD has removed his office to the rear of Ladd
Bros.' Drug Store, Leventritt's building.[430]

The Ladd Bros. mercantile business was insured and monitored
for its credit worthiness by a Northern firm of R. G. Dun &
Company.[431] Those reports expanded the information about the
Ladd Bros. business, including the fact that A. W. Ladd was in the
mercantile business before 1865. In fact, he had a partnership
before the war with W. B. McCreight from December 1858 to
February 1859 in a hardware and grocery business with about
$2,000 in capital. The agent for R. G. Dun rated the young men as
"of steady industrial habits and moderate capacity," in business but
a short time. The accidental death of W. B. McCreight was reported
in the newspaper in March 1859.

In 1865 the newly established Ladd Bros. dry goods store, Ladd
Bros. drug store, Mr. Daly's jewelry goods, and Dr. Charles Ladd's
medical office were all located in the Leventritt Building. R. G. Dun
& Co. gave their jobs as physician and former store clerk, "doing a
small business, are worthy young men, but think their means are
light indeed."

The newspapers carried notices of what kind of merchandise
was for sale by Ladd Bros., Commission House, dry goods and drug
store, including ads that featured these varied titles. Goods for sale
included drugs, medicines, medicinal whiskey (unless by the case),
cigars, smoking and chewing tobacco, dry goods, jewelry, printed
circulars,[432] Yankee notions, and country goods sold on
commission.

The year 1866 began for the Ladd Bros.', Cheap Cash Store,
with advertisements for fabrics and shoes.[433] In the spring, a new
shipment of spring and summer fabrics arrived, and the drug store
replenished supplies. Both Dr. Ladd and Dr. Aiken, who ran drug
stores in Winnsboro, stated that they sold and compounded drugs
"in strict accordance with the U.S. Dispensary of 1866." The
regulation and distribution of opiates was the business of the
United States Dispensary, but prescriptions were not *required* until
the 1900s.

At the end of the year in 1865, the former *Fairfield Herald and
Register*, then the *Winnsboro* [*sic*] *News* newspaper offices that
included town lot #40 (one-half an acre), buildings, and printing
press, were up for auction as part of the estate settlement of F.
Gaillard vs. R. S. Desportes. In May 1866, the office for the
Winnsboro *Tri Weekly News* by Gaillard & Desportes was "in the
rear of Ladd Bros. Drug Store where we will be found at all times."

The newspaper confirmed that A. W. Ladd continued as a
photographer in March 1866:

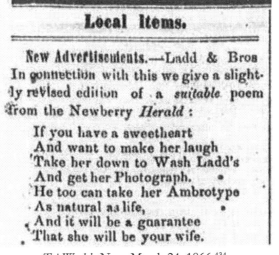

Local Items.

New Advertisements.—Ladd & Bros
In connection with this we give a slight-
ly revised edition of a *suitable* poem
from the Newberry *Herald* :

If you have a sweetheart
And want to make her laugh
'Take her down to Wash Ladd's
And get her Photograph.
He too can take her Ambrotype
As natural as life,
And it will be a guarantee
That she will be your wife.

Tri Weekly News, March 24, 1866.[434]

He also had other jobs in the spring of 1866:

> Our friend A. W. Ladd may still be found at the Drug Store
> where he is prepared to take pictures, deal out drugs, measure
> muslin and—2 doors South at the Ware Room—make
> "depositories" for victims of too much or too little drugs. See
> notice.[435]

So now there is a warehouse where A. W. is perhaps a coffin
maker?

At the end of May 1866, a confectionary and bakery of Townley
and Oxner was located next to Ladd Bros. Within a month, the
third Ladd brother, George D. Ladd, opened a new confectionary
in Thespian Hall, over the post office.[436] In July he advertised, "I
am now prepared to furnish gentlemen with Lunch, such as Pies,
Iced Milk, Cakes, Syrup, &c."[437] George D. Ladd's confectionary
moved from Thespian Hall to No. 1 Fairfield Hotel Range as
described under New Advertisements:

See the advertisement of G.D. Ladd & Co. All kinds of nice
things are kept on hand or prepared to order by this firm, and
"weddin fixins" &c. Call and see the handsome display of
confections &c., at G. D. Ladd & Co's.[438]

In his advertisement, George D. Ladd also offered candy in
bulk for country stores in twenty-five to one-hundred-pound
amounts. This was the last newspaper notice about his business,
which was not to say he discontinued to bake.

The summer advertisements enticed customers to purchase
summer goods at New York prices for cash. The problem of
purchasing items on credit was already presenting itself for the
owners. The flow of goods into new town businesses was
substantial, but the problem of how business owners could make a
profit with customers who paid mostly on credit was never solved.

The Ladd brothers published notices about credit and a new
partnership in the fall with R. A. Buchanan. "Ladd Bros. & Co.
notify the public of a new firm. May their shadow never grow less."
Ladd Bros. under the same heading calls on debtors to "pay" up.
May they all be able to "do just so." And further down the column,
"On Commission Ladd Bros. & Co. This firm has a fine assortment
of ready made clothing."[439] At the same time, A. W. Ladd traded his
interest as agent for a furniture store and shop to D. B. McCreight,
whose gin shop carried Fisk's Metallic Burial Cases.

For the year 1866, the Ladd Bros. dry goods mercantile store
was in the former Fairfield Hotel owned by Catharine. She
purchased the building and lot in January, no doubt motivating the
move there for the Ladd Bros. store and for the confectionary of
George D. Ladd. Along with the Thespian Hall building rental,
Catharine invested in the town's revival.

The next year, 1867, Ladd Bros. & Co. added a new partner,
William J. Egleston, and moved to No. 2 Bank Range, also owned
by their mother. Catharine did not lose a rented space in the

Fairfield Hotel building, however, because a young man, W. M. Nelson, moved in as a family grocer in December "where Ladd Bros. kept last year." A statement about the new grocer's service to the Confederacy promoted him to customers:

> His experience in business and his gallantry as a good
> Confederate soldier, as well as his excellent taste in the selection
> of stock of goods in the grocery line, will no doubt insure a
> good demand upon his stock.[440]

The Ladd Bros. declared themselves a specialty retailer, with a supply of shoes never offered in Winnsboro, and with the largest and most varied selections of goods since the war.

The Fairfield Herald promoted the use of a barometer for consulting the weather on display in the drug store of Drs. Aiken and Ladd, another partnership. The barometer was "constructed by our ingenious friend Dr. C. H. Ladd." [441]

However, in September, the partnership with Dr. Aiken ended when Ladd Bros. announced the buy-out of all the Aiken and Ladd drug store stock; the drug business continued in their former stand. There was a call for patrons of the former partnership to pay up contracts due. There was concern about the economy in the dry good business as well. Ladd Bros. & Co. announced sometime in that fall of 1867, "In consequence of the great decline in cotton we have this day marked down clothing, boots & shoes, Yankee notions, hats & caps at least fifteen per cent lower." [442]

Merchants Ketchin & McMaster printed a notice to their former customers that many had accounts still open and unresolved since 1860 and 1861. Daly's Jewelry Store stated, "I sell for cash and I work for cash!" In the fall of 1868, Ladd Bros. declined filling any orders unless accompanied with cash.

In 1868 they were described by the R. G. Dun agent as sober, industrious, and attentive to business, but had stock in trade as only means. In that same year, in November, they were operating out of a house lately purchased by them, but not yet paid for, "seem to be doing well," and had no debts except the house.

In 1869, the credit report noted the new partner, W. M. Dwight. Their business continued in dry goods and drugs through 1870.

In 1871, R. G. Dun & Company's agent reported that the Ladds were buying cotton and urging others to sell their cotton at home. Their worth was reported as $10,000. Their young partner Mr. Dwight had little means but was popular and influenced trade. The notes stated that the firm was doing well, that all the men were of good business habits and their credit was good.[443]

The co-partnership with Mr. Dwight was dissolved in 1873, and the firm of A. W. and C. H. Ladd was simply Ladd Bros.

In the fall of 1874, the agent reported that the Ladd Bros. were in business on their Flint Hill plantation, one hundred acres not fully paid for, but soon to be. The stated $10,000 in worth seemed to be tied to Catharine's holding the title to mortgage in town.

The following years through 1875 reported the Ladds making money, meeting their engagements promptly, and having their plantation nearly paid for. They were "honest, doing well," with a small stock worth about fifteen hundred, "mostly kept for Negro trade." [444] Among several additions to Ladd Bros. advertisements was, in 1877, "To Our Colored Friends."

Like online businesses today that broaden their outlay to increase appeal and sales, the Ladd brothers saw the new opportunities in customers. According to the above assessments by R. G. Dun and Company and the newspaper advertisement, from 1875 to 1877 their rural dry goods business was aimed at the Negro trade. The Ladd brothers saw how they could stay in business during the years of Reconstruction by directing their advertisements and stock to a large, newly freed population who sought to make their way as well.

LADD BROS.
WE have now completed one of the best stocks of
DRY GOODS, BOOTS and SHOES, HATS and CAPS, YANKEE
NOTIONS, CROCKERY, &c.
IN THE COUNTY.
We will not be undersold. Let us say, however, that our best Calicoes are 10
cents a yard. We cannot sell them lower and have a uniform profit on all Goods.
GIVE US A CALL.

TO OUR COLORED FRIENDS.
As you have always put confidence in us, we will state that you may depend on
getting goods at a regular even price.
No baits held out to anyone. nov30.

Transcribed from the *News and Herald* (Winnsboro, South Carolina)
February 15, 1877 [445]

As a farmer with property in Fairfield District, Dr. C. H. Ladd shared his experience of applying bone phosphate as manure to twenty acres. It was not adulterated, as were many of the fertilizers sold. He manufactured the phosphate "by himself from the skeletons of the numberless horses and mules that were killed by Sherman before crossing the river in his memorable raid."[446]

And in 1878, Ladd Bros. improved their customer service with the statement, "We intend to try to please you in prices, goods, and polite attention."

By 1879, they had "too much of everything" and "too many accounts unpaid. All persons not paid up by the first of January will be sued."[447]

These times were followed by the bankruptcy of the firm in town. Through the credit reports of R.G. Dun and Company it was learned that the dry goods store did continue in Winnsboro. The Ladds owned property in Fairfield District called Flint Hill plantation, and by 1874 had an additional location as reported by R. G. Dun and Company.

The credit report for 1876 stated their (Flint Hill) plantation was worth $10,000, with $3,000 still due. They owned horses, mules, and other personal property with a total worth of $18,000. In the winter of 1877 they also did business in Winnsboro.

It was learned that, in 1878, they secured debts on the store's stock by a mortgage on their personal property plus a mortgage on Catharine's house. Catharine provided collateral against their debt. The last report in September 1878 mentioned their stock in town was down about forty-five percent and about twelve percent at the country store at Flint Hill. They had an encumbrance, a mortgage on Flint Hill, and on two other tracts, a mortgage on Ridge Place and on their farm's cattle and stock.

Appendix A

Historical Timelines

Timeline, Prior to Birth of Catharine and George Ladd

KEY

Nation

State

Catharine Stratton and George Ladd

Ladd Children

1765	*Birth of Catharine, maternal grandmother of Catharine Stratton Ladd*
1783	**Sept 23 Treaty of Paris, End of Revolutionary War**
1783	Charleston, South Carolina incorporated as a city
1783	*Birth of Ann Collins, mother of Catharine Stratton Ladd*
1786	Capital of South Carolina moved to Columbia (from Charleston)
1786	*Marriage of maternal grandmother Catharine to John Collins*
1788	**George Washington elected President**
1790	**US Constitution ratified**
1790	United States Federal Census: SC

        140,178 white

        107,094 enslaved

          1,801 free black

        249,073 total

1792	**George Washington reelected President**
1794	*Death of John Collins, maternal step-grandfather of Catharine S. Ladd, Richmond, VA*
1796	**John Adams elected President**
1797	*Marriage Catharine Collins to Humphrey Dabney, Richmond, VA, maternal grandparents of Catharine*
1800	**Thomas Jefferson elected President**
1800	United States Federal Census: SC

        196,255 white

        146,151 enslaved

          3,185 free black

        345,591 total

Timeline for Catharine Stratton Ladd 1808–1899

KEY

Nation

State

Catharine Stratton and George Ladd

Ladd Children

1802	*June 21 Birth of George Williamson Livermore Ladd, Exeter, NH*
1802	Dr. David Ramsey introduced practice of smallpox vaccination in SC
1804	**Thomas Jefferson reelected President**
1805	College of South Carolina opened in Columbia
1807	*Dec 16 Marriage of Ann Collins to James Stratton, Henrico Co., VA, parents of Catharine*
1808	*Oct 28 Birth of Catharine Stratton, Richmond, VA*
1808	**End of foreign slave trade**
1808	**James Madison elected President**
1810	United Stated Federal Census: SC
	214,196 white
	196,365 enslaved
	4,554 free black
	415,115 total
1811	South Carolina Free School Act passed
1812	**War of 1812 with England**
1812	**James Madison reelected President**
1815	*George Ladd's first known portrait in miniature of Peter Townsend, New York*
1816	**James Monroe elected President**
1818	*George Ladd, age 16, merchant seaman, Plymouth, Boston, Savannah*
1818	Price of short-staple cotton in Charleston market at thirty-five cents a pound, highest price in antebellum period
1820	**James Monroe reelected President**
1820	**Missouri Compromise – issue of statehood and slavery**

1820	United Stated Federal Census: SC
	237,440 white
	258,475 enslaved
	6,826 free black
	502,741 total
1822	Slave insurrection in Charleston led by Denmark Vesey, free black; Denmark Vesey hanged
1824	**John Quincy Adams elected President**
1824	**Marquis de Lafayette's tour of American South**
1824	*Catharine Stratton, 16-year-old schoolgirl, meets Lafayette in Richmond, VA*
1825	Marquis de Lafayette tours South Carolina
1826	**Death of Thomas Jefferson**
	Death of John Adams
1827	*Sept 18 Marriage of Catharine Stratton , age 18, to George W.L. Ladd, age 25*
1828	**Andrew Jackson elected President; John C. Calhoun elected Vice President**
1828-29	*Catharine and George Ladd in Charleston with Ann Stratton member of household*
	George portraitist; Catharine teaching ornamentals to females
1829	*George Ladd itinerant portrait artist n New Bern, North Carolina*
	Catharine Ladd contributing to Charleston newspapers.
1830	*Catharine and George Ladd in Fayetteville, North Carolina; George in Nash County, North Carolina*
1830	United Stated Federal Census: SC
	257,863 white
	323,322 black
	581,185 total
1831	Price of short-staple cotton in Charleston market at nine cents a pound, bottom price
1832	**Andrew Jackson reelected President; John C. Calhoun Vice President**
1832	**John C. Calhoun resigned as Vice President to return to the US Senate**
1832	Ordinance of Nullification nullified the tariff acts of 1828 and 1832
1832-33	*Catharine teaching at Rolesville Female Academy, Rolesville, North Carolina*
1832	Carolina Gilman began editing *The Rose Bud or Youth's Gazette*, Charleston
	Catharine Ladd contributing to The Rose Bud
1833	Steam railroad from Charleston to Hamburg, South Carolina completed at 136 miles, the longest railroad in the world
1833	Ordinance of Nullification repealed

1835	*George Ladd portrait in miniature of Matthew F. Maury, VA; bust length portrait of William Rosborough, Chester, SC*
1835-37	*Catharine Ladd contributing poetry to a new Southern periodical, The Southern Literary Messenger, Richmond, VA*

1836   *Oct 15 Birth of A.W. Ladd, son of Catharine and George, Chester County, SC*

1836   **Martin Van Buren elected President.**

1837   **US Senator John C. Calhoun (SC) defended slavery as "a positive good" to the Senate**

1838   *Catharine teaching ornamentals at Macon Female Academy, Macon, Georgia*

1838   *Apr 1 Birth of Charles H. Ladd, son of Catharine and George, in Macon, GA*

1839   *George advertising portrait painting in Macon, Georgia*

1840   **William Henry Harrison elected President**

1840   United Stated Federal Census: SC
         259,084 white
         327,038 enslaved
           8,276 free black
         594,398 total

1840   United States Federal Census, *George Ladd owner of two enslaved females*

1840-42   *Catharine principal of Brattonsville Female Seminary at Brattonsville, York District, SC*

1842   Railroad service between Columbia and Charleston, SC

1843-44   *Catharine principal of Winnsboro Female Seminary, Winnsboro, SC*

1844   **James K. Polk elected President**

1844   *Dec 23 Birth of Josephine N. Ladd, daughter of Catharine and George, Feasterville, SC*

1845-48   *Catharine principal of Feasterville Female Seminary, Feasterville, Fairfield District, SC*

1845   *Oct-Dec Birth of George Douglas Ladd, son of Catharine and George, Feasterville, SC*

1844-1860   *George Ladd portraitist, seven portraits painted of planters of Fairfield District, SC*

1848   **Zachary Taylor elected President**

1848   Telegraph completed between Columbia and Charleston, SC

1849   *George Ladd deed of purchase of two town lots in Winnsboro, SC*

1849-62   *Catharine principal of Winnsboro Female Seminary/Winnsboro Female Institute (1860)*

1849   *Apr 18 Birth of Catherine Ladd, daughter of Catharine and George, Winnsboro, SC*

1850	United Stated Federal Census: SC
	274,563 white
	393,944 black
	668,507 total

1850 Missouri Compromise of 1850 – statehood and slavery

1850 United Stated Federal Census, George Ladd owner of seven enslaved persons

1851   *Nov 14 Birth of Annie J. Ladd, daughter of Catharine and George, Winnsboro, SC, last child born to the Ladds*

1852 George Ladd deed for purchase of Ketchin house, Winnsboro, SC for female institute

1855-63 George Ladd deeds of purchase for town lots in Winnsboro, SC

1860	United Stated Federal Census: SC
	291,300 white
	402,206 enslaved
	9,914 free black
	88 others
	703,708 total

1860 United States Federal Census, George Ladd owner of eight enslaved persons

1860 Abraham Lincoln elected President

1861 Feb 9 South Carolina joined other states to form Confederate States of America, Montgomery, AL

1861 March Catharine and George Ladd submit a proposal to the Committee on Flag and Seal for a design for the Confederate National Flag

1861 April 12 First shot fired on Fort Sumter, Charleston, SC

1861-1865 Civil War

1861-1865 A.W., Charles H., George D. Ladd serve in SC Volunteers, Confederate Army; Dr. Charles H. Ladd surgeon
Catharine Ladd, President of Ladies Relief Association of Fairfield; continues to teach; takes in boarders

1862 George Ladd deed of sale for Ketchin house
George Ladd deed of sale for two enslaved persons

1864 July 14 Death of George Ladd, Winnsboro, SC
George Ladd probate inventory of estate, owner of five enslaved persons

1865 February Union Brigadier General Slocum's Union troops occupied and burned sections of town of Winnsboro, SC including Catharine Ladd's house and contents

1865 April 14 End of Civil War

1865 April 14 Assassination of President Lincoln

1865-1877 Reconstruction in the South

1866-67 Catharine Ladd deeds of purchase from Dr. David Aiken estate, lots and buildings including the old Fairfield Hotel, for total of $15,000

1868 "New Improvement" editorial by Catharine Ladd

1868   New South Carolina Constitution of 1868 drawn up
        and general election held; Governor Robert K. Scott
        of Ohio

1868   Ulysses S. Grant elected President

1865-1880s Ladd Brothers and partners dry goods store in Winnsboro
        Dr. Charles H. Ladd, physician and pharmacist
          A.W. Ladd, photographer, dry goods store, furniture repairer
          George D. Ladd, confectioner (briefly), store clerk

1870   United Stated Federal Census: SC
                289,667 white
                415,814 black
                    125 others
                705,606 total

1870   Catharine living in Township 1, Fairfield with adult children in household

**1871   President Ulysses S. Grant suspended the writ of habeas corpus due
        to KKK-instigated violence, in nine upcountry South Carolina
        counties: Chester, Chesterfield, Fairfield, Lancaster, Laurens,
        Newberry, Spartanburg, Union and York**

*1872   Josephine N. Ladd deed of purchase for 18
        acres on Buena Vista plantation where she
        operated a mill*

1872   Ulysses S. Grant reelected President

*1875   Jan 12 Death of Annie J. Ladd Neil, Winnsboro,
        SC, daughter of G and C Ladd*

1880   United States Federal Census: SC
                391,105 white
                604,332 black
                    140 other
                995,577 total

1880s   Bankruptcy filed for Ladd Bros. stores

*1880   Oct 12 Death of Dr. Charles H. Ladd,
        Winnsboro, SC, son of G and C Ladd*

1890   United States Federal Census: SC
                462,008 white
                688,934 black
                    207 other
              1,151,149 total

*1891   Catharine Ladd becomes blind, continues to write and publish poetry,
        reminiscences for the Fairfield Herald*

1899   Jan 30 Death of Catharine Ladd, Fairfield County, SC

Appendix B

Genealogy Charts
for Stratton and Ladd Families

Genealogy Chart for Collins/Dabney/Stratton Family

I <u>Catharine (maiden name unknown) [Sears/Zahr; Miller; Foulk?] (husband unk)</u>
   b. 1765-69, Pennsylvania d. >1840 <1850 VA

                                                Henrico, VA
     <u>1. Ann Collins (adopted surname)</u> Dec. 16 1807 m. <u>James Stratton</u>
       b. 1783 d. 1856 Winnsboro, SC   b. Ireland
                                                d.>1810<1820
                                     Portsmouth, VA, at sea

          1. son Stratton?   2. Catharine Stratton
            d.>1810   b. Oct. 28, 1808 Richmond, VA

II <u>Catharine (maiden name unknown)   c. 1786 m. John Collins, Sr.</u>
                                       b. Ireland d. 1794,
                                      Richmond, VA

    <u>1. Jane Collins Oct. 24, 1805 m. William McCabe</u> 2. John Collins, Jr.
      b. 1787 Richmond, VA d. 1843 b. 1780 d. 1823   b. 1790 Richmond, VA
                                           d.>1815

                                 3. Adam Collins (nm)
                                   b. 1792 d. 1812 Richmond, VA

1. James Dabney McCabe   2. John Collins McCabe (Rev.)
  b. 1806 Richmond, VA   b. 1810 Richmond, VA
                             d. Feb. 26, 1875 Chambersburg, PA

3 .Josephine Augusta McCabe
  b. 1815 Richmond, VA

III   <u>Catharine Collins</u>c. 1797 m <u>Humphrey Dabney</u>
                           b. 1772-1776 VA
                           d. 1809 Richmond, VA

<u>1. Katharine Dabney 1814 m. John Brooks Prentis</u> 2. Mary Ann Dabney (nm)
   b. 1799   b. 1789 d. 1848   b. 1800

3. Sarah E. Dabney   <u>4. Albert Gallatin Dabney m. Susan Hill</u>
  b. 1801   b. 1804 d. 1884

 5. Susan Hill Dabney   1. Humphrey 2. Emma (nm) 3 Alberta
   b. 1805   4. John C. 5. David M. 6. Susan S.

Genealogy Chart for Ladd Family

Daniel Ladd   1801 m.   Lydia Dow
b. 1773 d. unk   b. May 7, 1776 Salem
     d. Oct. 1, 1811, Plymouth, N.H.

1. George Williamson Livermore Ladd   2. Permelia Ladd   3 Bela Orlando Ladd
b. June 21, 1802   d. July 14, 1864   b. 1803 d. 1804   b. 1805

4. William H. Ladd   5. Charles Ladd
b. 1807 d. 1886   b. 1809

Richmond, VA
George Williamson Livermore Ladd   m. Sept. 18, 1827   Catharine Stratton
June 21, 1802-July 14, 1864   Oct. 28, 1808-Jan. 30, 1899

1. Albert Washington Ladd   m. 1875   Mary Ann Owings
    b. Oct. 15, 1836 Chester, SC   b. May 22, 1855, SC
    d. Feb. 11, 1908, Fairfield, SC   d. Feb. 25, 1936, SC

2. Charles Henry Ladd (nm)   3. Josephine N. Ladd (nm)
    b. April 1, 1838, Macon, GA   b. Dec. 23, 1844
    d. Oct. 9, 1880 Fairfield   d. Jan. 14, 1912 Fairfield, SC

4. George Douglas Ladd   m.c. 1875   Louise Phillips
   b. Oct-Dec. 1845, Feasterville, SC   b.c. 1850
    d. 1910, Union Co., SC

5. Catherine Lydia Ladd   m. Oct. 19, 1866   Dr. James D. Cureton
    b. April 18, 1849 Winnsboro, SC   b. Aug. 6, 1830 Greenville, SC
    d. June 5, 1921 Pickens, SC   d. Nov. 11, 1904, Pickens, SC

6. Annie James Ladd m. 1874 John J. Neil
    b. Nov. 14, 1851 Winnsboro, SC
    d. Dec. 1, 1875 Fairfield, SC

Appendix C

Catharine Ladd Entry
in
Mary T. Tardy's
The Living Female Writers of the South

MRS. CATHARINE LADD.

THE name that heads this article will call a thrill of pleasure to
many hearts—for this lady is "one of the most noted and successful of the teachers of the State of South Carolina," and hundreds
of her old pupils, many of them now "teaching," scattered throughout
the land, remember her kindness and entire unselfishness. "She is
the most generous of women; her time, her talents, her worldly goods
are at the command of all her friends," says one of her ex-pupils.

Mrs. Ladd is a native of Virginia—was born in October, 1810—
married when eighteen years old to Mr. Ladd, a portrait and miniature painter. Her maiden name was Catharine Stratton.

For several years after her marriage Mrs. Ladd wrote poetry, which
was published in the various periodicals of the day. For three years
she was a regular correspondent of several newspapers, and published
a series of articles on drawing, painting, and education, which attracted considerable attention.

In 1842, Mrs. Ladd permanently settled in the town of Winnsboro',
South Carolina, where she established one of the largest institutions
of learning in the State, which sustained its well-deserved reputation
until closed, in 1861.

Mrs. Ladd has contributed tales, sketches, essays, and poems to
various journals under different *noms de plume*—as "Minnie May-
flower," "Arcturus," "Alida," and "Morna."

During the existence of the "Floral Wreath," published in Charleston by Mr. Edwin Heriott, Mrs. Ladd was a regular contributor.
Mr. Heriott, in a notice of the literary talent of the South, speaking
of Mrs. Ladd's poetical works, said: "They were sweet, smooth, and
flowing, particularly so; but, like Scotch music, their gayest notes
were sad."

In 1851, she with ardor took up the subject of education, home
manufactories, and encouragement of white labor, believing that the
ultimate prosperity of South Carolina would depend on it. She rea-
soned from a conviction that South Carolina could not long compete

62   489

490   LIVING FEMALE WRITERS OF THE SOUTH.

with the more Southern and Southwestern States in raising cotton, and an extensive system of slave labor would realize no profit.

Mrs. Ladd's plays, written at the solicitation of friends, and performed by them, were very popular. The "Grand Scheme" and "Honeymoon" were celebrated far and wide. The incidents and introduction of characters showed that she had more than ordinary talent for that species of composition. Mrs. Ladd has a wonderful knack of managing young people.

After the commencement of the war, Mrs. Ladd gave up everything to devote herself to the cause of the South. She lived for the soldiers! was elected President of the "Soldiers' Aid Association," which office she retained until the close of the war, and by her untiring exertions kept the society well supplied with clothing. Her pen was unused during the war, the needle and her personal supervision being constantly in demand. In Winnsboro', no church is built, no charity solicited, no ball, concert, tableaux, or fair — *nothing* goes on without her cheerful and ever-ready aid.

Mrs. Ladd is said to be "homely," and dresses to suit herself, never caring about the "latest fashions," ignores "hoops," and always wears her hair short. Her manner is abrupt and decided; but one instinctively feels it to be "kind."

The "Confederate flag" is said to have originated with Mrs. Ladd; the first one, we allude to. The fire of February 21st, 1865, destroyed the literary labor of thirty years. With the assistance of a Federal officer, Mrs. Ladd saved the jewels of the Masonic Lodge in the next house to hers; but the flame and smoke prevented her finding the "charter." By this time the fire had got so much ahead on her own premises, and the confusion was so great, that she lost everything.

It is said that outside of the walls of her school, Mrs. Ladd was the gay, social companion of every young lady under her charge. Following her to the school-room, you instantly felt the change: though not perhaps a word was spoken, every young lady felt it. She has a powerful will and habit of centring every thought and feeling instantly on the occupation of the moment. The confusion of voices or passing objects never seemed to disturb her when writing.

A friend of Mrs. Ladd says: "Her quick motions show the rapidity of thought. Even now, at the age of fifty-eight, were you walking behind her, you might mistake her, from the light buoyancy of step, for a young girl."

1862.   ◇

Appendix D

Brattonsville Female Seminary Advertisement

Transcription of Brattonsville Female Seminary Advertisement in *The Compiler*, Yorkville, South Carolina, August 22, 1840

Brattonsville Female Seminary
Mrs. C. Ladd, Principal

This institution is situated midway between the Villages of Yorkville and Chesterville, on the main stage road.

As an instructress Mrs. Ladd is well known; therefore it will be useless, again to enumerate the high testimonials of her qualifications.

Arrangements have also been made by Dr. Jno. S. Bratton whose residence is nearly opposite the Seminary to accommodate with board, all young ladies who may wish to become pupils of this institution. Board can also be had at the residence of Mr. Samuel Moore, situated about half a mile from the Seminary.

The course of study in the English Department will comprise all branches that belong to a thorough English education, in all its parts. In this department no pupil will be allowed a choice of studies, but all will be examined and classed accordingly; and so long as they continue pupils of the institution, they will by its rules, be required to go on with their studies by a regular course.

RATES OF TUITION, PERTERM, OF TEN MONTHS

Orthography[1], Reading, & Writing	$12.00
Arithmetic, Grammar, Geography, and History	$20.00
The studies of this Class (including the above) will consist of the following Branches: Rhetoric, Astronomy, Natural and Moral Philosophy, Algebra, Geometry, &c	$32.00
Modern Languages	$35.00
Tuition in the Musical and Ornamental Departments, Music on the Piano Forte	$50.00
Guitar	$45.00

---

[1] Orthography was the 19th century term for spelling.

Pencil Drawing and Landscape Painting in the Water Colours	$24.00
Oil and Miniature Painting	$32.00
Ornamental, Needle, and Fancy Work	$20.00
For the use of the Piano	$ 4.00
Use of the Guitar	$ 2.00
Tuition is required to be paid in advance	
Boarding including: Rooms, Fires, Washing, Candles, &c	$ 8.00

No corporeal punishment will be allowed; and pupils over the age of twelve, who cannot be managed by the force of reason, will be expelled. No superfluous expense will be allowed in dress; and pupils will be required to be neat but plain. No pupil will be admitted for a less time than a half term of five months.

Persons wishing their children or wards instructed in Music, Painting, &c, as well as the English, and entering them by the Term, will only be charged $100 per term. The above named sum if entered for the time specified, or until they graduate, shall cover every expense of Tuition per term. Pupils entered as above, who have never studied Music, will be kept at the Piano for one term, after that time will receive instruction on both Piano and Guitar, the price continuing the same. In the Painting Department, the pupils will be required not only to be good drawers, but to understand the principles of the art well before being put to colouring; will then receive instruction both in Oil and Water Colours.

Fuel in the Seminary 50 cts. Per quarter.

We feel no hesitation in saying that this Seminary will be equal to any in the State. The English Department will embrace a thorough collegiate course. The Ornamental Department will also include all the branches generally learned by young ladies.

John S. Bratton, M.D.
James Moore

N.B. – No pupil who is a boarder will be allowed to go in debt for articles of clothing, beyond the sum of $25 per term without orders from their parents or Guardians.

Appendix E

George Ladd's Last Will and Testament

George Ladd's Last Will and Testament[448]
The State of South Carolina

I George W. Ladd, of the Town of Winnsboro, in the State aforesaid, being of sound and disposing mind and memory, do make and declare the following as and for my last will and testament.

1. I will, bequeath, and divide the whole of my estate, both real and personal to my beloved wife for life, with full power during her life, by will or otherwise to dispose of any or all of my estate among our children, according to their necessities, to be judged by her.

2. Should it become necessary in the life time of my wife to sell or exchange any part of my property, she is hereby fully authorized and empowered to make such sale or exchange the proceeds of such sale or the property acquired by such exchange to be held by her for life, with the power during her life, to dispose of the same as provided for in the first clause of this will.

3. Lastly I nominate and appoint my wife executrix of this my last will and testament. Witness my hand and seal this thirtieth day of September in the year eighteen hundred and fifty-nine.

 George W. Ladd

Signed, sealed and declared by
 George W. Ladd to be his
last will and testament
in our presence.

J. S. Stewart
H. L . Elliott
J. B. McCants

Appendix F

Catharine Ladd's Proposal Letter
for the
Confederate National Flag

Catharine Ladd's Proposal Letter for the Confederate National Flag

664   Southern Confederacy.
                  Winnsboro S.C. Feby. 10, 1861

Hon. W. W. Boyce,
                    Sir,
                          Enclosed I send to you
a Flag for the New Republic designed
by Mr. Ladd which is simple as all
national flags should be, it is Tri Colored,
with a Red Union, seven Stars, and the
Cresent moon.
            It was all the design of Mr. L—
with exception of the Stars in a circle or
wreath and placing the Cresent Moon
among them, which I thought would
be a fit emblem of our young Republic,
and by placing the Stars in a wreath others
could be added forming a large wreath
as the other States came in.
            I am vain enough if you please
to term it so, (but I term it patriotism)
to feel that I would wish no greater honor
than to see the slightest thing I had a hand in,
adopted by the Southern Confederacy.

We have three boys to give to our country; words could not express the glow of pride that throbbed our bosoms, when I saw them ready to respond to their country's call, my boys are a part of a mother's jewels, freely given when needed, my next greatest glory would be to see the design adopted, and flung to the Breeze.

May it yet be unfurled, floating proudly and free o'er the bright sunny South, and on the dark rolling sea.

Our great Washington fought for the principles we are now contending for, and thought he had secured them; — may our young republic honor his memory with the name of Washington Republic, dating from the 22 of February, the day would then be kept to celebrate two great events.

Just as I finished the word events — I heard the news, that Mr. Davis had been elected President, — glorious news, we are free, we have Institutions of our own, a

country that we can call our own — rulers
from among our own people, — there is not
a Southern woman, wife, mother, or maid,
but what feels prouder to day of their country,
knowing as we do that we have fathers, husbands, sons and brothers, who are willing
to sacrifice all to duty and honor.

In peace or war you have with
you the prayers and sympathies of
every woman who glories in saying
I am a woman of the South.

Yours &c.

Mrs. C. Ladd

P.S. We shall need your services to
defend the Flag & the Boys ____ in
the course of ten days.

Transcription of Catharine Ladd's Proposal Letter for the Confederate National Flag

Southern Confederacy
Winnsboro S.C., Feby. 10th, 1861

Hon. W. W. Boyce
            Sir,
                        Enclosed I send to you a flag for the new Republic designed by Mr. Ladd which is simple as all national flags should be, it is Tri Colored, with a Red Union, seven stars, and the Crescent moon.

It was all the design of Mr. L — with the exception of the Stars in a circle or wreath and placing the Crescent Moon among them, which I thought would be a fit emblem for our young Republic, and by placing the Stars in a wreath others could be added forming a large wreath as the other States came in.

I am vain enough if you please to term it so, (but I term it patriotism) to feel that I would wish no greater honor than to see the slightest thing I had a hand in, adopted by the Southern Confederacy.

We have three boys to give to our country; words could not express the glow of pride that throbbed our bosoms, when I saw them ready to respond to their country's call, my boys are part of a mother's jewels, freely given when needed, my next greatest glory would be to see the design adopted, and flung to the Breeze.

May it yet be unfurled,
            floating proudly and free,
O'er the bright sunny South
            and the dark rolling sea.

Our great Washington fought for the principles we are now contending for, and thought he had secured them; — may our young republic honor his memory with the name of Washington Republic, dating from the 22^d of February, the day would then be kept to celebrate two great events.

Just as I finished the word events — I heard the news, that Mr. Davis had been elected President, — glorious news, we are free, we have Institutions of our own, a country that we can call our own — rulers from among our own people, there is not a Southern woman, wife, mother, or maid, but what feels prouder to day of their country, knowing, as we do that we have fathers, husbands, sons and brothers, who are willing to sacrifice all to duty and honor.

In peace or war you have with you the prayers and sympathies of every woman, who glories in saying I am a woman of the South.

                                    Yours, &c.,
                                    Mrs. C. Ladd

Appendix G

List of Catharine Ladd's Known Writings, 1835-1898

Year	Title	Genre	Periodical	Place
1835	*Lines: The dove of my bosom lies bleeding*	poem	The Southern Literary Messenger; devoted to every department of literature and the fine arts	Richmond, VA
1835	*To H. W. M.*	poem	The Southern Literary Messenger	Richmond, VA
1835	*Song*	poem	The Southern Literary Messenger	Richmond, VA
1836	*Unknown Flowers*	poem	The Southern Literary Messenger	Richmond, VA
1836	*Ianthe*	poem	The Southern Literary Messenger	Richmond, VA
1837	*Lines*	poem	The Southern Literary Messenger	Richmond, VA
1837	*To ------*	poem	The Southern Literary Messenger	Richmond, VA
1839	*Lines*	poem	Macon Georgia Telegraph newspaper	Macon, GA
1841	*Mother and Child*	prose	The Ladies Garland	
1841	*Oh! Do Not Say Again Love's Blind*	poem	Godey's Lady's Book	Philadelphia, PA
1844	*Ode,* Sung at the Celebration of the Anniversary of Lafayette Lodge, NO. 8 L.O.O.F. at Winnsboro (S.C.) August 2nd, 1844	song	The Symbol, and Odd Fellow's Magazine	
1850	*Tales: William Brown, or the Reward of Virtue*	short story	Rural Repository A Semi-monthly Journal, Embellished with Engravings	Hudson, NY
1852	*Our Cousin Ellie*	prose	The Ladies Repository: a monthly periodical, devoted to literature, arts and religion	Cincinnati, OH
1853	*The Grand Scheme*	play	unknown	Winnsboro, SC
1861	*Hurrah for Bethel*	poem/set to an air	Weekly State Journal newspaper	Raleigh, NC
1866	*Sweet Whispering Winds*	poem	News and Herald newspaper	Winnsboro, SC
1867	*I Am Growing Old*	poem	The Fairfield Herald newspaper	Winnsboro, SC
1868	*I Love God's Beauteous World*	poem	The Fairfield Herald newspaper	Winnsboro, SC
1868	*The Village Where I Was Born*	poem	The Fairfield Herald newspaper	Winnsboro, SC
1868	*New Improvement*	editorial	unknown	Winnsboro, SC

1868	The Legend of St. Nickolas/ For the Christmas Tree *Hurrah for the Christmas Tree*	prose and poem	The Fairfield Herald newspaper	Winnsboro, SC
1894	*The Gates Ajar*, A Hymn by Mrs. C. Ladd in Her 86th Year	hymn	newspaper	Winnsboro, SC
1894	*The Old Grist Mill*	poem	Fairfield News and Herald newspaper	Winnsboro, SC
1894	*Ned and Nell or, Nellie Don't Say No*	song	Fairfield News and Herald newspaper	Winnsboro, SC
1895	*Come Unto Me, I Will Give You Rest*	poem	The Baptist Courier newspaper	Spartanburg, SC
1895	Obituary for James Stratton Ratterree with poem	poem	newspaper	Chester, SC
1895	*Alpha and Omega*	poem	News and Herald newspaper	Winnsboro, SC
1895	*God Is Love*	poem	News and Herald newspaper	Winnsboro, SC
1896	*Never-More*	incomplete poem	News and Herald newspaper	Winnsboro, SC
1897	*Death of the Old Year*	poem	News and Herald newspaper	Winnsboro, SC
1897	*Pat Present and Future*	incomplete poem	News and Herald newspaper	Winnsboro, SC
1897	*The Rod of Life*	poem	Fairfield News and Herald newspaper	Winnsboro, SC
1897	*Memories*	poem	Fairfield News and Herald newspaper	Winnsboro, SC
1897	*I Cannot Love Again*	poem	News and Herald newspaper	Winnsboro, SC
1898	*All Things Pass Away*	poem	Fairfield News and Herald newspaper	Winnsboro, SC
	Mrs. J's Wax Works	play	unknown	Winnsboro, SC
	Ruth, Naoma and Orpah	play	unknown	Winnsboro, SC
	Sweet Mary Gray	song	News and Herald newspaper	
	Sweet Katy Did	poem		
	Not Changed But Glorified	poem		
	A Dream of the Past	poem		
	The Raven	poem		
	The Boys Soliloquy	poem		

Images from *A Relentless Spirit*

Endnotes & Index

Endnotes

Abbreviations:
MESDA=Museum of Early Southern Decorative Arts
SCDAH=South Carolina Department of Archives and History
SCL=South Caroliniana Library

---

[1] William Floyd Jackson to Mother, May 13, 1862, Civil War Letters of William Floyd Jackson, Private Collection.

[2] *Ibid.*, October 24, 1862.

[3] William Floyd Jackson to Sister Ema, May 1862, Civil War Letters of William Floyd Jackson, Private Collection.

[4] https://en.m.wikipedia.org/wiki/Slave_Narrative_Collection

[5] C. Vann Woodward, ed. *Mary Chestnut's Civil War.* (New Haven: Yale Univ. Press, 1981), 15-16.

[6] Diary of Mrs. W. W. Boyce. *The News and Herald. Memorial Edition.* (Winnsboro, SC), May 25, 1910.

[7] John F. Marszalek, ed. *The Diary of Miss Emma Holmes.* (Baton Rouge: Louisiana State Univ. Press, 1979), 13.

[8] Image provided compliments of David M. Rubenstein Rare Book & Manuscript Library, Duke University, Durham, North Carolina.
Emma Edwards Holmes, Diaries, 1861-1862.

[9] *Edgefield (South Carolina) Advertiser,* 17 April 1861. It is noted that at least one article was negative about the Confederate flag design, it being criticized for its similarity to the American flag. *Richmond (Virginia) Dispatch*, 7 December 1861.

[10] Devereaux D. Cannon, Jr., "The Genesis of the 'Stars and Bars'," (paper presented at the 38th NAVA Meeting, Indianapolis, Ind., October 2004; received the Captain William Driver Award for best presentation), 1-26.

[11] Cannon, *The Flags of the Confederacy: An Illustrated History.* (Gretna, LA: Pelican Publishing, 1988), 10-12.

[12] For the purpose of this discussion only the proposal submitted by Catharine Ladd and relevant facts will be considered. For a full discussion of the adoption of the Confederate national flag see Mr. Cannon's article and references, "The Genesis of the Stars and Bars," and his other writings listed in these notes and bibliography. Further, see references and articles from the web site of NAVA. www.nava.org

[13] *Chronicle & Sentinel* (Augusta, Georgia), 16 February 1861. Catharine's flag proposal was published in the Augusta newspaper as part of the proceedings of the Provisional Government of the Confederate States.

[14] Cannon, "Genesis," 17-18 n, 52, 53.

[15] War Department Collection of Confederate Records, Confederate Flag Designs, RG 109, National Archives, Washington, D.C.

[16] *Webster's Collegiate Dictionary*, 2nd ed., s.v. "rectangular division occupying one-fourth or less of a flag, usually in the upper corner near the staff and containing the national or other device."

[17] Cannon, "Genesis," 19.

[18] Cannon, "Genesis," 6, n, 22.

[19] Wikipedia contributors, "Flags of the Confederate States of America." *Wikipedia, The Free Encyclopedia* https://en.wikipedia.org/w/index.php?title=Flags-of-the-Confederte-States-of-America&oldid=867948768 (accessed Nov. 13, 2018)

[20] Cannon, "Genesis," 19-20, 22.

[21] In coping with confusing family stories, one source of reliable information was the MESDA in Winston-Salem, North Carolina. That repository has extensive files on early Southern craftsmen. In searching those files for George Ladd as an itinerant portrait artist in the South, by cross reference, the name of Catharine's mother, Ann Collins Stratton, appeared as an heir of her step-father, John Collins. John Collins was a prosperous house carpenter and land owner in Richmond, Virginia. Craftsman files of John Collins contained his will with the names and dates of Catharine Stratton's maternal family: her grandmother, two step-grandfathers, mother and father, aunts, uncles, and cousins. While clearly rich in detail, there were also unsolved mysteries regarding the birth father of Ann Collins, the details of which are discussed in this chapter. By the time the John Collins estate was settled in 1809, Ann was married to James Stratton. That meant her husband received the inheritance with her.

[22] In the 1810 United States Federal Census James Stratton is listed as head of household, with other family members: a male child under 10 years, a male adult between 26-44, a female child under ten years, and a female adult age between 26-44. If Catharine had a male sibling in 1810, there was no future reference to this fact. However, FamilySearch.org revealed a file on James and Ann Stratton that listed a male sibling (1005-1822) who would correspond to the entry in 1810.

[23] 1820 United States Federal Census records do not list James Stratton in 1820 as head of a household in Richmond City or Henrico County, Virginia.

[24] Collins, John(I), carpenter, Richmond, August 29, 1794, Virginia Wills and Administrations, Richmond City Hustings Deeds No. 2, 1792-1799, 135. Craftsman Database, MESDA at Old Salem, Winston-Salem, NC.

[25] Dabney, Humphrey, carpenter, lumberyard proprietor, Richmond, 1803, Craftsman Database, MESDA at Old Salem, Winston-Salem, NC.

[26] Humphrey Dabney was cited for his faithful service in John Collins' will, to inherit three books on architecture and a case of instruments with a silver plate to be inscribed "John Collins to Humphrey Dabney."

[27] Collins, John (II), carpenter, Richmond, Hustings Deeds No. 6, 6 February 1810. Craftsman Database, MESDA at Old Salem, Winston-Salem, NC. John Collins (I), had a son John who was underage (not twenty-one) at this time. His son John inherited architecture books from his father, studied in Philadelphia, and returned to Richmond to practice his trade by 1810.

[28] Dabney, Humphrey, lumberyard proprietor, Richmond, 1804, Craftsman Database, MESDA at Old Salem, Winston-Salem, NC.

[29] Dabney, Humphrey, lumberyard proprietor, Richmond, 1804, Craftsman Database, MESDA at Old Salem, Winston-Salem, NC.

[30] Dabney, Humphrey, lumberyard proprietor, Richmond, 1805, Craftsman Database, MESDA at Old Salem, Winston-Salem, NC.

[31] Dabney, Humphrey, carpenter, lumberyard proprietor, Richmond, post-[3 July 1809], Craftsman Database, MESDA at Old Salem, Winston-Salem, NC. As per a newspaper notice, Catharine did not apply for administration of his estate, which as a result was disposed of by sheriff Hezekiah Henley.

[32] Catharine Dabney lost her husband John Collins in 1794. It is unknown if her first husband was deceased, was divorced from her, or other circumstances by 1809. Since Ann Collins did receive a settlement in the John Collins estate, she must not have received the withheld inheritance from her birth father, Catharine Dabney's first husband..

[33] James Stratton and Ann Collins married in 1807. Ancestry.com *Virginia Marriages 1740-1850* [database on-line], Provo, UT, USA. (accessed April 23, 2008)

[34] Hustings Court Order bk. 8, 11 Sept 1809, p. 353, Collins, John (I), carpenter, Richmond, post-1794, Craftsman Database, MESDA at Old Salem, Winston-Salem, NC.

[35] Cities in Virginia are separate governmental entities from counties.

[36] Adam died by 1812, underage. Collins, John (I), carpenter, Richmond, 1813, Craftsman Database, MESDA (MESDA) at Old Salem, Winston-Salem, NC.

[37] 1810 United States Federal Census.

[38] Deed Book No. 5, 1796-1800, 7 Oct 1799, Craftsman Database, MESDA at Old Salem, Winston-Salem, NC. Humphrey and Catharine Dabney owned some property in Henrico Country which they sold in 1799.

[39] The Mutual Assurance Society Against Fire on Buildings of the State of Virginia, Library of Virginia, Richmond, Virginia. Microcards 47839. (accessed April 08, 2008). These records show the lots, the buildings, and the values of each for fire insurance for tenement and other properties under guardianship for John Collins' underage children.

[40] Dabney, Humphrey, carpenter, lumberyard proprietor, Richmond, post-[3 July 1809], Craftsman Database, MESDA at Old Salem, Winston-Salem, NC.

[41] 1830 United States Federal Census.

[42] 1840 United States Federal Census. In that same household were two enslaved females, a child and an adult, and a female free person of color.

[43] With no official record of marriage, Stratton and Ladd family history give conflicting dates of 1827 and 1828 for the marriage of Catharine to George Ladd. Ancestry.com sourced their marriage, George W. L. Ladd to Catharine J. Stratton on 19 November 1828 in Richmond, Virginia, to *Virginia, Compiled Marriages, 1740-1850.* The original data was from Dodd, Jordan R., *Early American Marriages: Virginia to 1850.* Bountiful, Utah, Precision Index Publishers. These sources are no longer available online or otherwise through the Mormon Church. (accessed June 12, 2018) Family Search (Mormon Church) records submitted by family members record a date of September 1827. Both are plausible; however, I chose to use the 1827 date in this book.

[44] Emma Dabney was first cousin to Catharine Ladd and second cousin to Catharine and George W. Ladd's children.

[45] A.W. Ladd was a son of George and Catharine Ladd.

[46] W. J. Bennett, Engraver, and G. Cooke, *Richmond from the hill above the waterworks/engraved by W.J. Bennett from a painting by G. Cooke.* James River Richmond Virginia ca. 1834. New York: Published by Lewis P. Clover. Photograph. Retrieved from the Library of Congress, https://www.loc.gov/item/96510852/. (accessed April 07, 2018.)

[47] Agnes M. Bondurant, *Poe's Richmond* (1978 ; reprint, Richmond: Edgar Allan Poe Museum, 1999), 1.

[48] https://www.nps.gov/nr/travel/richmond/VirginiaStateCapitol.html (accessed April 07, 2018)

[49] Mr. W.H. Fitzwhyllson was one of the witnesses to John Collins' will. He was perhaps the same Fitzwhyllson who conducted Fitzwhyllson's English School for young ladies and gentlemen from 1787 to 1824 in Richmond. There were opportunities in Richmond for Ann Collins and her siblings to attend this academy or another one.

[50] Margaret Meagher, *The History of Education in Richmond* (Richmond: Works Projects Administration, 1939), 14.

[51] Bondurant, 14 n, 60.

[52] Bondurant, 141.

[53] Mary T. Tardy, ed. *The Living Female Writers of the South* (Philadelphia, PA: Claxton, Remsen and Haffelfinger, 1872), 489-490.

[54] Kimberly Smith Ivey, "First Effort of an Infant Hand: An Introduction to Virginia Schoolgirl Embroideries, 1742-1850," *Journal of Early Southern Decorative Arts* 16, no. 10 (1990): 79-89. See also Agnes M. Bondurant, *Poe's Richmond* (1978: reprint, Richmond: Edgar Allan Poe Museum, 1999), 87.

[55] *Charleston (South Carolina) Courier*, December 13, 1828.

[56] By comparing the 1819 City Directory for Richmond, the 1820 census, the Mutual Assurance fire insurance records, and Catharine's reminiscences of her Richmond childhood, we know that the extended Collins/Dabney/Stratton family lived near the Canal Basin, east of Shockoe Slip, at the James River. This helped analyze the persistent story that Catharine was a playmate of Edgar Allan Poe. In 1820 Poe lived with the Allan family some ten blocks northwest of where the Dabney/Stratton family resided in 1810. However, in 1820, Catharine lived with her grandmother and mother beyond Richmond City in the adjacent county.

[57] Secular Sunday Schools were elementary level schools established mainly to give instruction in the Bible, but as well to accomplish basic literacy for the poor. They were also intended for "respectable children, for here was an opportunity to gain religious training." Sunday Schools in Richmond began about 1817 and were taught by women at no charge. Bondurant, 75.

[58] Bondurant, 60.

[59] *Ibid.*, 75.

[60] The American Missionary Fellowship or American Sunday School Union was a missionary movement begun in 1817 to organize Sunday schools in rural areas. It also rewarded memorization of Scripture and published books. http://en.wikipedia.org/wiki/American_Missionary_Fellowship

[61] *The Richmond Dispatch*, October 30, 1898.

[62] *History, Art & Archives, U. S. House of Representatives,* "Gilbert du Motier, Marquis de Lafayette," http://history.house.gov/Collection/Detail (September 16, 2018)

---

[63] Christie Anne Farnham, *The Education of the Southern Belle* (New York: New York University Press, 1994), 7.

[64] 1790-1820

[65] Christie Anne Farnham in *The Education of the Southern Belle* (New York: New York University Press, 1994), 12 n, 15-16, refers to the classic study of this ideology by Barbara Welter, "The Cult of True Womanhood," *American Quarterly* 18 (Winter 1966): 151-169.

[66] Keep within Compass and you shall be sure, to avoid many troubles which others endure. 1935, 0522.3.63AN274586001 http://britishmuseum.org (accessed June 2, 2018)

[67] "Circular of the Alexandria Boarding School for the Twentieth Annual Session, Ending Seventh Month, 1844," (Alexandria, Virginia: William S. Hough, 1844). The James S. Hallowell Collection, Box 132. Alexandria Public Library, Alexandria, Virginia. http://www.alexandria.lib.va.us/lhsc_online_exhibits/letters/abs.html (accessed November 05, 2001)

[68] Catherine Clinton, "Equally Their Due: The Education of the Planter Daughter in the Early Republic," *Journal of the Early Republic* 2 (April 1982): 48-52.

[69] The Rolesville Academy was an exception with the examination review in June 1833; however, the Trustees stated that the second session would begin June 24, 1833.

[70] Reputable and popular academies with large enrollments like Salem Girls' Boarding School in Salem, North Carolina had graduation and examinations in the spring. Enrollment occurred year-round.

[71] Farnham, 52-53.

[72] Poonah painting was "painting on rice or other thin paper in imitation of oriental work, by the application of thick body-colour, with little or no shading, and without background." *The Shorter Oxford English Dictionary*, 3rd ed. rev. addenda (London: Oxford University Press, 1956), 1544.

[73] Theorem painting was achieved by applying paint on silk velvet or silk satin through stencils of flowers or fruit so that shading was accomplished. The result was a still life that lacked dimension.

[74] *Charleston Courier,* December 15, 1828.

[75] Fairfield County Historical Society Collection (2002.4.2)

[76] *Charleston Courier,* December 13, 1828.

[77] Mary T. Tardy, ed. *The Living Female Writers of the South* (Philadelphia: Claxton, Remsen and Haffelfinger, 1872), 489-490.

[78] In April 1830 on the occasion of a Thomas Jefferson birthday celebration in Washington, D.C., President Andrew Jackson toasted, "Our Federal Union-It must be preserved." George C. Rogers, Jr. and C. James Taylor, *A South Carolina Chronology 1497-1992*, 2nd ed., (Columbia: University of South Carolina

Press, 1994), 81. Catharine Ladd was a believer in the preservation of the national Union, and for a time, the Confederate States.

[79] Dead letters were correspondence that remained unclaimed at the post office. The addressees' names were published in the newspaper for a definite period of time. These lists could be used as documentation for a resident's movement or departure.

[80] *Newbern Spectator (New Bern, NC)*, October 3, 1829.

[81] *Carolina Observer* (Fayetteville, North Carolina), March 25, 1830.

[82] https://en.wikipedia.org/wiki/Fayetteville,_North_Carolina#Antebellum (accessed April 23, 2018)

[83] "Ladd, Catherine," Anne King Gregorie, *Dictionary of American Biography*, vol. 10 (New York: Charles Scribner's Sons, 1946-1958). Gregorie's account claimed that the Ladds were in Augusta, Georgia when a great fire drove them out in 1829. However, there is no documentation for the Ladds being in Augusta, so perhaps it was Fayetteville in 1831.

[84] There were only two male children, both under five years, living in the Ladd household in 1840. 1840 United States Federal Census.

[85] 1830 United States Federal Census. Nash County is east of Raleigh, North Carolina.

[86] Charles L. Coon, *North Carolina Schools and Academies 1790-1840* (Raleigh: North Carolina Historical Commission, 1912).

[87] *The Star,* December 23, 1832 and June 21, 1833.

[88] Natural philosophy included astronomy, chemistry, and physics.

[89] Rolesville is northeast of Raleigh with less than fifty miles distance east to Nash County.

[90] Filigree work was open work decoration made out of very fine threads and usually minute balls of silver or gold used in jewelry. The work was embroidered with silk thread wrapped in gold or silver. Bronzing and gilding were methods of applying a gold surface to an object or textile by rubbing or painting with a bronze or gold powder. John and Hugh Honor Fleming. *Dictionary of the Decorative Arts* (New York: Harper and Row Publishers, 1877), 29. In Fayetteville George Ladd's advertisement stated that paintings were displayed at his residence and also at "Mr. J. Campbell's Jewelry store," but if there were an association with a jeweler is not clear. Engraving was part of a jeweler's craft. Engraving and gilding as well as decorative painting were all part of the itinerant artists' expertise.

[91] *The Star,* June 21, 1833.

[92] Patricia V. Veasey, "Samplers of the Carolina Piedmont: The Presbyterian Connection and the Bethel Group," *Journal of Early Southern Decorative Arts* XXXI:II (Winter 2005-Winter 2006): 103-148.

[93] Farnham, 107. Many Northern teachers-in-training practiced in the South where compensation was higher than in the North.

94 Anna Wells Rutledge, "Samuel F. B. Morse," in *Artists in the Life of Charleston: Through Colony and State from Restoration to Reconstruction* (Columbia: University of South Carolina Press, 1949), 130.

95 Alan Burroughs, *John Greenwood in America, 1745-1752* (Andover, MA: Addison Gallery of American Art, 1943)., See also, "Portraiture in a Developing Nation," Currier Museum of Art Online Curriculum, online: http://curriculum.currier.org/portraiture/the_context.html and http://curriculum.currier.org/portraiture/the_artists.html (accessed December 12, 2017).

96 For instance, writing as a profession was acceptable because it was a "cottage" employment.

97 Emily Bingham and Penny Richards, "The Female Academy and Beyond: Three Mordecai Sisters at Work in the Old South," in *Neither Lady nor Slave: Working Women of the Old South*. Susanna Delfino and Michele Gillespie, ed. (Chapel Hill: University of North Carolina Press, 2002), 171.

98 *Ibid*, 188.

99 L.E.L. or Letitia Elizabeth Landon (1802-1838) was a talented young English writer whose family fell into poverty due to her father's financial speculation and death. The Landon family depended on Letitia's income as a successful and popular writer. Angela Leighton, "L.E.L.," in *Victorian Women Poets* (Charlottesville: University Press of Virginia, 1992), 46-48.

100 For a thorough discussion of Catharine Ladd as a writer, see Part Two.

101 *Georgia Messenger (Macon)*, June 7, 1838.

102 Sally G. McMillan, *Motherhood in the Old South* (Baton Rouge: Louisiana State University Press: 1990), 60-61. McMillan goes on to say that while mothers were welcome in the birthing chamber, husbands were not.

103 There are no accounts of Catharine's confinements during pregnancy, childbirth, or her child-rearing years in conjunction with teaching. See Sally G. McMillan, *Motherhood in the Old South* (Baton Rouge: Louisiana State University Press: 1990), 80.

104 *Macon Georgia Telegraph,* May 14, 1839; *Georgia Messenger (Macon)*, May 16, 1839.

105 *Macon Georgia Telegraph*, January 1, 1839.

106 *Ibid.*

107 Farnham, 57.

108 Younger boys were sometimes taught the rudiments of arithmetic, reading and writing in a female school, particularly when the instruction was at home. Thomas Bratton, the youngest child, joined his sisters at Brattonsville Female Seminary in 1843.

109 Tuition at Salem Girls' Boarding School in Salem, North Carolina was $35. to $47. per quarter during the 1840s plus electives and contingent costs for supplies and sundries. Expenses ranged from $150 to over $200 a year for each girl. Salem Girls' Boarding School Bill Book #14, October 1838-May

1841; Bill Book # 16, July 1844-June 1848, Salem College Library, Salem College, Winston-Salem, NC.

[110] The Bratton in-laws, the Raineys, sent all of their daughters to Salem, and a future Bratton daughter-in-law Mary Rebecca Massey from Lancaster, South Carolina, attended Salem. A first cousin to the Bratton girls, Martha Elizabeth Steele, attended Salem from 1839 to 1841, then for a time in 1842 she returned home to attend Brattonsville Female Seminary. Martha Steele's father sent her to boarding school in Columbia in 1842. From 1820 until the Civil War, over forty girls from York County attended Salem. Patricia V. Veasey conducted this research on York County girls who attended SGBS, 1791 to 1857, as a recipient of the Madelyn Moeller Research Fellowship, MESDA, in June 2008.

[111] Presbyterians dominated the settlement of York County from the 1760s, establishing meeting houses and academies with equal rapidity. Presbyterians were a denomination that required an educated clergy both in Scotland and America.

[112] Christy A. Farnham, *The Education of the Southern Belle: Higher Education and Student Socialization in the Antebellum South,* (New York: New York University Press, 1994), 64.

[113] It is not known if the enslaved females were inherited as property of the Strattons before Catharine's marriage, or were the property of George Ladd prior to or after marriage.

[114] Ann Collins Stratton was Catharine Ladd's mother.

[115] Bratton Family Papers, General store account book, 6 August 1839, South Caroliniana Library, University of South Carolina, Columbia.

[116] George Williamson Livermore Ladd signed his name various ways in business accounts and on his portraits: G. W. Ladd, G. W. L. Ladd, Geo. W.L. Ladd, G. W. Ladd pinxt (painter), and Ladd, pinxt.

[117] This type of coarse, durable cloth was used for slave clothing. Typically the cloth was cut by the mistress like Mrs. Stratton and then sewn by the enslaved woman. Without further documentation this is based on inference derived from other plantation accounts like those of John Springs of York District.

[118] In the accounts were plain and fancy dishes, cutlery, iron pots and tin pans, cups and tumblers (glasses), gallon jars, a sieve, bowls, buckets, a tea kettle, coffee mill and coffee pot, ladle, pitchers, steel snuffers, candlesticks, andirons and a chamber pot.

[119] Those listed were bed ticking (linen twill), twenty-two yards; a variety of homespun (linen or cotton), mostly unbleached, fifty-three yards; calico (plain weave cotton), twenty-three yards; and one yard of moreen (worsted [wool] for bed furnishing).

[120] At Salem Girls' Boarding School the girls did employ their time in sewing items of clothing such as aprons, cloaks, dresses, documented by headmaster

Steiner's letter books that recorded correspondence with parents. The teachers also spent long hours sewing caps and other small clothing accessories for the girls to purchase in the store. *Abraham Steiner Letter Books Concerning the Boarding School, 1804-1816*. Salem Academy & College Archives, Salem College Library, Winston-Salem, North Carolina.

[121] Textile purchases from Brattonsville store by George W. Ladd, March, 1841. Bratton Family Papers, South Caroliniana Library, Columbia, South Carolina.

[122] *The Compiler*, Yorkville, SC, August 22, 1840.

[123] See Appendix D for a full transcript of the Brattonsville Female Seminary advertisement.

[124] A quire of paper amounted to twenty-four to twenty-five pages.

[125] *The Compiler* (Yorkville, South Carolina), August 22, 1840.

[126] *Ibid.*

[127] Miss Bates was the daughter of Rev. Dr. Bates formerly President of Middlebury College, Vermont. She presided over the female seminary in Pendleton, South Carolina.

[128] Miss Mary Bates, "Female Education," *The Magnolia* (Charleston: Burgess & James, November 1842): 65. See also satirical essays on female education, "A Leaf from Punch, Preparatory Schools for Young Ladies," *Harper's New Monthly Magazine* (New York: Harper & Bros., 1851): 285-286.

[129] Documentation for these numbers were found in the Bratton Family Papers in letters, tuition bills, Bratton store ledgers, and public records like the United States Federal Census, probate court, and genealogy sources like the Hart Collection at the York County Historical Center in York, South Carolina. Dr. John Bratton's letter of 1842 stated that there were "upwards of 30 scholars."

[130] *Godey's Lady's Book,* August 1841. https://babel.hathitrust.org

[131] Commissioners of Free Schools Report, York District, 1840. South Carolina Department of Archives and History, Columbia, South Carolina.

[132] Taken from the book title *We Lived in a Little Cabin in the Yard: Accounts of Slavery in Virginia*. Belinda Hurmence, ed., (Winston-Salem, North Carolina: John F. Blair, 1994).

[133] Archaeologist Monica Beck's conclusions are from her study of the outbuilding footprint at the Col. William Bratton home. Monica Leigh Beck, "Servant to Chattel: African American Slaves and Their Masters on an Upcountry Plantation," (MA Thesis, University of South Carolina, 1996).

[134] Martha Bratton to John Bratton. February 12, 1842. Bratton Family Papers, South Caroliniana Library, University of South Carolina, Columbia (hereafter cited as SCL). In 1842 the Ladds were in Fairfield County, South Carolina.

[135] Farnham, 57.

[136] Susan Delfino and Michelle Gillespie, ed., "Neither Lady or Slave," in *Working Women of the Old South*. (Chapel Hill: University of North Carolina Press, 2002), 190. The Mordecai daughters Ellen and Caroline proved that teaching

could pay, "and in later years when family members protested that they did not need to earn an income and should not live or work away from home," they made independent decisions about their teaching roles elsewhere.

137 Gloria Seaman Allen, "Needlework Education in Antebellum Alexandria, Virginia," *The Magazine Antiques* CLIX, no. 2 (February 2001): 335.

138 Miss Lambert, *The Handbook of Needlework, Decorative and Ornamental* (1846; reprint, Piper Publishing, 2003), 219.

139 A possible exception may be the portrait of Dr. John Bratton's oldest brother, physician William Bratton who lived in Winnsboro, South Carolina. The portrait is not signed.

140 Martha's letters began in 1840 and continued through 1843, except for the year 1841.

141 Martha Bratton to John Bratton. January 11, 1840. Bratton Family Papers. SCL.

142 John S. Bratton was a brother of Martha Bratton. This is the first recorded instance of Martha addressing her brother John as Jack.

143 George Steele was the brother-in-law and mercantile partner of John Bratton, Sr.

144 Martha E. Steele was first cousin to Martha, daughter of George and Mary Bratton Steele. She attended school in Columbia, South Carolina in 1842.

145 This was the music teacher at Brattonsville Female Seminary, possibly Signor Pucci.

146 Martha Bratton to John Bratton, February 16, 1843, SCL.

147 Efforts to positively identify M.R. of the poem failed. Several Bratton relations were possible.

148 The *Compiler* (Yorkville South Carolina), December 19, 1840.

149 John S. Bratton Sr. to John Bratton, Feb. 8, 1842, Bratton Family Papers, SCL.

150 Martha Bratton to John Bratton, February 16, 1843, Bratton Family Papers, SCL.

151 Apparently they could not secure Mr. Mayer referred to in Dr. John's letter in February.

152 "Old lady" was a term of respect for their mother, Harriet Bratton. Living to an old age was considered fortunate.

153 Martha Bratton to John Bratton, March 5, 1842, Bratton Family Papers, SCL.

154 The only known surviving piece of needlework from Mrs. Ladd's students from all of her academies is the Berlin work by Elizabeth Bratton. In a study of education and needlework from York County, South Carolina and Mecklenburg, North Carolina, surviving examples of needlework far exceeded schoolgirl paintings. Patricia V. Veasey, "Samplers of the Carolina Piedmont: The Presbyterian Connection and the Bethel Group," *Journal of Early Southern Decorative Arts* XXXI, no. 11, XXXII, no. 1 and 2 (Winter 2005-Winter 2006): 103-148.

155 Norman Laliberte and Alex Mogelon. *Painting with Crayons.* New York: Reinhold Pub., 1967, 15. Crayon work included chalk, pencil, pastel, charcoal, and crayons.

156 See image of wax work p. 57, 101.

157 *Georgia Messenger (Macon)*, December 27, 1838.

158 To view color images of schoolgirl art accomplished by Brattonsville Female Seminary students and from Catharine Ladd's academies in Fairfield County, go to www.chmuseums.org/brattonsville/ and click on History, Catharine Ladd.

159 Neither the theorem painting nor the landscape of Brattonsville was signed but both were attributed to Martha Bratton. The original theorem painting is retained by Bratton descendants.

160 As part of museum collections today, schoolgirl art is considered folk art.

161 The needlework counterparts to the paintings, needle pictures, were stitched on silk in silk thread to mimic the painting and might be mistaken for a painting at a distance.

162 In order to have an unobstructed view a cleared field must have existed between the artist and the academy. A tree stump and ruts of a plowed field are visible in the painting foreground.

163 Harriet Bratton to My Boys [John, Rufus and Samuel Edward Bratton], July 30 1839, Bratton Family Papers, SCL.

164 Interview and analysis of the painting by D. Shawn Beckwith, Preservation Coordinator/Restoration Specialist, Historic Brattonsville, December 21, 2014.

165 The mural is painted in oil on canvas that was glued to the four walls, covering the wooden paneling from the wainscoting to the ceiling. This mural is in a plantation home parlor in Lowrys, Chester County, South Carolina. Lowrys is located several miles south of Brattonsville. Mrs. Ann Stratton possibly boarded temporarily with the McNeels of Lowrys.

166 These included two yards of linen (flax), colored (linen) canvas, silk velvet, and silk satin, in addition to silk ribbon, tape (linen), and lace, which could be used to embellish needlework pieces.

167 This amount of worsted indicated instruction of numerous students.

168 Berlin work was accomplished by stitching the Zephyr wool into a linen ground cloth with a regular thread count to the inch, using a printed pattern as a guide. The patterns were printed in color on a grid. Each square on the grid represented one thread in the ground cloth vertically and horizontally. Stitches used were cross or tent (half cross) over one or two threads, similar to what became known as needlepoint. In some cases the entire canvas was filled in with stitches.

169 *Georgia Messenger (Macon)*, December 27, 1838.

[170] Perforated paper was card stock weight paper perforated with holes in a grid pattern for needlework.

[171] Estate of Dr John S. Bratton to Hugh A. McWhorter Jr., November 10, 1843, Bratton Family Papers, SCL. Dr. John Bratton died in April 1843.

[172] See page one for courses under the English Branches.

[173] Martha Bratton to John Bratton, February 16, 1843, Bratton Family Papers, SCL.

[174] Dr. John Bratton to John Bratton. February 8, 1842, Bratton Family Papers, SCL.

[175] Like the Ladds, the McWhorters remained for two years before leaving to teach in Chesterville in 1844. For the next two years Mary A. Poulton was principal/teacher. Mary [Ann] Poulton was enrolled in Brattonsville Female Seminary from its beginning as a student/assistant who stayed on after the Ladds departed; she was frequently named in Martha Bratton's letters to her brother John. A school at Brattonsville was not documented again in the Free School Reports until 1854. Whether a school existed in the interim period 1845-54 is questioned, but possible. The later academy in 1854 had both male and female pupils.

[176] Rev. McWhorter's mother was a daughter of Rev. Samuel Watson, a renowned Presbyterian family of York County. Rev. Samuel Watson was the fourth minister of Bethel Presbyterian Church (1764) serving for forty two years.

[177] *South Carolinian (Columbia)*, October 31, 1844.

[178] This letter very likely revealed the cause of Dr. Bratton's death the following month. An astounding fact was that measles were not mentioned in Martha Bratton's letter to her brother John dated Feb. 16, 1843. Epidemics in the nineteenth century could last for as long as a year and spread beyond the local community. It could have caused Martha "Mattie" Steele's death, a first cousin and best friend of Martha Bratton, on Sept. 17, 1843.

[179] Dr. John Bratton to John Bratton. February 10, 1843. Bratton Family Papers, SCL.

[180] South Carolina's Free School Act of 1811 provided education for a limited number of poor, white children. The records documented academies and teachers where indigent children were in attendance. Academies that did not enroll indigent children did not receive a county stipend, and therefore were not documented.

[181] Suzanne Lebsock, *The Free Women of Petersburg, Status and culture in a Southern Town, 1784-1860* (New York: W. W. Norton & Company, 1984), 174-175.

[182] It was not uncommon in the 19th century for concerned parents to send ill children to live with a physician's family. Mrs. David de Verill Walker, Sr., "A Short Sketch of Mrs. Katharine Ladd." *Fairfield Herald,* before 1940.

[183] *Ibid.*

[184] Return of Commissioners of Free Schools for Fairfield District for year 1843, South Carolina Department of Archives & History, Columbia, South Carolina.

[185] Library of Congress, www.loc.gov (accessed October 30, 2018)

[186] In 1831 R. D. Coleman, a Feaster relative, was an agent for spreading Universalism/Unitarianism. Papers of the Coleman Feaster, and Faucette Families, 1787-1943, Collection Description, MSS 12663, SCL. http://library.sc.edu.sc/socar/uscs/1998/colema98.html (accessed April 28, 2018)

[187] The Feaster plantation was situated about twenty-two miles northwest of the town of Winnsboro, or a day's travel.

[188] Etta A. Rosson, "The Feasters (Pfister) and Feasterville," in Julian Stevenson Bolick, *A Fairfield Sketchbook* (Clinton, South Carolina, 1963), 266-269.

[189] *South Carolinian* (Columbia), October 17, 1844.

[190] Papers of the Coleman, Feaster, and Faucette Families, 1787-1943, MSS 12663, SCL.

[191] Rosson, 268.

[192] *South Carolinian* (Columbia), October 17, 1844.

[193] *Ibid.*

[194] Papers of the Coleman, Feaster, and Faucette Families, 1787-1943, MSS 12663, SCL.

[195] Papers of the Coleman, Feaster, and Faucette Families, 1787-1943, MSS 12663, SCL.

[196] "To printing 100 circulars on super fine French paper," Oct 18, 1847. Papers of the Coleman, Feaster, and Faucette Families, Manuscript #12663, SCL.

[197] "For two days' hauling and six days labor by slave Dave at $.50 per day," November 18, 184, Papers of the Coleman, Feaster, and Faucette Families, 1787-1943, MSS 12663, SCL.

[198] These charges were likely for labor hired to achieve the tasks. It seemed counterintuitive for the Ladds to install a fence and gate around property they did not own. It may be that George Ladd helped in the construction of the academy buildings in a supervisory role

[199] Drucilla Feaster b. 1834, was a daughter of John Mobley Feaster, brother to Andrew.

[200] Unlike Brattonsville Female Seminary, there are no known surviving family letters that enhance an understanding of the experience at Feasterville Female Seminary. Instead the writer relied on the Feaster family documents, Feaster family genealogy, Ladd family genealogy and history, United States Federal Census, newspaper advertisements, and a few surviving works of schoolgirl art to interpret the Feasterville years.

[201] Rosson, 268. Mrs. Jennie I. Coleman's record is in *The Robert Coleman Family* by J.P. Coleman.

[202] *The Compiler* (Yorkville, South Carolina), August 22, 1840.

[203] In the mid-nineteenth century an interest in displays from nature grew to the Victorian obsession with collections displayed in cases or shadow box frames, including taxidermied specimens.

[204] Fairfield County Historical Society Collection (2002.4.3)

[205] The painting was inscribed at the bottom, *Mary A. Feaster, 1848.* She was probably the daughter of Jacob Feaster, brother of Andrew. Mary Andrews Feaster was born in 1836, making her age twelve in 1848. A Mary Feaster enrolled in Catharine Ladd's school in Winnsboro in 1850 at age fourteen. Yet, it is a bit confusing. There is no Mary listed in the Feaster accounts for instructional fees to Catharine Ladd 1846-1848. The daughter of Andrew Feaster named Mary, born in 1828, was Mary Drusilla Feaster. The painting was quite sophisticated and accomplished for girl of twelve.

[206] Papers of the Coleman, Feaster, and Faucette Families, 1787-1943, MSS 12663, South Caroliniana Library, University of South Carolina, Columbia.

[207] Brattonsville Female Seminary students boarded on the Bratton plantation and with their neighbors, the Moore family.

[208] Calculating an average yearly tuition income of $90.-$100. per pupil, the Ladds could realize $1800. a year for twenty pupils, not counting the income for indigent students.

[209] To George W. Ladd from Caleb Clark, Sr., February 10, 1849. Book A I, 104-105 Winnsboro town lots 19, 20, South Carolina Department of Archives and History, Columbia, South Carolina. (hereafter known as SCDAH)

[210] *South Carolinian,* (Columbia), November 17, 1848.

[211] 1850 United States Federal Census.

[212] Farnham, 70.

[213] *Ibid.*

[214] On loan to the Fairfield County Historical Society, Private Collection.

[215] The greatest number of known portraits by George Ladd were those of Fairfield County residents.

[216] 1850 United States Federal Census.

[217] Cheryl Junk, "'To Become a Power in the Land:'" "The Burwell School and Women's Education in Antebellum North Carolina, 1837-1857," in *Hillsborough Historical Society Journal* 2.1 (July 1999): 36.

[218] Katharine Theus Obear, *Through the Years in Old Winnsboro,* (Spartanburg, SC: The Reprint Company, 2002), 27.

[219] Farnham, 107. This statement referred specifically to academies on the seminary or collegiate level, for which Winnsboro Female Institute qualified.

[220] *South Carolinian,* November 7, 1848.

[221] *Fairfield Herald* (Winnsboro, South Carolina), January 16, 1851.

[222] F. D. Jones and W.H. Mills, eds., *History of the Presbyterian Church in South Carolina Since 1850* (Columbia: R. L. Bryan Company, 1920), 449. and http://wc.rootsweb.ancestry.com (accessed January 13, 2016)

[223] *The Fairfield Herald*, January 16,1851.

[224] "John Schorb Photography Collection," Dacus Library Archives. Winthrop University.
www.winthrop.edu/dacus/about/archives/collections/johnschorb.htm (accessed January 11, 2016)

[225] *Ibid.*

[226] 1850 United States Federal Census.

[227] The Henry Harrisse Papers, 1853-1924, The New York Public Library, Manuscripts and Archives Division. MSSCol 133. www.nypl.org (accessed January 11, 2018)

[228] Farnham, 72.

[229] The Commissioners of Free Schools Report for Fairfield County, 1849, 1850, 1858. SCDAH.

[230] Mrs. David de Verill Walker, Sr., "A Short Sketch of Mrs. Katharine Ladd." *Fairfield Herald,* before 1940.

[231] To George W. Ladd from Richard Cathcart, March 29, 1852, Book T T, 191-193, Winnsboro town lo #53 (Ketchin house and lot), SCDAH.

[232] Walker, *op. cit.*

[233] *Yorkville Enquirer,* (South Carolina), December 17, 1857.

[234] Ibid., December 16, 1858.

[235] See Part Two, p. 161-166, for the description of entertainments in Winnsboro's Thespian Hall following the war. Catharine Ladd favored producing tableau as exhibitions, and May Day 1869 was a prime example of her talents.

[236] *Yorkville Enquirer* (South Carolina), June 2, 1859.

[237] *Ibid.*, December 16, 1858.

[238] *Ibid.*

[239] *Ibid.,* Another advertisement noted in the *Yorkville Enquirer,* the *Edgefield Advertiser,* and the *Abbeville Banner* was for First Class Piano Fortes with makers listed from Boston and New York. One maker from Boston consistently listed was A. W. Ladd. This gentleman was a relative of G. W. Ladd, possibly his contact in the business of furnishing musical instruments for pupils.

[240] Josephine Ladd was sixteen years old.

[241] There was however an account of George Ladd painting a regimental flag for Col. McCorkle's 34th Regiment of Militia of York in 1856. "We saw yesterday a very beautiful flag painted by our fellow townsman Mr. Ladd." The ladies of York worked on a palmetto tree (embroidery), over which Mr. Ladd painted

an appropriate and handsome national design. *Yorkville Enquirer* (South Carolina), August 21, 1856, from the *Winnsboro Register.*

[242] Refer to the former advertisement of December 16, 1858 for Winnsboro' Female Institute with a Miss E. Crossitt as an instructor in the musical department.

[243] 1860 United States Federal Census.

[244] The Nortons advertised for their female academy in 1848 and 1849, but in 1850 they lived in Montgomery, Alabama. 1850 Unites States Federal Census for Montgomery, Alabama.

[245] Obear, 4.

[246] Note in the reminiscence by Katharine Obear that Miss Parish apparently did not teach music.

[247] Mrs. Julia Obear played piano, harp, guitar and organ.

[248] Obear, 26.

[249] Walter Edgar, South Carolina A History (Columbia: University of South Carolina Press, 1998), 286.

[250] *Ibid*

[251] This estimate was based on computing forty years of teaching at a minimum of twenty students per year, equaling eight hundred students. Consideration was given to several years of no teaching balanced against the facts of enrollment from 1850 to 1860 of up to one hundred pupils a year.

[252] To Catharine Ladd from Heirs of David R. Aiken, January 1, 1866, Book W W, 574-575, lot formerly known as Fairfield Hotel property with all buildings, SCDAH. The purchase price was $5,000.

[253] *Tri Weekly News* (Winnsboro, South Carolina), December 14, 1865.

[254] *Tri Weekly News* (Winnsboro, South Carolina), December 25, 1866.

[255] 1870 United States Federal Census.

[256] Rev. James Douglass served as one of three principals at Winnsboro Female institute for the 1859 session.

[257] *Fairfield Herald*, December 5, 1866.

[258] To Catharine Ladd from Heirs of David Aiken, January 1,1867, Book A E, 134-135, Winnsboro town lot #44, adjacent South of the Court House on Congress St., SCDAH. The purchase price was $10,000.

[259] *Tri Weekly News* (Winnsboro, South Carolina), December 5, 1866. Catharine Ladd must have counted from 1843 when she first began in Winnsboro through the war years to calculate 43 sessions past (at two sessions a year). It would add up to between eighteen and twenty years as principal and teacher of her own school.

[260] Rev. Josiah Obear was the Episcopal clergyman who established St. John's Episcopal Church in Winnsboro. He died in 1882.

[261] *Fairfield Herald* (Winnsboro, South Carolina), January 5, 1870.

[262] *Ibid.*, January 12, 1870

263 *Ibid.*

264 *Fairfield Herald* (Winnsboro, South Carolina), June 9, 1869.

265 *News and Herald* (Winnsboro, South Carolina), February 28, 1878.

266 *Ibid.*

267 See the Prologue.

268 Catharine Ladd to Hon. W. W. Boyce, February 10, 1861. NWCT1R-601, National Archives and Records Administration, Washington, D. C. The letter was also printed in the *Weekly Chronicle & Sentinel* (Augusta, Georgia), February 16, 1861. Hargett Rare Book and Manuscript Library, University of Georgia, Athens.

269 *Ibid.*

270 See Appendix F for a copy of the original hand-written letter and a transcript.

271 Cynthia A. Kierner, *Southern Women in Revolution, 1776-1800* (Columbia: University of South Carolina Press, 1998), 101.

272 Flag ceremonies at Southern female academies during the antebellum period were a fixed part of May Day celebrations. "Next to the coronation itself, the most important part of the ceremony was the May queen's speech as she presented a flag or banner on behalf of her school or class to the uniformed young men who attended her." Farnham, 170.

273 *Georgia Messenger (Macon)*, 7 May 1838.

274 "Presentation of Flag to Boyce Guards," *Winnsboro Register*, February 1861, Reprint. *News and Herald.* (Winnsboro, S.C.), Memorial Edition, May 25, 1910

275 Mrs. W. W. Boyce's diary, March 15, 1861, Reprint. *News and Herald* (Winnsboro, South Carolina), Memorial Edition, May 25, 1910.

276 Devereaux D. Cannon, Jr., "The Genesis of the 'Stars and Bars'," 12 (2005): 1-26.

277 Walter Clark, ed.*, Histories of the Several Regiments and Battalions from North Carolina in the Great War, 1861-'65* 3, (Goldsboro, North Carolina: Nash Brothers, Book and Job Printers, c. 1901), 593.

278 William Floyd Jackson to Mother, Near Orange C.H., Virginia, March 23, 1862, Civil War Letters of William Floyd Jackson, Private Collection

279 William Floyd Jackson to Mother, nd., Civil War Letters of William Floyd Jackson, Private Collection.

280 William Floyd Jackson to Father, Centerville, Va., February 25, 1862, Civil War Letters of William Floyd Jackson, Private Collection.

281 William Floyd Jackson to Mother, 1862, Civil War Letters of William Floyd Jackson. Private Collection.

282 William Floyd Jackson to Mother, Camp near Richmond, Virginia, July 10, 1862, Civil War Letters of William Floyd Jackson, Private Collection.

283 Minutes of the Ladies' Relief Association of Fairfield. The Work at Fairfield, in *South Carolina Women in the Confederacy,* Mrs. Thomas Taylor, ed. et.al. (Columbia: The State Company, 1903), 36-53.

284 Mrs. K.L. Cureton, "How Mrs. Ladd Saved the Masonic Jewels," *Recollections and Reminiscences 1861-1865 through World War I* 3, (Columbia: South Carolina Division, United Daughters of the Confederacy, 1992), 308.

285 William Floyd Jackson to Sister Ema [sic], July 31st, 1862, Civil War Letters of William Floyd Jackson. Private Collection.

286 George W. Ladd to Philip E. Porcher, Deed Book WW, p. 353 354, December 2, 1862, SCDAH.

287 Field schools were neighborhood schools that students attended during the day and provided the rudiments of learning: reading, writing, and ciphering (mathematics).

288 William Floyd Jackson to My Dear Mother, December 30, 1862, Civil War Letters of William Floyd Jackson, Private Collection.

289 1860 United States Federal Census. Robert Fishburne, fifty year old planter of Charleston, listed his real estate value at $35,000. and his personal property value at $85,000. He had eleven additional members of the household with the oldest being a twenty-eight year old daughter. Also listed were his son Francis, ten years old, and his son Julian, the youngest, at nine years old. His wife Harriet A. Fishburne was listed in 1850, but not in the 1860 list.

290 To Messers Simons and Simons from Mrs. C. Ladd, Mrs. C. Ladd legal correspondence, 1867-1868, (431.01 (C) 02 (L) 01), South Carolina Historical Society, Charleston, South Carolina.

291 Abraham LaMasters debts due John S. Bratton for Bratton & Erwin and Bratton& Rainey, Test by Geo. W. Ladd, 20 March 1841, Bratton Family Papers, Caroliniana Library,(Columbia: University of South Carolina).

292 Summary Process Rolls, Court of Common Pleas, #5286, March 16, 1861, SCDAH.

293 Philip E. Porcher, Trustee of Martha Egleston, to George W. Ladd, Conveyance of Real Estate in Trust, December 2, 1862, Town of Winnsboro, South Carolina, SCDAH.

294 Thomas H. Christmast and A. W. Ladd to George W. Ladd, Deed Book W W, p. 393-394, June 8, 1863, SCDAH. This same property was purchased by Thomas H. Christmast and A. W. Ladd in February 1861 from Francis Elder in February 1861.

295 It is possible, but unknown, that Josephine was staying with a member of the Feaster family. This idea is based on inference from Feaster family stories, 1860 United States Federal Census of Feasters in Florida, the Ladd connection with the Feasters from 1844 to 1848 when Catharine led the Feasterville Female Seminary, and Josephine Ladd's real estate purchases and sales with the Feasters following the war. By the 1870 United States Federal Census Josephine Ladd was living in Fairfield District.

296 Joe (Josephine) Ladd may have been staying with some of the Feasters. In the 1860 census for Florida, John Mobley Feaster, his wife, and nephew Jacob N.

Feaster lived in Alachua, Florida and John Mobley's son John Pickett Feaster, his wife, and two children lived in Marion, Florida.

297 A. W. Ladd to Josephine Ladd, July 24, 1864. Fairfield County Museum, Winnsboro, South Carolina.

298 See Appendix E for a full transcript of George Ladd's last will and testament.

299 Deeds searched were located at SCDAH.

300 Edgar, 285.

301 Last Will and Testament of Richard Watson, Fairfield District, South Carolina, 1859, SCDAH.

302 Last Will and Testament of John Campbell, Fairfield District, South Carolina, 1859, SCDAH.

303 The United States Federal Census slave schedules gave estimated ages.

304 The destruction of her life's literary works along with other documents of the school, personal letters, and business correspondence left a large gap in understanding the Ladds' personal lives.

305 W.W. Lord, Jr., "In the Path of Sherman," in *Harper's Monthly Magazine* (New York: Harper & Brothers Publishers, 1910), 441.

306 *Ibid.,* 443-444.

307 *Ibid.,* 444.

308 In 1862 George Ladd sold the three-story brick building that was the Winnsboro Female Institute along with the land (four town lots). Therefore where the students met for class after that time is uncertain. Perhaps Catharine rented space in the building since the purchaser, Philip E. Porcher, was from Charleston.

309 Mrs. K. L. Cureton, "How Mrs. Ladd Saved the Masonic Jewels," *Recollections and Reminiscences 1861-1865 through World War I* 3, (Columbia: South Carolina Division, United Daughters of the Confederacy, 1992), 307-310.

310 *Fairfield News and Herald* (Winnsboro, South Carolina), January 8, 1890.

311 See the extensive curriculum listings of Brattonsville Female Seminary in Appendix D.

312 *The Star* (Wake County, North Carolina), December 23, 1832.

313 *The Star* (Wake County, North Carolina), June 21, 1833.

314 The Osmund Woodward family of Winnsboro, South Carolina, sent an ailing young daughter to live with the Dr. Bratton family and subsequently enrolled several daughters in Brattonsville Female Seminary.

315 In the newspaper advertisement for Brattonsville Female Seminary it was stated: "The English Department will embrace a thorough collegiate course." *Compiler* (Yorkville, South Carolina), August 22, 1840.

316 Farnham, 105.

317 *Ibid.,* 106.

318 *South Carolinian (Columbia),* October 31, 1844.

319 *Charleston Courier,* December 26, 1828.

[320] *Georgia Messenger (Macon),* December 30, 1838

[321] M. E. Bratton to My dear Brother (John Bratton), March 5, 1842, SCL.

[322] *Daily Register* (Winnsboro, South Carolina), March 1, 1854.

[323] *Daily Register* (Winnsboro, South Carolina), December 20, 1860.

[324] To Messers Simons and Simons from Mrs. C. Ladd, Mrs. C. Ladd legal correspondence, 1867-1868, (431.01 (C) 02 (L) 01), South Carolina Historical Society, Charleston, South Carolina.

[325] Last Will and Testament of George W. Ladd, SCDAH.

[326] Joyce W. Warren, *Women, Money, and the Law: Nineteenth Century Fiction, Gender, and the Courts,* (Iowa City: University of Iowa Press, 2005), 52. (Accessed July 2018)

[327] This was sold by the heirs of David R. Aiken.

[328] Heirs of David R. Aiken to Catharine Ladd, January 1, 1867, Deed Book A E, p. 134-135, Lot #44, SCDAH. This was known as the Bank Range. She advertised that her school was located there in 1867.

[329] *Fairfield Herald* (Winnsboro, South Carolina), January 9, 1867.

[330] Regarding the security of specie, in the inventory of George Ladd's estate there was a safe appraised at three dollars.

[331] Etta A. Rosson, "The Feasters (Pfister) and Feasterville," in Julian Stevenson Bolick, *A Fairfield Sketchbook* (Clinton, South Carolina, 1963), 266-269.

[332] *Fairfield News and Herald* (Winnsboro, South Carolina), January 8, 1890.

[333] Cokie Roberts, *Capital Dames: The Civil War and the Women of Washington, 1848-1868* (New York: Harper, 2015), 2-3.

[334] See Part 3 for a detailed discussion of Catharine Ladd as an author.

[335] *Tri Weekly News* (Winnsboro, South Carolina), August 7, 1866. Thespian Hall was located above the Post Office.

[336] *Tri-Weekly News* (Winnsboro, South Carolina), March 6, 1866.

[337] *Tri-Weekly News* (Winnsboro, South Carolina), Aril 24, 1866.

[338] Was Catharine Ladd's inspiration her youthful exposure to Edgar A. Poe in Richmond?

[339] Advertisement Mr. Jededian Bobbins Singin Skule, Broadsides, South Caroliniana Library, Digital Collections, University of South Carolina, Columbia (accessed November 17, 2918).

[340] *Fairfield Herald* (Winnsboro, South Carolina), July 27, 1870.

[341] *Tableau vivant,* lit. 'living picture': a representation of a personage, character, scene, incident, etc., or of a well-known painting or statue, by one person or a group of persons in suitable costumes and attitudes, silent and motionless. *The Shorter Oxford English Dictionary*, 3rd ed., s. v. "tableau."

[342] *News and Herald* (Winnsboro, South Carolina), June 28, 1877.

[343] *Ibid.,* October 20, 1877.

[344] *Ibid.,* December 11, 1883. Catharine Ladd's residences were in the United States Federal Census for Fairfield County. In 1880 Catharine Ladd and her

unmarried daughter Josephine lived in the household of unmarried son and brother Dr. Charles H. Ladd, Township 1, near Buckhead. Dr. Charles Ladd died of consumption (tuberculosis) on October 12 of that year. The 1890 United States Federal Census was destroyed. In 1900 Josephine Ladd, fifty-six years old, lived in Township 1, with her nephew, Richard Wilks, head of household, and his family. A. W. Ladd married Mary A. Owings in 1875 and lived with his family in Township 13 in 1880 and 1900.

[345] *Tri Weekly News* (Winnsboro, South Carolina), March 15, 1866.

[346] In the 1860 United States Federal Census George W. Ladd as head of household reported $7,000. in real estate and $10, 756. in personal estate which included eight enslaved persons.

[347]She lived with her family in Township 5, Fairfield. Eventually the Curetons settled in Pickens County, South Carolina.

[348] For a detailed discussion of the Ladd brothers' post-war business, see the Postscript, p. 224.

[349] William B. Atkinson, M.D., ed., *The Physicians and Surgeons of the United States* (Philadelphia: Charles Robson, 1878), 481.

[350] Katharine Theus Obear, *Through the Years in Old Winnsboro* (Spartanburg: The Reprint Company, Publishers 2002), 129-130.

[351] Angela Leighton. *Victorian Women Poets: Writing Against the Heart.* Charlottesville and London: University Press of Virginia, 1992.

[352] Agnes M. Bondurant, *Poe's Richmond.* (Richmond: The Edgar Allan Poe Museum, 1999), 183.

[353]Benjamin Blake Minor, *The Southern Literary Messenger 1834-1864* (New York: The Neale Publishing Company, 1905), 57.

[354] See Appendix G for a complete list of Catharine Ladd's known writings with dates of publication and names of periodicals.

[355] Jane Turner Censer, *The Reconstruction of White Southern Womanhood 1865-1895* (Baton Rouge: Louisiana State University Press, 2003), 214.

[356] Mary T. Tardy, ed. *The Living Female Writers of the South* (Philadelphia: Claxton, Remsen and Haffelfinger, 1872), 489.

[357] Junk, 17, fn 10 on Hannah More.

[358] A full text of the biographical entry by Mary Tardy is in Appendix C.

[359] Edwin Heriott, ed., *The Floral Wreath and Ladies' Monthly Magazine* (Charleston:

[360] Tardy, 489. No examples of these articles in newspapers identified as her writing were found.

[361] *Shorter Oxford English Dictionary*, 3rd ed., s. v. "littterateur," a literary man.

[362] George A. Wauchope, *The Writers of South Carolina* (Columbia: The State Co. Pub., 1910), 11-12.

[363] Caroline Howard Gilman, ed. *The Rose Bud or Youth's Gazette* (Charleston: J.S. Burges, 1832-1833). In 1834 it became the *Southern Rose Bud*, then the *Southern*

Rose, 1832-1839, both edited by Caroline Gilman, and published by W. Estill in Charleston. In 1841 *The Rose-Bud Wreath* was edited by Caroline Gilman and published by S. Babcock & Co. in Charleston. A search of the existing editions of these periodicals in digital versions resulted in no contributions by Catharine Ladd, but many of these publications did not publish the writer's names. www.https://babel.hathltrust.org (accessed August 2018)

364 Miss Mary Bates, "Female Education," *The Magnolia* (Charleston: Burgess & James, November 1842) 65.

365 The 1830 United States Federal Census, Fayetteville, North Carolina recorded a male child less than five years of age living in their household but no children were documented in family records until 1836.

366 Tardy, 490.

367 Minor, 21.

368 Minor, 187.

369 "…one of the leading female seminaries in early nineteenth-century Richmond. This institution might be cited for its high standards in scholarship and its claims to social distinction." Bondurant, 88.

370 *Ibid.*

371 Norman Foerster, *American Poetry and Prose* (Boston: Houghton Mifflin Company, 1957), 261.

372 Meter of verse is measured in a foot consisting normally of one accented syllable and one unaccented syllable. The secondary term of measurement is the line, naming the number of feet in it. Iamb meter has an unaccented syllable followed by an accented one. Pentameter has five feet to a line. Laurence Perrine, *Sound and Sense, An Introduction of Poetry*, 6th edition (NY: Harcourt Brace Jovanovich Publishers, 1982), 167-168.

373 Ianthe, meaning purple or violet flower; or from mythology, a Cretan girl who married Iphis after Isis turned Iphis from a woman into a man; or, a water nymph. Wikipedia https://en.wikipedia.org/wiki/Ianthe (accessed September 1, 2018)

374 The 1830 United States Federal Census for Fayetteville, North Carolina listed a male child under the age of five in the George Ladd household.

375 Tardy, 489.

376 Leighton, 5.

377 These two lines are like her expression of *unknown flowers* in her poem with that title.

378 Morna, "To H.W.M.," *The Southern Literary Messenger* Vol. 1, Issue 1, July 1835. Richmond, Virginia. 634-635.

379 "Wildwood Flower," originally "I'll Twine 'Mid the Ringlets" (1860) composed by Joseph Webster to a Maud Irving poem. Fiona Ritchie & Doug Orr, *Wayfaring Strangers: The Musical Voyage from Scotland and Ulster to Appalachia* (Chapel Hill: University of North Carolina Press, 2014), 259.

[380] Rev. John Collins McCabe was Catharine's cousin, a son of her mother's step sister Jane Collins (therefore Catharine's aunt Jane) who married William McCabe. See Appendix A for the Collins-Dabney family genealogy.

[381] Lord Byron, "Adieu, adieu! my native shore," Canto the First, IV, *Childe Harold's Pilgrimage (1812).*

[382] Read the critique and listen to the reading at http://www.bostonliteraryhistory.com/chapter-3/mrs-c-ladd-"oh-do-not-say-again-love's-blind"-godeys-ladys-book-and-ladies-american.html.

[383] Mr. C. M. Ladd, "Ode," Sung at the Celebration of the Anniversary of Lafayette Lodge, No. 8, I.O.O.F. at Winnsboro', (S.C.), August 2nd, 1844. Rev. E.H. Chapin, ed., *The Symbol, and Odd Fellow's Magazine* Vol. III (Boston: Thomas Price, Publisher, 1844),*414.* www.https://babel.hathitrust.org (accessed September 1,2018)
To clarify, *our* in line two did not include Catharine, a female, in this male-only Masonic organization. For her point of view to be consistent, instead of *Their* faith in line four, it should have been *our.*

[384] Mrs. C. Ladd, "Hurrah for Bethel," *Weekly State Journal* (Raleigh, North Carolina), September 4, 1861. www.newspapers.com (accessed May 26, 2017).

[385] See comments in the next section on plays written by Catharine in which she included a character "Ku Klux."

[386] Mrs. C. Ladd, "Hurrah for Bethel," *Weekly State Journal* (Raleigh, North Carolina), September 4, 1861. www.newspapers.com (accessed May 26, 2017). The *Weekly State Journal* is not available on the Library of Congress web site *Chronicling America,* nor is it in a list of repositories.

[387] *News and Herald* (Winnsboro, South Carolina), December 18, 1897.

[388] Arcturus, "Mother and Child," *The Ladies' Garland* Vol. IV (Philadelphia: J. Van Court, April 20, 1841), 244. www.https://babel.hathitrust.org (Accessed March 1, 2018)

[389] Joyce W. Warren, *Women, Money, and the Law: Nineteenth Century, Fiction, Gender, and the Courts* (Iowa City: University of Iowa Press, 2005), 52.

[390] Warren, 71.

[391] Alida, "Our Cousin Ellie," *The Ladies' Repository: A Monthly Periodical Devoted to Literature, Arts, and Religion* Vol. 12 (Cincinnati: Methodist Episcopal Church, October 1852), 389. Making of America Journal Articles, www.quod.lib.umich.edu. (accessed July 30, 2007)

[392] See Part Two regarding performances in Thespian Hall.

[393] *The Grand Scheme,* 1853, act 1, scene 1, hand-written play script attributed to Catharine Ladd, Fairfield County Museum, Winnsboro, South Carolina.

[394] *Mrs. J's Wax Works,* a hand-written play script, unsigned, Mrs. Ladd's Scrapbook, Fairfield County Museum, Winnsboro, South Carolina.

[395] Censer, 214.

[396] Ida Raymond is named as the author under this title; Ida Raymond was a pseudonym for Mary T. Tardy.

[397] Tardy, 489. Unfortunately, neither the dates nor the newspapers were specified.

[398] *Ibid.* Subsequent volumes under the title of *Living Female Writers of the South* by Mary T. Tardy were published, however it is known by the comments of one author, Mrs. William Rives of Virginia, that some writers were not aware of being included in the volumes, and the sources of the information provided were anonymous. Mrs. Rives stated that no members of her own family contributed to the biographical information, although she did not alter its contents. www.booktraces.org (accessed January 6, 2019) This is to say that the reliability of the biographical sketch of Catharine Ladd is unknown; however her editorial, "New Improvement" does contain subjects and opinions that correspond to Mary Tardy's information.

[399] *Tri Weekly News* (Winnsboro, South Carolina) Dec. 13, 1866.

[400] *Fairfield Herald* (Winnsboro, South Carolina), August 12, 1868.

[401] Catharine's prose included characters who suffered when family members succumbed to drink. For example, see discussion of *William Brown, or the Reward of Virtue*, p. 220.

[402] *Fairfield Herald*, January 13, 1869.

[403] *Fairfield Herald*, January 27, 1869.

[404] *Tri Weekly News* (Winnsboro, South Carolina), June 30, 1866.

[405] Edgar, 337.

[406] For more background, see Lewis P. Jones, Chapter 12, "Brinksmanship," in *South Carolina, A Synoptic History for Laymen* (Orangeburg, SC: Sandlapper Publishing, Inc., 1971), 138-147.

[407] Walter Edgar, *South Carolina A History* (Columbia: University of South Carolina Press, 1998), 280.

[408] Edgar, 281.

[409] Edgar, 383-384.

[410] Dr. Carolyn Sung spent extensive time comparing the handwriting in the editorial to other examples of Catharine Ladd's handwriting. Dr. Sung is well-qualified for the analysis. She is retired from the Library of Congress where over the years she examined hand-written manuscripts. Her dissertation subject was printer Peter Force, 1818-1850. In her opinion the manuscript may not be a draft in Catharine Ladd's hand, but rather a hand-written copy reproduced by a printer's assistant expressly for typesetting before printing. She believes the cipher at the end of the manuscript is possibly CL.

[411] This editorial was transcribed using original punctuation and spelling. In some cases the original spelling is followed by [sic]. You will notice instead of a period Catharine used a comma to separate her thoughts. The grammar including subject-verb agreement was left as written. Words and letters were

inserted within brackets where missing or unreadable. Blank spaces indicate missing sections. The larger damaged sections with words missing were left as in the original.

[412] Catharine Ladd, "New Improvement," MS RG-2, 1999.013, Ladd Letters, Historical Center of York County, York, South Carolina.

[413] Mr. Francis Elder advertised his products in the Winnsboro newspaper. He invented a spring bedstead in 1860 and in 1868 received a patent for his new churn.

[414] 1860 United States Federal Census.

[415] Edgar, 323.

[416] Paul Johnson, *A History of the American People* (New York: Harper Collins Publishers, 1997), 387.

[417] Edgar, 323.

[418] Catharine Ladd, "New Improvement," MS RG-2, 1999.013, Ladd Letters, Historical Center of York County, York, South Carolina. All remaining directly-quoted passages of the editorial are from the same source.

[419] See essays on the economics of slavery in Hugh G. J. Aiken, ed. *Did Slavery Pay?* (Boston: Houghton Mifflin Co., 1971).

[420] Catharine intended sarcasm here with the adjective *talented* to describe the state legislature. She used it for emphasis on the importance of voting for whom, in her opinion, would be responsible legislators. She was passionately in favor of a literate, well-educated citizenry.

[421] Catharine Ladd included a wax museum figure named Ku Klux in her satirical play about a visit to a wax museum, further making known her negative opinions about the KKK. See p. 194-195.

[422] Lou Faulkner Williams, *The Great South Carolina Ku Klux Klan Trials 1871-1872*. (Athens: University of Georgia Press, 1996), 27.

[423] In York County the Ku Klux Klan trials involved prominent families such as the Brattons who had previously been patrons of the Ladds. The Brattons had immediate family members in Winnsboro; in fact, Gen. John Bratton and Dr. Rufus Bratton were first cousins. Rufus Bratton' s implication in the murder of Jim Williams in 1871, a black militia leader, caused him to flee to Canada. See Lou Faulker Williams, *The Great Ku Klux Klan Trails 1871-1872,* 76-80. See also Jerry L. West, *The Reconstruction Ku Klux Klan in York County, South Carolina, 1865-1877*(Jefferson, North Carolina: McFarland and Company, Inc., Publishers: 2002.

[424] Williams, 32.

[425] Farnham, 199 n 13.

[426] Victoria E. Bynum, *Unruly Women,* (Chapel Hill: University of North Carolina Press, 1992), 56.

[427] "Plymouth Rock and Democracy," Speech delivered by Henry W. Grady to the Bay State Club, Boston, December 1889 as in Edwin Dubois Sherter, ed.,

The Complete Orations and Speeches of Henry W. Grady (New York: Hinds, Noble & Eldredge, 1910), 229-230. https://babel.hathitrust.org (accessed January 7, 2019)

[428] Emily Bingham and Penny Richards, "The Female Academy and Beyond: Three Mordecai Sisters at Work in the Old South," in *Neither Lady nor Slave: Working Women of the Old South*. Susanna Delfino and Michele Gillespie, ed (Chapel Hill: University of North Carolina Press, 2002), 171.

[429] Harvey S. Teal, *Partners with the Sun: South Carolina Photographers 1840-1940* (Columbia: University of South Carolina Press, 2001), 123. A. W. Ladd reopened the photography gallery in 1866.

[430] *Tri Weekly News* (Winnsboro, South Carolina), September 4, 1865. The jewelry store was "next to his old stand-opposite the Bank."

[431] I would like to thank Alex Moore, former editor with the University of South Carolina Press, for directing me to the R.G. Dun & Co. collection at Harvard University, Harvard Business School, Baker Library.

[432] For example, one published circular by P. Walsh was on how to vote and how to obtain pardon.

[433] *Tri Weekly News* (Winnsboro, South Carolina), February 27, 1866.

[434] https://chroniclingamerica.loc.gov/ (accessed October 29, 2018).

[435] *Tri Weekly News* (Winnsboro, South Carolina), May 24, 1866. The notice stated, "prescriptions filled all hours of the day and night." Druggist Fred Moss of Gastonia suggested "depositories" might be a couched term for coffins? A. W. was a furniture repairer and agent at one time.

[436] *Tri Weekly News* (Winnsboro, South Carolina), June 30, 1866.

[437] *Ibid.*, July 21,1866.

[438] *Ibid.*, October 25, 1866.

[439] *Fairfield Herald*, (Winnsboro, South Carolina), October 10, 1866.

[440] *Ibid.*, December 18, 1867.

[441] *Ibid.,* June 26, 1867.

[442] *Ibid.*, November 6, 1867.

[443] Ladd Bros. & Co., Fairfield County, South Carolina, 9 b, p. 108D, February 23, 1871, R.G. Dun & Co. Collection, Harvard Business School, Baker Library, Harvard University, Cambridge, Massachusetts.

[444] *News and Herald* (Winnsboro, S.C.), February 15, 1877.

[445] *News and Herald* (Winnsboro, S.C.), May 15, 1877, https://chroniclingamerica.loc.gov/ (accessed October 30, 2018)

[446] *Ibid.*, May 15, 1877.

[447] *Ibid.*, January 11, 1879.

[448] Ladd, George W., September 13, 1859, Fairfield County Probate Court, Estate Papers, Box 22, Pkg 207, South Carolina Department of Archives and History, Columbia, South Carolina.

Index

Made in the
USA
Lexington, KY